Photoshop for Landscape Photographers

Art and Techniques

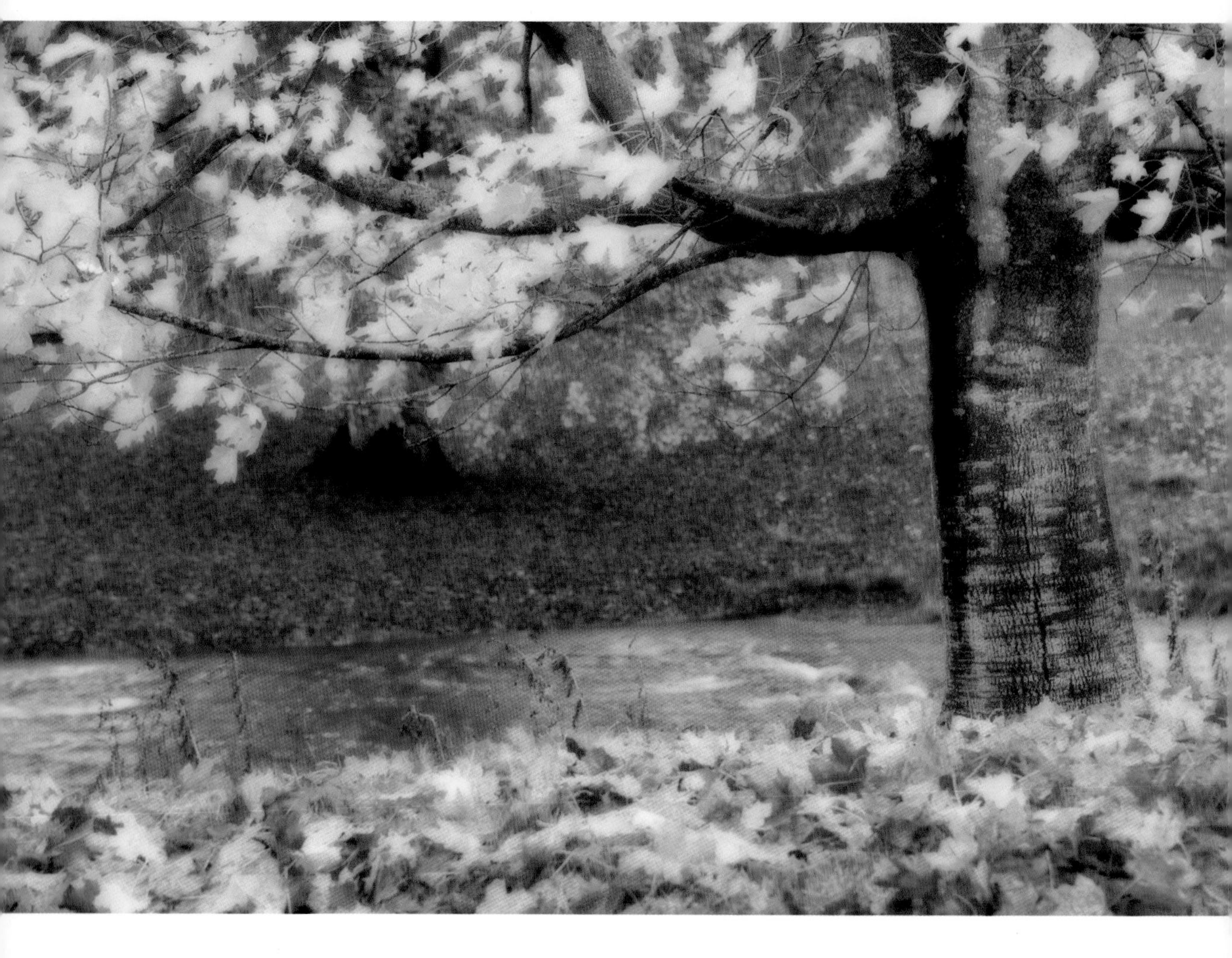

Photoshop for Landscape Photographers

Art and Techniques

John Gravett

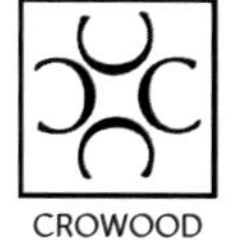

CROWOOD

First published in 2017 by
The Crowood Press Ltd
Ramsbury, Marlborough
Wiltshire SN8 2HR
www.crowood.com

British Library Cataloguing-in-Publication Data
A catalogue record for this book is available from the British Library.
ISBN 978 1 78500 118 5

Graphic design and layout by Peggy & Co. Design Inc.
Printed and bound in Malaysia by Times Offset (M) Sdn Bhd.

CONTENTS

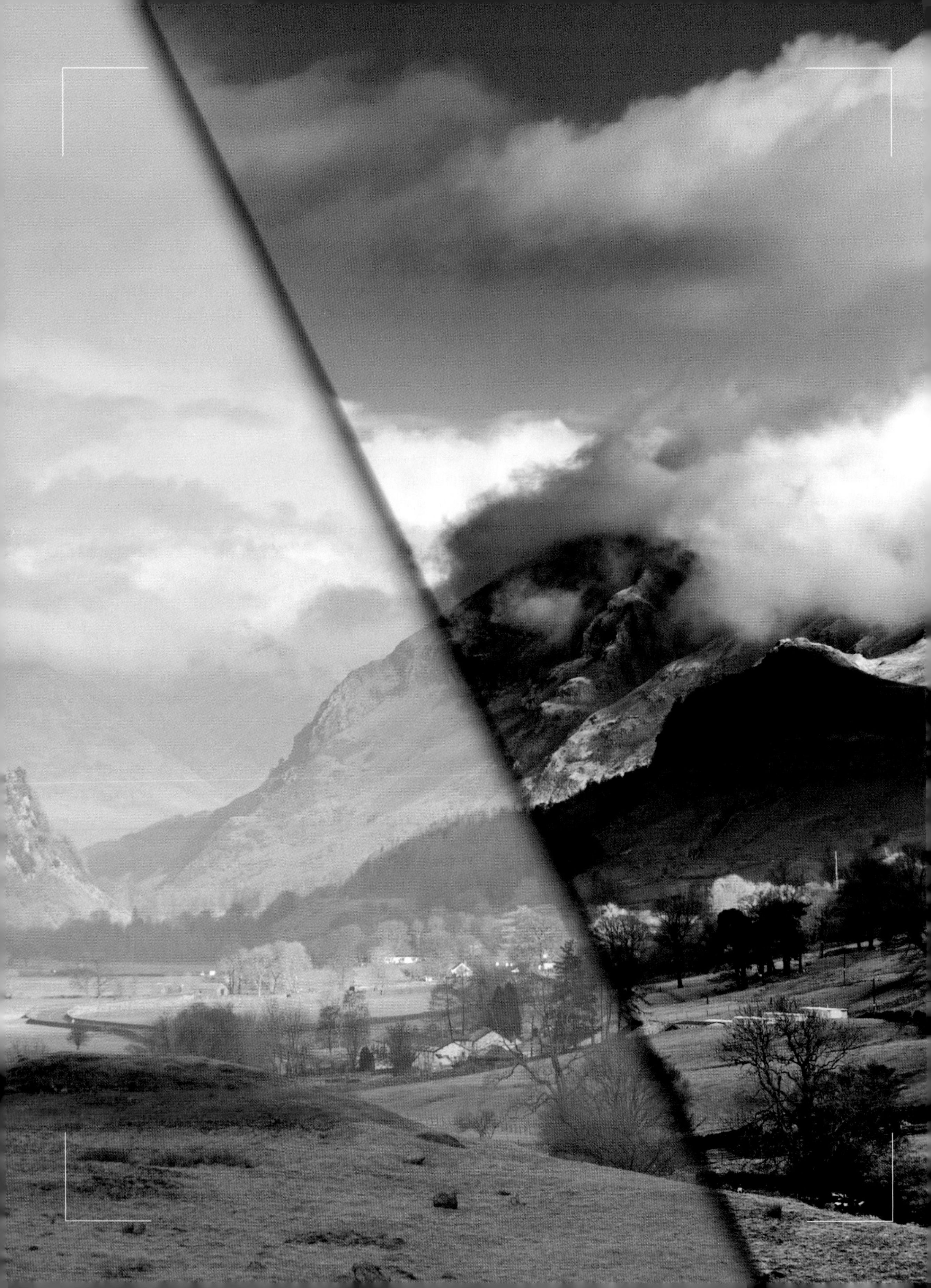

Chapter 1

Photography and Photoshop

As landscape photographers, we should be using editing software like Photoshop to improve and enhance photographs rather than rescue poor images. There is an old adage – rubbish in, rubbish out – and this applies to the photographic process as much as anything else.

The photographic process doesn't start with importing the pictures into editing software, but right back at the beginning, with the initial exposure. In the days of film, we talked about going out and taking photographs. Now it might be more relevant to talk about shooting data, as the more data we can capture at the taking stage, the better our final image quality will be. Some photographers these days refer to 'making photographs' and that is what editing software gives us the ability to do.

I started really looking at the histogram on the back of my camera a few years back, not just to see if the exposure was 'acceptable' but to see if I could maximize the data in my file by improving the exposure. Changing from slide film to digital was a real step change for me. With slides, the initial exposure produced the final shot – no further adjustments were possible. With digital, the greatest aggregation of data occurs at the right end of the histogram, so pushing the histogram to the right (by maximizing exposure) will give more data to work with. In doing this, it is of course vital that you retain highlight detail, and don't clip your highlights, but getting into the habit of this will give greater data with significantly improved shadow detail. Over-lightening dark shadows in Photoshop is a sure-fire way to create poor images with noise.

Although the dynamic range of the human eye is only about 7 stops, as we scan a scene the eye constantly adjusts and the brain pieces together

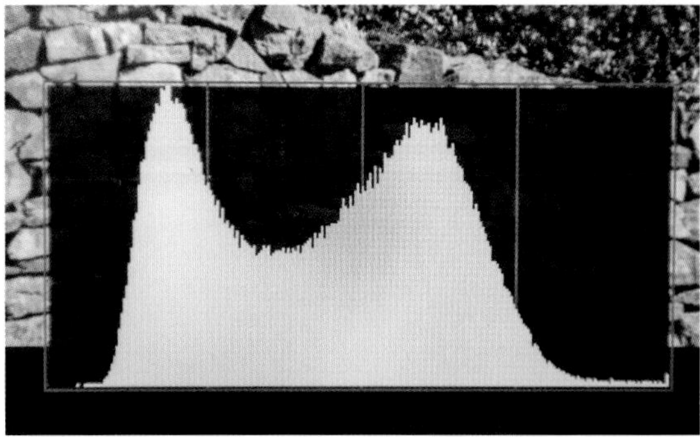

▲ Fig. 1.1
The histogram showing the spread of data from dark tones (on the left), to highlights (on the right).

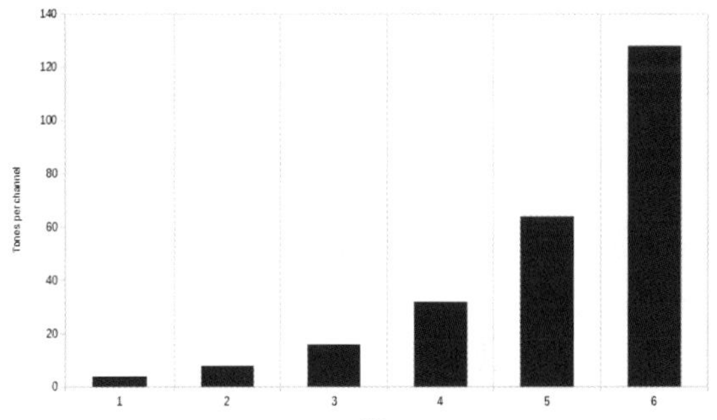

▲ Fig. 1.2
Data spread over the 6 stops of the dynamic range of a typical digital camera – showing that the right-hand stop of the histogram holds 50% of the total available data.

the information, giving us an effective dynamic range of in excess of 20 stops. The digital image recorded in-camera has a dynamic range of about 6 stops; this works well with most subjects, but where the dynamic range exceeds the capabilities of the camera, either highlight or shadow detail will be lost. Getting round this problem is something we will be looking at in Chapter 8. On a typical scene though, where there is a bit of leeway at each end of the histogram, positioning makes a huge difference.

If we look at the spread of data across the histogram first (and these numbers relate only to

WHAT SHAPE SHOULD A HISTOGRAM BE?

A question I get asked time and time again – 'Should a perfect histogram be high in the middle and low at each end – a classic bell-shaped histogram?'

The answer is of course that there is no correct shape for a histogram, it merely shows the distribution of the brightness across an entire image. But as far as exposure is concerned, we are striving to keep the brightest highlights towards the right end of the histogram.

If the image is predominantly dark, with a few light areas, the majority of the histogram will be to the left, but those few bright areas will be towards the right, and we endeavour to push them as far to the right as possible without clipping the highlights.

the JPEG image – RAW files have significantly more data), there are 256 tones in each of the red, green and blue channels, from white through to black. These however are not spread evenly across the 6 stops of the histogram. The extreme right-hand (lightest) stop holds 50 per cent of the information, in other words 128 tones, the next 64, then 32, 16, 8 and 4 respectively.

It follows therefore, if you lighten dark shadows excessively, you are pushing data from an area which contains say, 4 tones per channel, into an area that requires 8 or 16 tones per channel, effectively trying to create new data, which is achieved simply by creating noise. Pushing your histogram as far to the right as possible at the taking stage should give you more data, *as long as you retain highlight detail.*

RAW FILES V JPEGS

The debate on what type of file to shoot – RAW or JPEG – has raged since digital photography has been about, and will doubtless continue forever. The simple answer is – whichever suits you best. Both have their advantages, both their disadvantages. For me, one clearly outweighs the other, but this is dependent upon your priorities.

JPEGs

Shooting an 8-bit JPEG will give you a relatively small file size, minimizing the space taken up on your computer. A certain amount of processing can occur in-camera – maybe not as sophisticated as doing it in Photoshop, but the downloaded thumbnails will have a more 'complete' look than with RAW, possibly encouraging you to look at them further, and certainly for those without the inclination to process pictures this may be the better option.

The downside of JPEGs is that the way they are written to the computer means they are compressed to take up as little space as possible. As the JPEG format is a lossy format, every time a JPEG file is written to, data is compressed in slightly different ways, losing (destroying) the quality of the image.

Lightening shadow details on JPEG files is more likely to cause noise due to the lack of information present in the original data. Similarly, trying to create texture in relatively smooth areas, such as cloudy skies, is more likely to create artefacts and banding (lines across areas that should be a smooth transgression of tones) in the image, compromising the quality. That said, if editing is kept to a minimum, JPEGs can still produce superb results.

RAW files

RAW files have a greater bit depth, typically 14-bit, though some older cameras shoot in 12-bit. When imported into Photoshop, they open up as 16-bit files, with 32,769 tones per channel (as compared to the JPEG's 256) clearly containing significantly more data. More data can ultimately lead to a better-quality print. They have more shadow detail, and areas of dark shadows or slightly blown highlights can be recovered in processing. File sizes are significantly larger, so fewer images will fit on your card in-camera, and they will take up significantly more space on your computer. They have to be processed, as in-camera settings for increased contrast and so on are never applied to the RAW file – that's just what it is, RAW data. No applied colour space, nor contrast or sharpening enhancements, just basic data. To truly assess your picture, a modicum of processing needs to be applied; in addition files need to be sharpened. Other benefits include the ability to alter the white balance within the RAW converter; if the original photo was shot on the incorrect colour balance (or even AWB) the changes can be easily applied.

Whether you choose to shoot JPEGs or RAW files, I would tend to set the camera up in the same way:

Shoot in Adobe RGB colour space

Shoot with the appropriate white balance (rather than AWB).

Use the most neutral colour setting. It will have no effect on the RAW file, but the review image you get on the back of the camera appertains to the JPEG data; if you shoot at a 'Vivid' or 'Landscape' setting, the RAW file you download will be totally different from the image you reviewed on the back of your camera. If you shoot a JPEG, you have far more sophisticated means of altering colour and contrast in Photoshop than in the camera.

I know many photographers who swear by either. Indeed, I know of some internationally famous photographers who shoot JPEGs very successfully, and many keen amateurs who win medals in international exhibitions from images shot as JPEGs. If the original file is well exposed and correct, there is no reason why very high-quality prints cannot be made from JPEGs. Most photographers are of the opinion that you're only serious about your photography if you shoot RAW files – I might go as far as saying RAW files make it easier to cover up your mistakes, by allowing more control and recovery at the initial processing stage. Remember, photography is more about *choice* than about rights and wrongs.

Personally, I shoot RAW files.

Below, I set out a comparison of two photos – both from the same file. The first is the unprocessed RAW out of the camera; the second is the edited version, in this case converted to monochrome. This book sets out to explain each stage of the editing process to enable the reader to achieve similar results with their own photographs. Each chapter will describe, with examples, each of the stages of the editing process, to enable you to get consistent and repeatable results in your own picture editing.

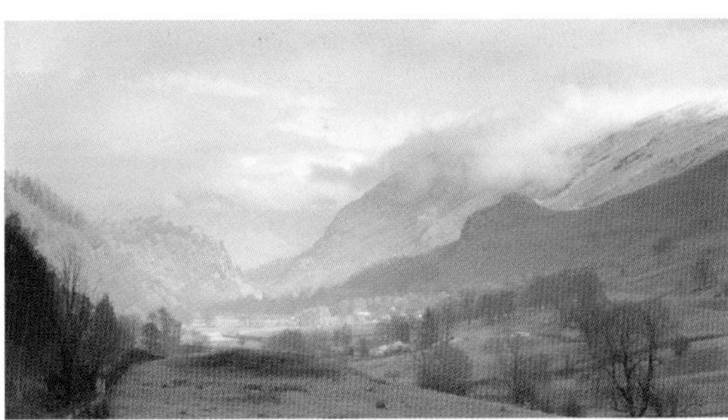

▲ Fig. 1.3
The unedited file straight out of the camera – the image appears washed out and flat with no great separation of tones and little contrast.

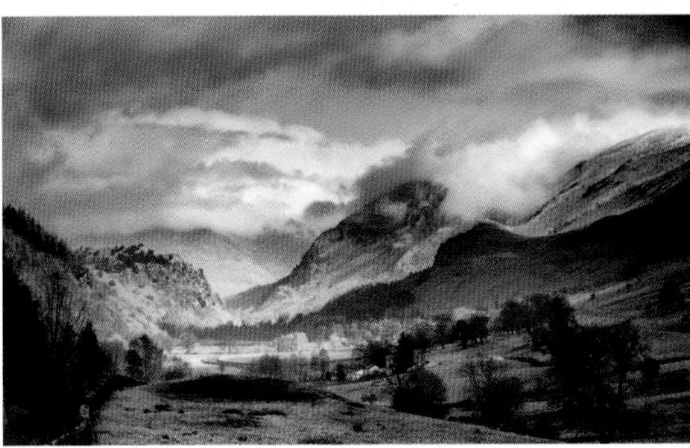

▲ Fig. 1.4
The fully processed file, converted to monochrome, showing a full range of tones, dynamic contrast and more drama than the original file. A conversion like this is possible because the original file was exposed to retain detail in the highlights and to preserve as much shadow detail as possible.

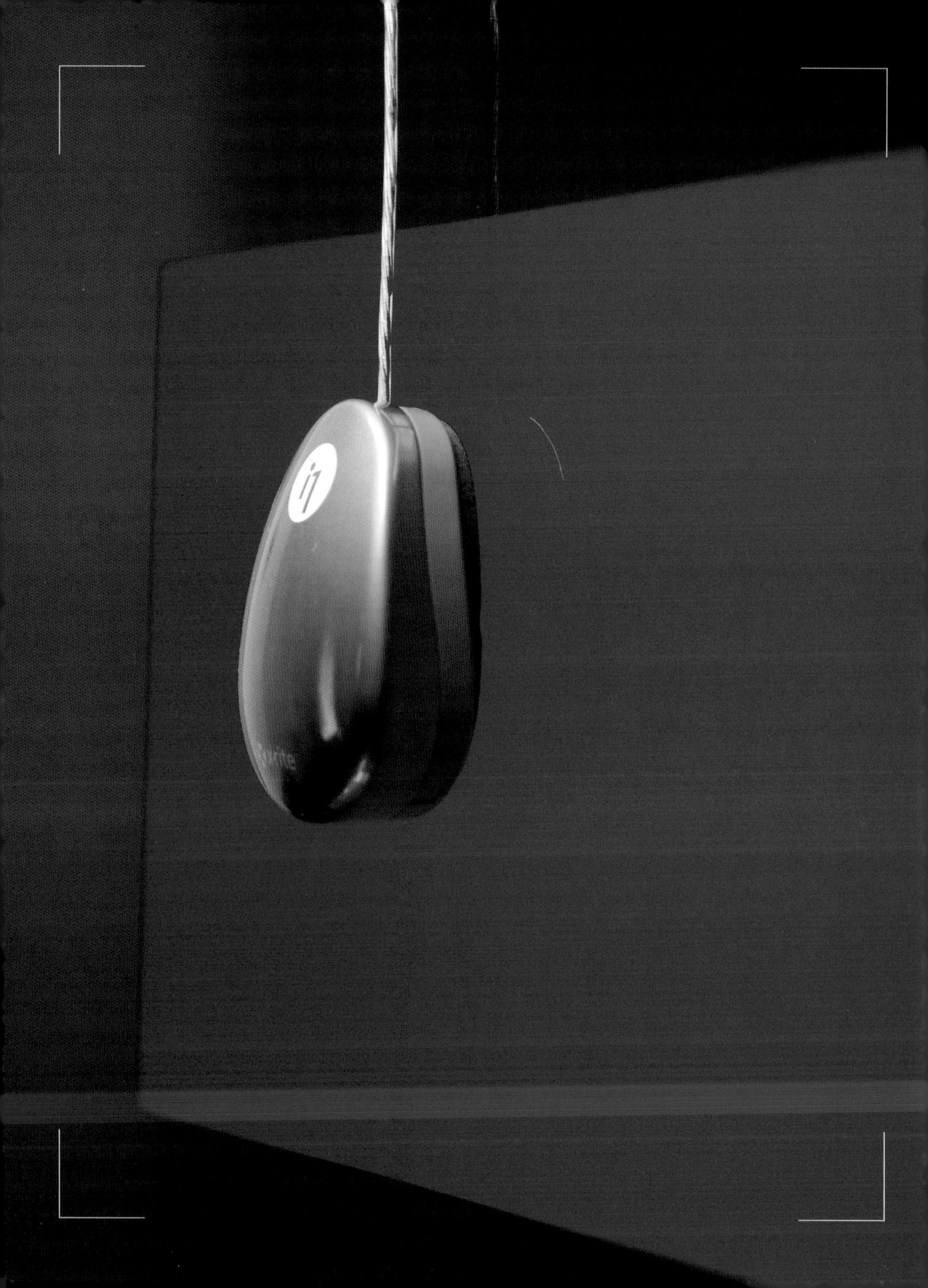

Chapter 2

Photoshop set-up and layout

Photoshop was originally developed as a graphic design tool, and its original palette layout was more suited to the graphics industry than to photographers. Over the past few generations, Photoshop has gradually improved its palette options, now offering a range including motion, typography, painting and photography-designed palettes – which work as a good starting point.

This chapter provides a step-by-step guide to the palettes; which ones I normally have visible, how to hide palettes, and save the layout you want. We'll also take a look at the Photoshop tools, and will mention shortcut keys. Hopefully, by the time you've worked your way through the book, you'll be using shortcut keys for most actions. I started a few years ago, trying to learn them to speed up my workflow. Now, I struggle to use the drop-down menus for everything I do on a day-to-day basis.

There is a list of shortcut keys at the end of the book.

STEP-BY-STEP AROUND THE PALETTES

Tools palette

Just to take the tools (particularly the ones I use) and summarize their uses (and shortcut keys – most are very obvious). If you need a reminder of the shortcut key, hover the cursor over the tool, and the tool name and shortcut key (in brackets) will show.

From the top:

Move tool (V): Not the most obvious shortcut; the move tool is simple, allows you to move things around – selections from one image to another, whole images, all sorts. There is another way of temporarily invoking the move tool; simply hold down the Ctrl key (Command on a Mac) and irrespective of what tool is currently in use, whilst that key is held down, the move tool is activated.

Marquee tool (M): More logical on the shortcut; the marquee tool is one of the multitude of selection tools. It allows rectangular, square, elliptical or round selections. It can be useful in certain circumstances.

Lasso tool (L): A tool for literally 'lassoing' around selections. By clicking on the corner of the logo, (or by holding the Shift key and tapping 'L') you can scroll through the other lasso options. The straight lasso tool allows you to draw freehand shapes of selection areas, good if you have a steady hand, or if you are roughly selecting something. The polygonal lasso tool links selections by straight lines, simply by clicking on each anchor point. Finally, the magnetic lasso tool allows the user to trace round the edge of a selection area, and the lasso tool sets its own anchor points according to the contrast locally.

Wand tool (W): Usually called the magic wand tool. Allows selection of pixels of similar tone to be selected. The sensitivity of the tool can be adjusted using the tolerance slider on the tool options, and selection can be applied locally, by ticking the contiguous box, or over the whole image area, by de-ticking it. The quick-selection tool under it (Shift-W) works in a similar way, but by clicking and dragging across the image.

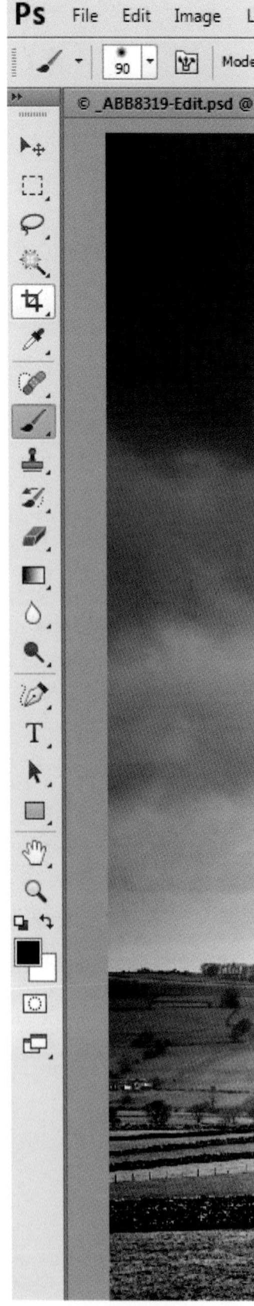

▲ Fig. 2.1
The tools palette, situated on the left side of the screen, with the tools arranged vertically; selection tools at the top, brush tools in the middle and other tools at the bottom.

Crop tool (C): A selection of crop tools, allowing the user to crop the image to the desired shape, including to preset and user-defined formats, to correct perspective.

Eyedropper tool (I): Also the shortcut for colour sampler tool, ruler tool and notes tool (why?). Allows you to select a foreground colour from part of the image/to put a marker on a point within the image from which you can monitor changes/ to measure and correct off-horizontal/vertical lines (straighten crooked horizons) etc.

Healing brush/spot healing brush/patch tool/content-aware move tool (J): Yes – another strange shortcut key – the healing brush and patch tool are used for removing marks and blemishes on the image. The content-aware move tool can be used for moving elements within the picture.

Brush tool (B): Although there are other options on this button, the brush tool is the most useful tool in Photoshop, allowing you to paint with a brush size from 1 pixel to 5,000 pixels wide, and with soft or hard edges. Why you would wish to paint on your photographs may seem an alien concept, but the brush tool is superb when working with certain selection tools, as well as on layer masks.

Clone stamp tool (S): Due to the shortcut key, I try to refer to it as a stamp tool rather than the more usual clone tool description. Photoshop's original tool for covering up blemishes and marks, by simply copying parts of the existing image over the offending area.

History brush tool (Y): Can be used in conjunction with the history palette to fade effects and bring them back selectively. Due to the way I tend to use Photoshop, it isn't a tool I use much at all.

Eraser tool (E): Used to erase parts of the image – more useful when working on layers than on the background layer, otherwise parts of your picture simply disappear!

Gradient tool (G): Enables you to create a gradient across the picture/mask in use. It is one of the tools I find people struggle with the most to grasp the concept of, but one of the most useful tools in the whole palette. I use the gradient tool a lot as both a selection tool, and in conjunction with layer masks.

Blur tool/sharpen tool/smudge tool (No shortcut key): Maybe the reason I never use it. Allows you to blur, sharpen or smudge parts of the picture with a brush-like interface.

Dodge/burn tool (O): For the shortcut key, think of a dodging tool from a darkroom; it would be the same shape as an 'O'. Again, with my ways of working, a rarely used tool.

Pen tool (B): I tend not to use it – more graphic design.

Text tool (T): Used to add text layers – great for greeting cards and the like, but hardly the landscape photographer's number one tool!

Path selection tool: I tend not to use it – more graphic design.

Rectangle tool: I tend not to use it – more graphic design.

Hand tool (H): Allows you to navigate around the image when zoomed in to greater than full screen. The 'H' shortcut key, although logical, I rarely use, as the tool can be temporarily invoked from any other tool simply by holding the space bar down, clicking and dragging on the image to navigate around the picture.

Zoom tool (Z): Used for zooming into and out from the picture to smaller areas, for detailed working. Other options for zooming are possible and will be covered elsewhere.

Below the regular tool icons are three further icons:

Foreground/background colours: The foreground colour is the colour the brush tool would use to paint on any layer. The background colour is the colour the canvas would be if you extended canvas size greater than that of the picture area. Default colours are black/white, and can be reset either by clicking on the small black/white logo above and to the left of the icon, or by simply hitting the default colours button 'D'.

To exchange the colours (to make the foreground colour the background, and vice versa), again either click on the logo to the top right of the foreground/background colours icon, or simply hit 'X' to 'eX-change' colours. (Simple, isn't it!)

Quick mask tool (Q): Designed as a tool for masking parts of the picture, leaving other areas selected. I turn things around and use it as a selection tool, which will be dealt with fully in Chapter 3.

Screen mode (F): The last button on the palette, this cycles through the different screen modes; standard/full screen with menu bar/full screen. This facility is useful when you've finished working on a picture – you can easily view it full screen against a black background.

GENERAL SET-UP

The majority of the Photoshop set-up works pretty well straight out of the box, but there are a few changes I would recommend:

Preferences modifications

Under *Edit>Preferences*: Going through the menus from top to bottom:

General: Leave most as set, but as I use a mouse with a scroll wheel, I do tick 'zoom with scroll wheel'.

Interface: No changes.

File handling: No changes.

Performance: Traditionally, Photoshop used to be set to use only 50 per cent of the computer's available RAM – newer versions up it to 65 per cent. That means if you have 32Mb of RAM, Photoshop is only using 20Mb of RAM – that's a lot of RAM to buy not to use. Now, using all 100 per cent will stop your machine working completely, as it won't be able to process anything else, but assuming you're using either Lightroom or another viewing package, and running a couple of other pieces of software simultaneously, there would be no problem pushing the percentage of RAM used up to 75 or

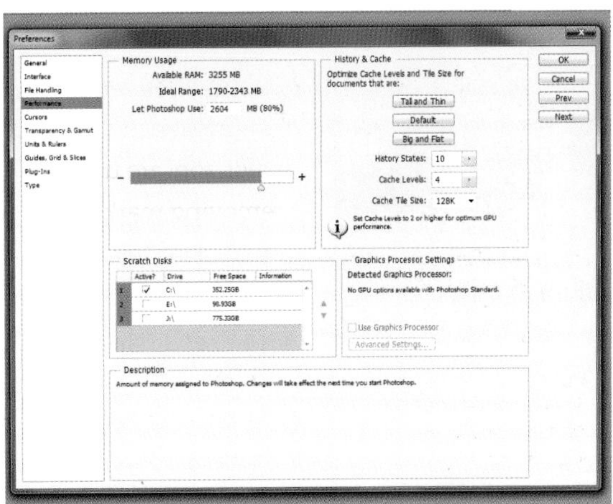

▲ Fig. 2.2
The Preferences menu (Edit>Preferences) on a PC, (Photoshop>Preferences) on a Mac, showing the performance screen, with memory usage set to 80% of available RAM.

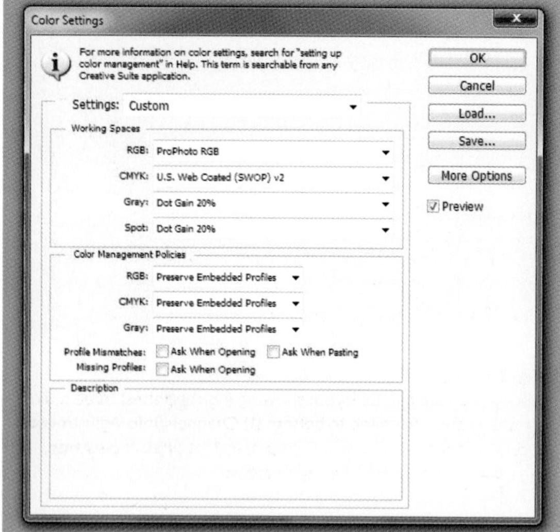

▲ **Fig. 2.3**
The colour settings menu (Edit>Colour settings) showing the RGB set to ProPhoto RGB (best for use with RAW files).

even 80 per cent. Clearly, the less RAM you have, the greater percentage you would have to leave spare to run other software, but the out-of-the-box settings are very cautious.

Scratch disks: If you have two disks in your computer, set the scratch disk to the one that does not have the programme loaded onto it.

History states: The number of history states are adjustable from 1 to 1,000, but the more history states you have set, the more memory you use, and the slower your computer will process each step. Because I work on layers for everything, I don't need the ability to undo many steps, so I set mine at 10.

Cursors: Two types, painting and other. I set painting to normal brush tip, with a cross hair. With a soft brush, this will set the edge of the round brush-cursor at the 50 per cent opacity point of the feather. The full-size brush tip sets the cursor size to the outer dimension of the feather. To me, this makes the brush look larger than I see it, but some users prefer this. Try both and see which suits you.

With normal cursors, the default setting is for an icon of the tool in use. With the crop tool, this is a confusing cursor, not at all clear as to the exact point at which the crop starts or ends. None of the other cursors are any better. Change the option to precise, and each tool will have a cross-hair cursor. More accurate by far, and much easier to use.

Transparency and gamut: I leave alone.

Units and rulers: Personal choice; cm or inches are useful if you print a lot; if you are working for electronic display, try pixels.

Guides, grids and slices: No change.

Plug-ins: No change.

Type: No change.

Colour settings

Under *Edit>Colour Settings*

One area that causes huge confusion in Photoshop is colour settings. Essentially there are three colour settings out of the plethora of available settings to choose from:

- sRGB
- Adobe RGB
- ProPhoto RGB

sRGB was a colour space introduced in 1995 by Microsoft and Hewlett Packard. Developed primarily for the internet, it has a relatively small colour gamut (small number of tones which can be accurately reproduced in printing).

Adobe RGB was introduced (by Adobe) three years later in 1998. It is an extended colour space, which more closely matches the output of a colour printer, meaning the colours contained within the image are more accurately printable.

ProPhoto RGB was introduced three years later in 2001, by Kodak, and is specifically designed for digital photography. It has the largest colour gamut of the three, and usually will match more closely the output of a RAW file.

If you are a JPEG user, set your camera to Adobe RGB colour space, and set Photoshop to the same. That way, you will be both shooting and editing in the same extended colour space.

If you shoot RAW files, they are independent of the colour space settings in-camera (I still set Adobe RGB in camera in any case, just in case I need to shoot a JPEG); set Photoshop to ProPhoto RGB, and maximize colour data in your image.

General palettes

Palettes are found under the *Window* drop-down menu. If you click on the drop-down, you'll be confronted with twenty-four different palettes. Needless to say, if you have all of these on display, you'll have such a cluttered workspace you won't have room to see a photo.

What palettes you set on permanent display is a personal thing, but the ones I refer to mostly, and therefore always have (broken into three sets) are:

Channels: Useful for black and white conversions, to compare the red, green and blue channels, and their different effect on the mono image.

Info: To me, an essential palette – enables precise measurement of colour and brightness on any part of the image, useful for colour balancing, and fine checking exposure.

Adjustments: Gives a one-click adjustment layer for levels, curves, etc.

Actions: If there is a set of repeatable actions you carry out on a number of pictures (for example resizing them for projection, or the internet), they can be stored as a single-button action. Saves time, and maintains repeatability.

History: Allows you to step back in stages to undo actions taken.

Histogram: Shows the histogram for the RGB, red, green and blue channels.

Properties: displays the active adjustment layer (levels, curves and so on).

Layers: No brainer – has to be on display at all times.

Should I need any of the other palettes, they are easy to open, and subsequently close.

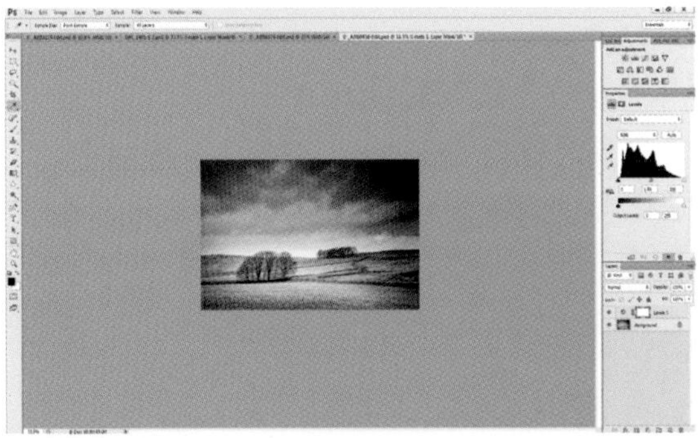

▲ **Fig. 2.4**
Recommended palette layout showing (right palettes) three main palette groups, from top to bottom (1) Channels/Info/Adjustments/Actions/History/Histogram (2) Properties (3) Layers. If preferred, Channels can be put in the Layers group.

SHOULD I PROFILE MY MONITOR?

A question I am constantly asked, the answer to which is a categorical yes! Monitors as supplied are not colour-balanced for photographic purposes, and even in use, the colours change periodically. The easiest way to 'profile' the colour of your monitor is to use one of the many different types of profiler that are available on the market. When properly set up, colours on the screen should perfectly match colours on the print. This is not only important if you print your own photographs, but also if you send them to an external printer. I do find that the image on the screen is typically lighter than the subsequent print, but it is important to realize that all computer screens work with transmitted light, and prints work by reflected light, so there are inherent differences anyway.

The profilers, irrespective of make, are very easy to set up and use. As profiles do go 'off' after a while, I reprofile my monitor about once a month, to make absolutely sure that I'm working to a constant accuracy.

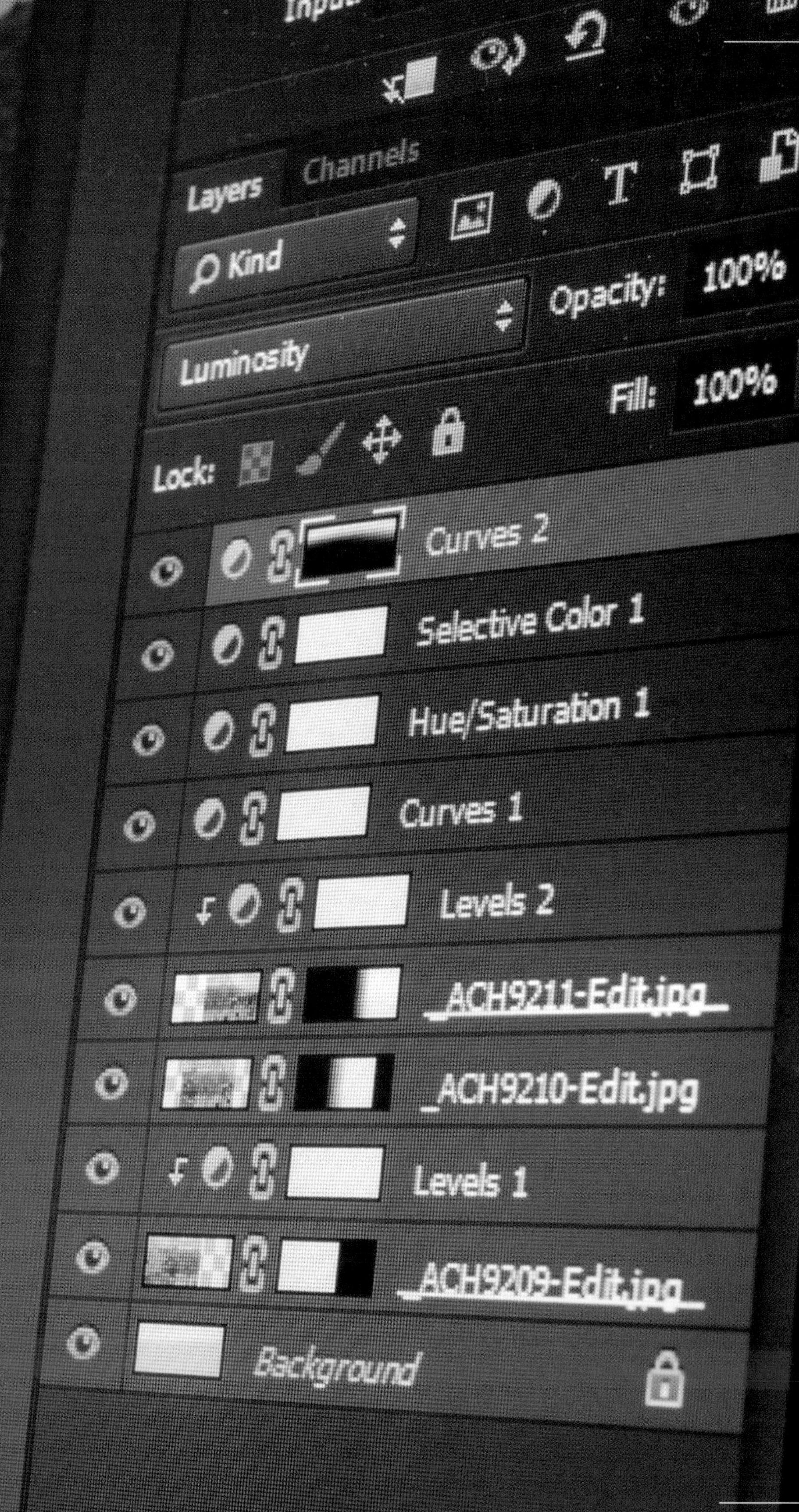

Input: 172
Channels
Layers
Kind
Opacity: 100%
Luminosity
Fill: 100%
Lock:
Curves 2
Selective Color 1
Hue/Saturation 1
Curves 1
Levels 2
_ACH9211-Edit.jpg
_ACH9210-Edit.jpg
Levels 1
_ACH9209-Edit.jpg
Background

Chapter 3

Working with layers

Layers are the absolute backbone of Photoshop. Everything to be adjusted on a picture – cloned, repaired, sharpened, added or taken away – is done on a separate layer, either on an adjustment layer (curves, levels and so on) or on what can be referred to as a pixel layer (that being a layer that will take colours in the form of photographic layers, or paint from the foreground colour box).

HOW MANY LAYERS DO I HAVE TO LIMIT MYSELF TO?

The chances of you running out of layers on a single image in Photoshop are pretty slim. Photoshop limits the number of layers that can be added to a picture to 9,999, yes – almost 10,000 layers. So the chances of you getting anywhere near that number are pretty slim. So never let numbers of layers worry you. Typically, most photographs never exceed ten to fifteen layers; speaking personally, the most I've ever managed on a complicated composite picture was 300 layers, and that involved about five hours of work.

In this chapter we're going to cover all aspects of layers, from adjustment layers to pixel layers; and methods of selection of areas within your landscapes to ensure you get results that enhance and improve your landscape photographs, which look natural, yet fit in with your visualization.

The most important thing about working with layers is not to be phased by them. They really aren't difficult to understand, yet people get so concerned about using them. The benefit is that you leave the original picture sitting at the bottom of the stack – untouched – so the pixels remain unchanged and quality remains high throughout the process.

Exercise 1 – adding pixel layers

Let's just try a simple example of pixel layers and how they relate to each other on a pile of other layers. This is something many people initially get confused over, but it is really very simple. Figure 3.1 shows an opened file – add a simple pixel layer to it by clicking on the new layer logo, at the bottom of the layers palette – second from right. This adds 'Layer 1' above the background layer, and the thumbnail looks like a grey and white chequerboard. This is currently a transparent pixel layer. It contains nothing – and your file size hasn't increased at all. For those of you who remember them, think of it as an overhead projector, with a single clear acetate laid on top of a projector slide – it adds nothing. If however you wrote on that gel, it would appear on the projection. But, you can move the gel about independently of the slide below and the writing on the gel moves with it. The same can be done on a separate pixel layer. So add a layer, and select the brush tool (B). You will notice that Layer 1, which you have just added, has become the active layer, because the Layer 1 'bar' is coloured (usually blue).

Select a colour for your brush tool by clicking your cursor on the foreground colour box near the bottom of the tool palette. You will pull up the colour picker – choose any colour, and you will see that the foreground colour box has changed. Paint a stripe

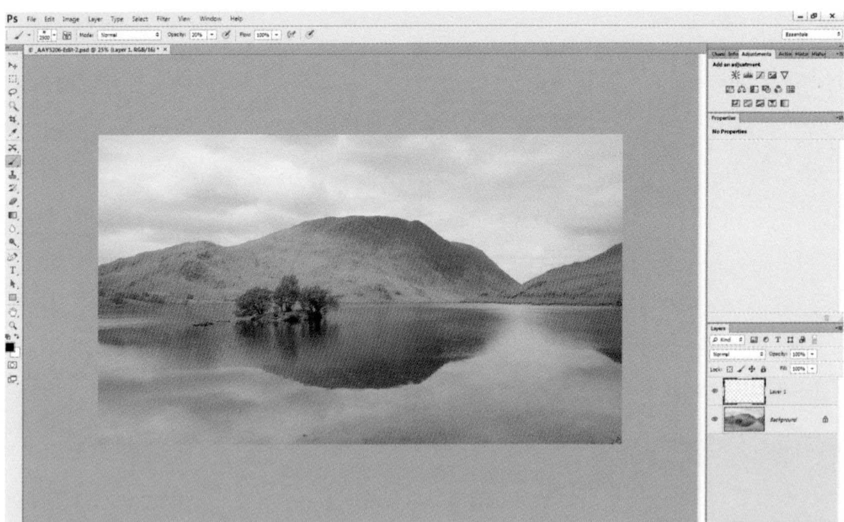

Fig. 3.1
Opened file, with empty (transparent) layer added.

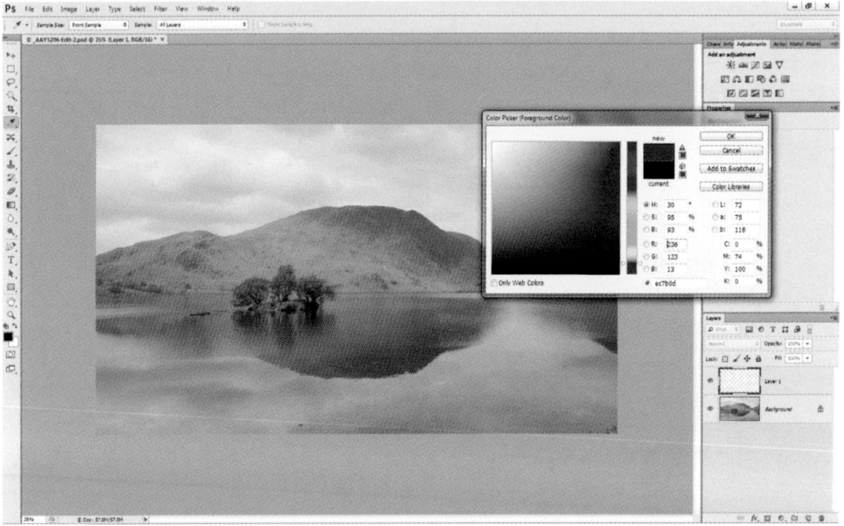

Fig. 3.2
Colour Picker activated by clicking on the foreground colour box.

across the picture – you can change the size of the brush tip by using the square brackets – the left bracket ([) will make the brush smaller, whereas the right bracket (]) will make the brush larger.

Paint a line across the image on the screen – you will see a stripe appear, apparently across the image. Now, on the left of the layer, on the palette, there is a small eye logo (just to the left of the layer thumbnail); click on it, you'll see the eye vanish, and the paint stripe disappear from the picture. The eye allows you to switch on and off any different layer. To get rid of any layer, simply place the cursor over the layer bar (you will see a hand with a finger raised), left-click the mouse (the hand turns into a gripping hand) and drag the layer to the bin, in the lower right of the layer palette.

Many people get confused by layer order. It's actually very straightforward. If you have a number of pixel layers with colour on them – it's the same as looking at a pile of prints – you'd only see the top print, rather than all those below it, so you only see the top layer. If you switch the layer off, erase part of it, or reduce its opacity, you can see part or all of the layer below.

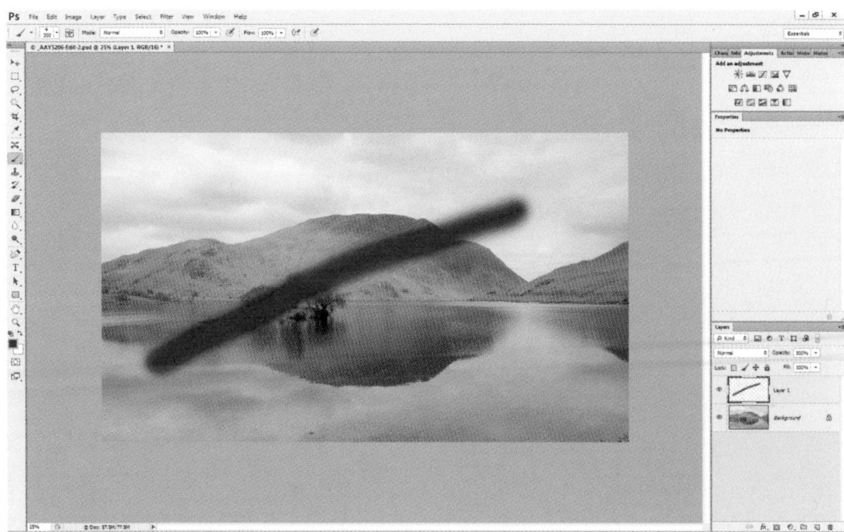

Fig. 3.3
Stripe added by using the brush tool on Layer 1.

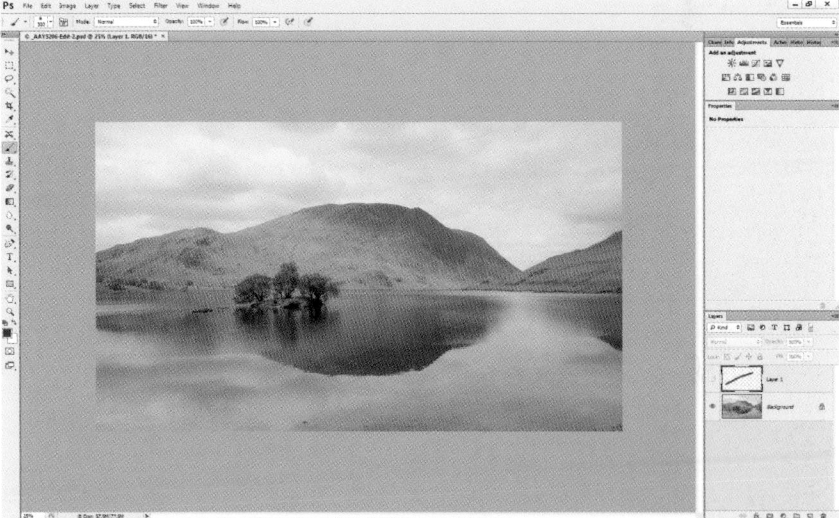

Fig. 3.4
Stripe turned off by clicking on the eye logo on Layer 1 – hiding the layer. The stripe remains as shown on Layer 1, but is no longer visible.

So with a picture of say three pixel layers, if they were all visible (eyes turned on) and at 100 per cent opacity, the only layer you would be able to see on the main image is the top one, although in the layer palette, all three layers would be visible.

ADJUSTMENT LAYERS

Adjustment layers are the most important part of Photoshop bar none. This is the *most important* part of the book. Newcomers to Photoshop often make adjustments to the picture via the top drop-down menu *Image>Adjustments>Levels/Curves/* and so on. The problem with working in this way is that it doesn't add an adjustment layer, it applies the adjustment directly to the pixel layer, modifying

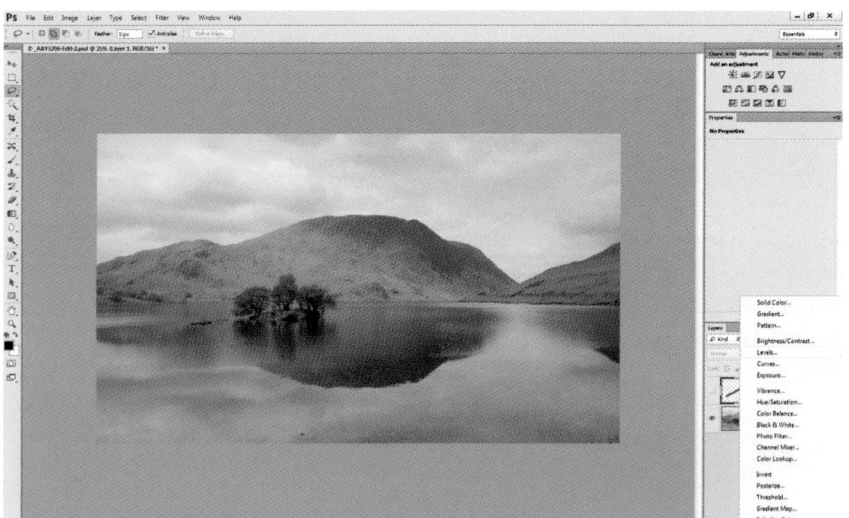

Fig. 3.5
Adjustment layer pop-up menu accessed by clicking on the 'create new fill or adjustment layer' icon (black/white divided circle) at the bottom of the layers palette

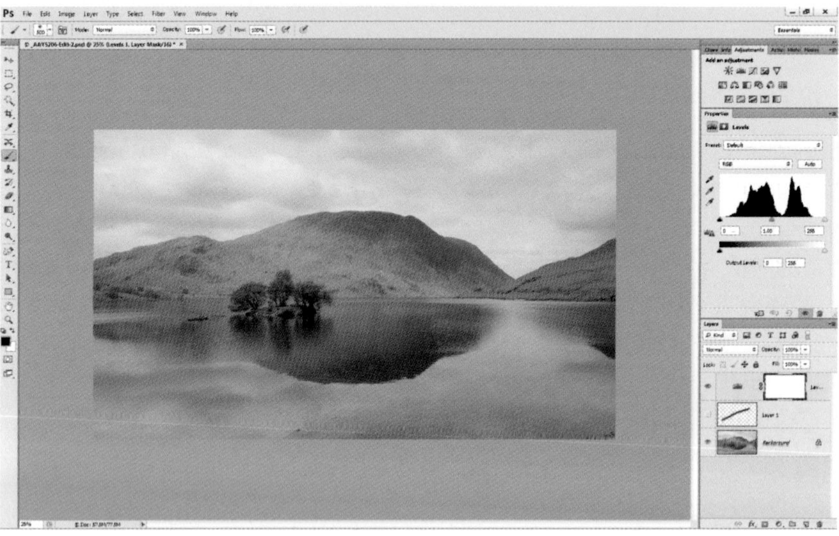

Fig. 3.6
Levels adjustment layer added to layer stack; the adjustment layer is positioned immediately above the layer that was active (blue) when the adjustment layer was selected. Any adjustments will affect all pixel layers below the adjustment layer.

the pixels and preventing later overall or localized changes to the image.

At the bottom of the layers palette, there is an icon to pop up the menu to 'create new fill or adjustment layers' (it's the centre icon – a circle of half black/half white). Click on this and the adjustment layer menu pops up. Choosing any one of these menus (try levels) will add a separate adjustment layer with its associated layer mask.

Newer versions of Photoshop offer an adjustments palette, with the icon of each adjustment layer shown. A simple click on the appropriate icon will create the adjustment layer. The only downside is that you have to remember the picture icon for each layer – use those you remember, use the pop-up menu from the layers palette for others.

The adjustment layer sits immediately above the layer that was active when it was invoked, and will affect all pixel layers below it, unless it is 'clipped' to a particular layer. Adjustments can be clipped to the pixel layer (so they only affect that layer), by clicking on the 'clip to layer' button at the lower left of the properties palette.

THE MOST USEFUL ADJUSTMENT LAYERS

To affect the brightness and contrast of the picture, surprisingly, don't use the 'brightness and contrast' adjustment. It's OK for a quick fix, but gives you far less control than the levels (brightness) and curves (contrast) adjustment layers. The levels work by making changes to a histogram – identical to the one you can see on the LCD panel on your camera.

HISTOGRAMS

The word 'histogram' can strike concern into many photographers, thinking it's something technical and complicated. In effect a histogram is no more than a bar chart showing the quantity of pixels of every tone, from black (left-hand end) to white (right-hand end). A picture of pure black would have a histogram of a single, vertical line at the extreme left end of the axis. Pure white, the same vertical line, but to the right, and mid-grey would be bang in the middle of the chart. There is no such thing as a correct shape for a histogram – it entirely depends on the tones within a picture. For example, a snow scene with a few skeletal trees will have a very right-heavy histogram (Figure 3.7) whereas a night sky with stars will be an overall dark image and the histogram will be correspondingly weighted to the left (Figure 3.8).

Using the levels adjustment layer

Add a levels layer (as described above) to a fairly low-contrast image, like the one here (Figure 3.9). The histogram that you see in the properties window falls short of each end of the available axis, therefore there is no real black, nor any pure white – the photo generally looks flat, and low in contrast. Surprisingly, this is not a bad thing, and gives us a spread of data that we can really work with. My workflow means I almost always start with a basic levels layer.

Starting at the left-hand side of the histogram, grab the small black triangle (known as the shadow slider) with the cursor, and slide it to the right until it reaches the edge of the histogram, but be careful not to go too far, or you will lose all shadow detail. A good way of checking this is as you move the shadow slider, hold down the Alt key. The whole image will go white, until you reach the edge of the histogram, when the clipped areas will show. It's important not to clip the shadows, so back it off just a little.

Now do the same with the highlight slider. These adjustments have ensured that we have a range of tones from black through to white across the image, helping to make the picture really come alive.

Curves layers

So many people who move from Elements to Photoshop are reluctant to try curves, because they don't fully understand them. It's hardly surprising, as initially we are confronted by a graph with a straight line, not a curve, and an X- and Y-axis that look to be identical. To the uninitiated, 'input levels' and 'output levels' don't help much either.

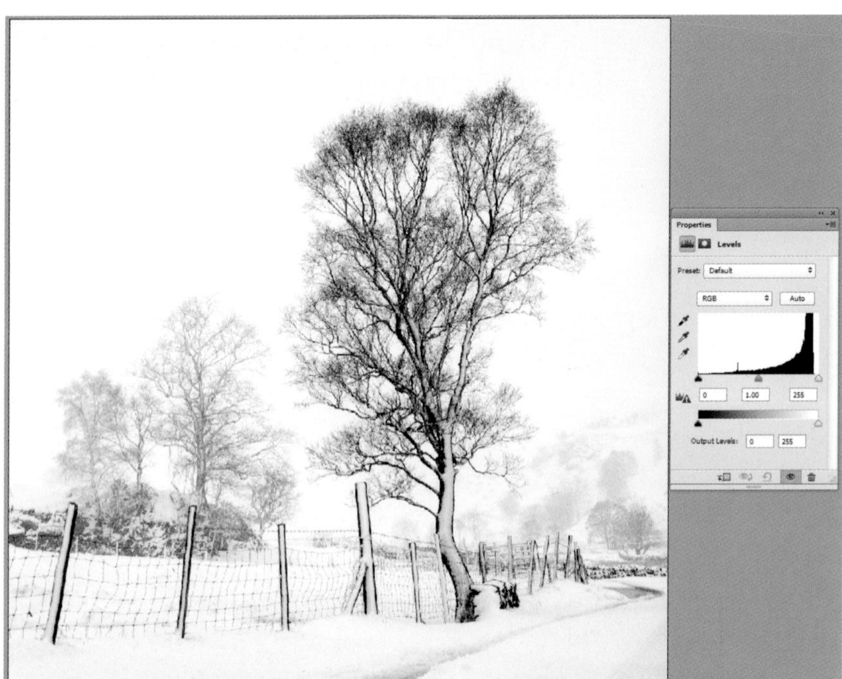

Fig. 3.7
Light-toned histogram showing the greater amount of tones to the right of the axis.

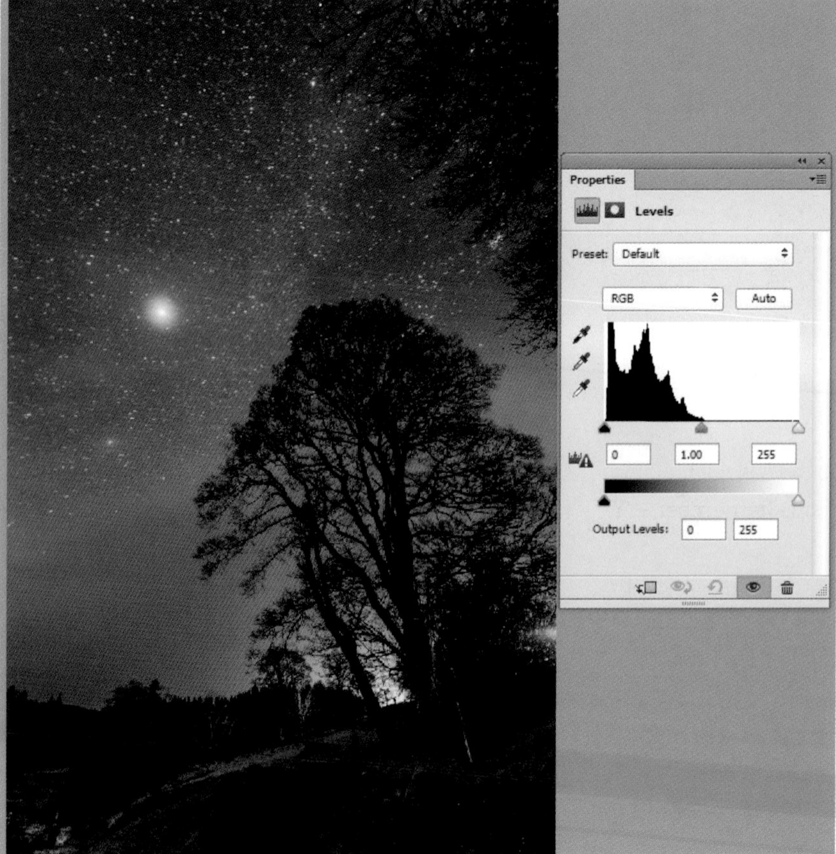

Fig. 3.8
Dark-toned histogram showing almost all the tones between black and mid-grey – the histogram is set almost entirely on the left side of the axis.

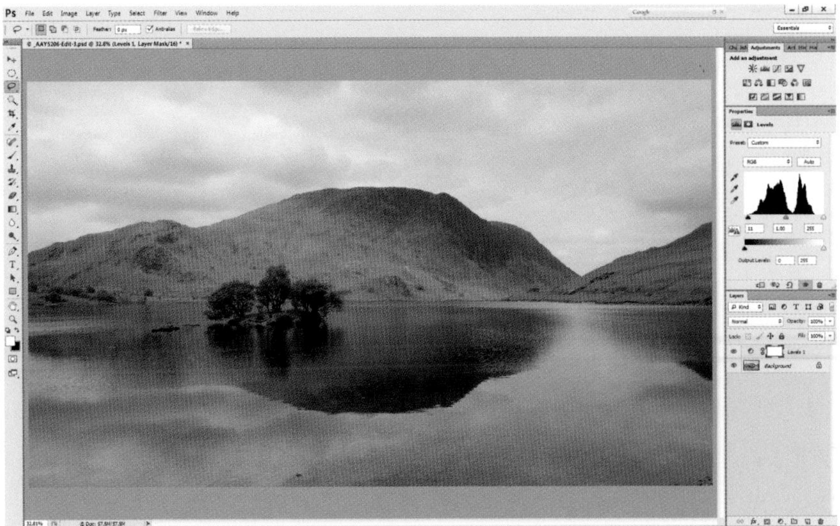

Fig. 3.9
Levels layer added (Levels 1).

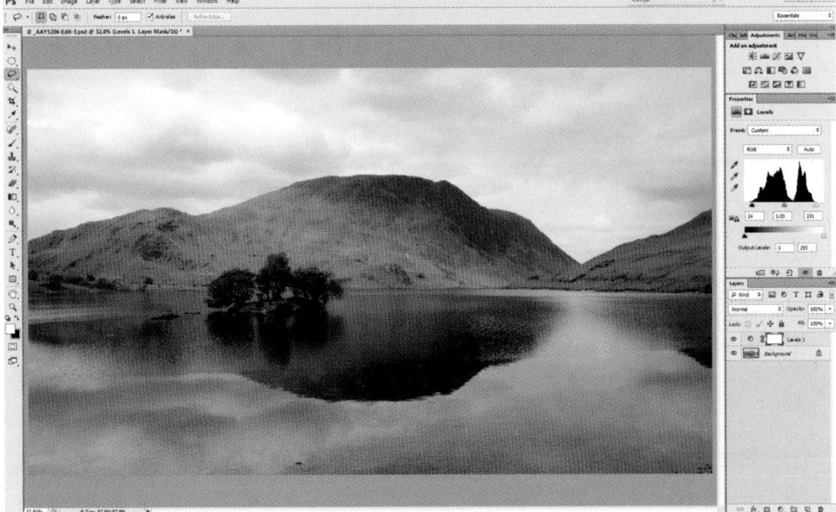

Fig. 3.10
Highlight and shadows sliders adjusted to deepen the shadows and increase the highlights, by pulling the sliders in to the ends of the body of the histogram.

Basics:

- The X-axis is the one along the base of the graph, the Y-axis is the one at the side (remember – 'Y' points to the sky).
- The X-axis represents input levels, which means the tones you start with, without changes.
- The Y-axis represents output levels, which show the changes you apply by moving the 'curve'.
- The curve itself is the diagonal straight line across the graph; you can click and drag the ends around, or click anywhere along its length and bend the line – into a curve!
- The way the shape of the line can affect brightness and especially contrast in the picture can be demonstrated simply: if you lift the black point (bottom left) halfway up the Y-axis, and drop the white point (top right) halfway down the Y-axis, you will end up with a horizontal line (curve) right across the mid-grey point of the graph. You'll notice the change it makes to the photo is pretty extreme – *all* contrast has gone and you are left with a completely grey photo.

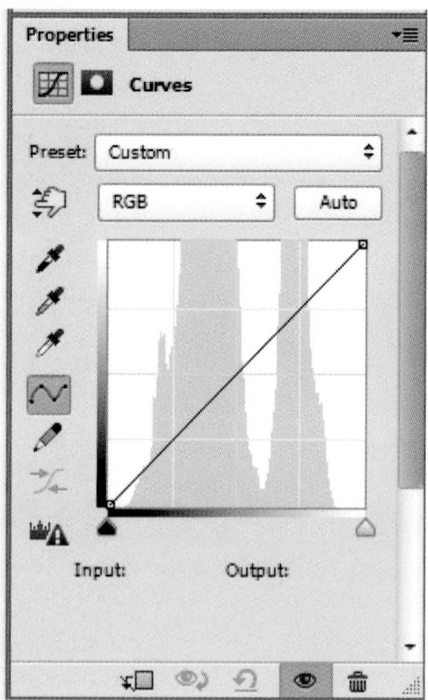

▲ Fig. 3.11
Unadjusted curves layer showing the straight, diagonal 'curve' overlaying the histogram of the image.

▲ Fig. 3.12
Curves adjusted to a horizontal line has made the image grey.

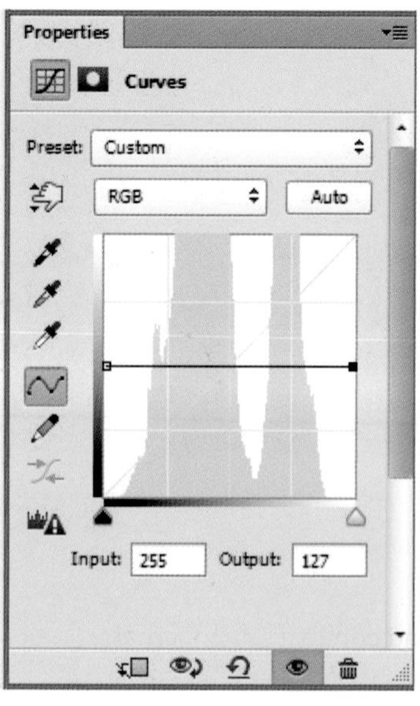

▲ Fig. 3.13
Curves line made horizontal has reduced contrast to nothing.

On the other hand, if you slide the black and white points in to create a line (curve) as vertical as possible – the contrast goes to the other extreme.

Clearly, both these extremes give ridiculous results, but they do serve to illustrate the basics of 'curves'. The flatter the curve line, the lower the contrast; the steeper, the higher the contrast. Using curves to increase contrast within a photo often needs only small changes to the line – and it can be a single point added to the centre of the line, it does not have to imitate a classic S-curve. Levels and curves are used a lot in working on landscapes, but often only on a part of the image.

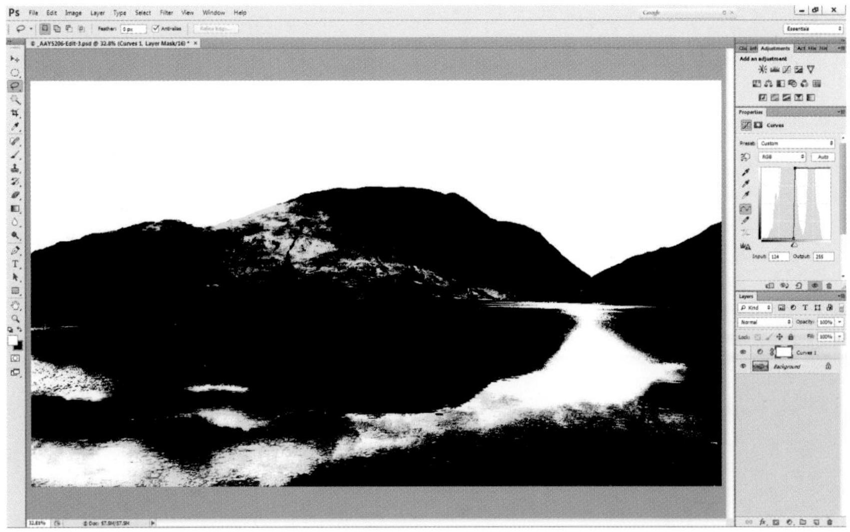

Fig. 3.14
Curves layer at maximum contrast by making the curve as vertical as possible – the vertical line is set close to the centre of the histogram giving roughly equal amounts of black and white within the picture.

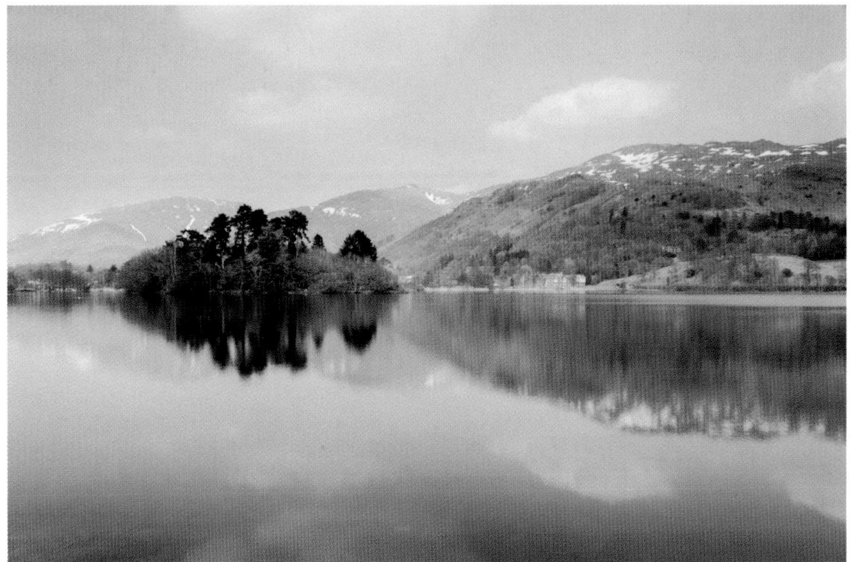

Fig. 3.15
Original, unedited photo of Grasmere, with an overall lack of contrast, particularly in the sky and reflections.

SELECTING PARTS OF THE PICTURE TO WORK ON

Different selection tools suit different selection types, and although they are all interchangeable, and can be used in conjunction with each other, everyone develops ways of selecting that suits them.

In the photo of Grasmere, the sky, and to some extent, reflections, are very light and could do with some darkening, and contrast enhancement.

There are a number of selection tools within Photoshop that it would be possible to use to select the sky. Some may work better than others:

The magic wand tool (W)

The wand tool will select pixels in adjacent areas of similar tone. When you select the tool, a tool options bar is displayed at the top of the screen. The four left-hand boxes define the selection method; if the

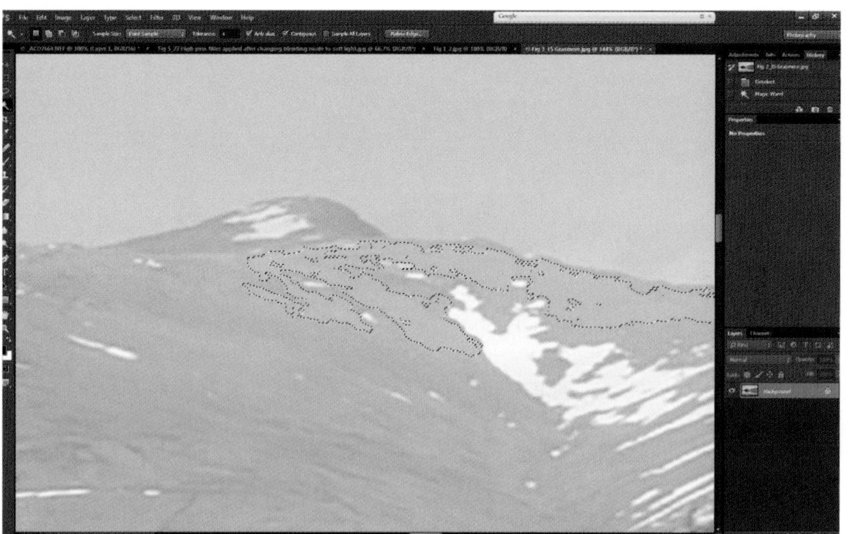

Fig. 3.16
An example in close-up of the selection of the fells with tolerance on the magic wand tool set to 4.

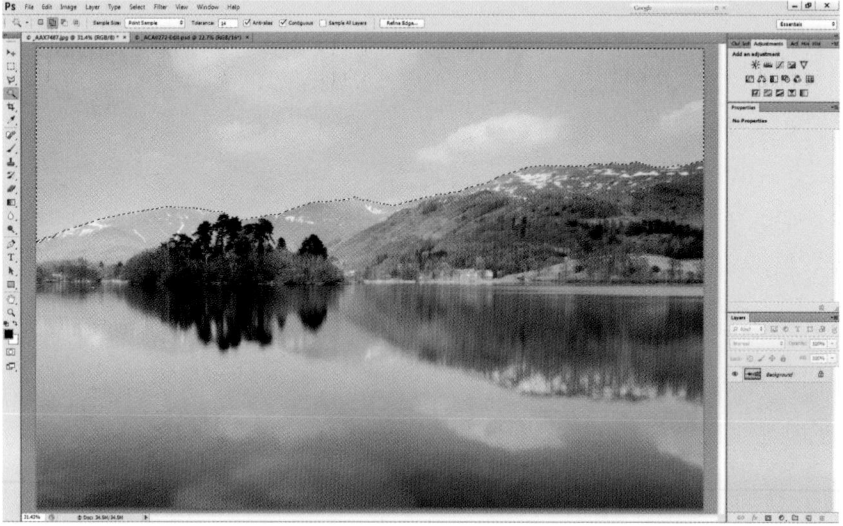

Fig. 3.17
The magic wand tool used to select the sky, using a tolerance of 15, and contiguous selections, building up the selected area until the whole sky is selected.

first (plain square) is selected, each click of the wand tool on the picture will start a new selection. The second, each click will add to the previous selection, allowing you to build up the selected area a bit at a time. The third box allows you to subtract from the existing selection, the fourth allows only an intersection of selected areas. These four option boxes are the same across selection tools (marquee tool, lasso tool and wand/quick selection brush tools). The most useful option is to add to the existing selection (second box).

The sample size relates to the area clicked on – in fact for a sky, a larger sample than 'point sample' (the default) might work well, but leave it for the moment.

The tolerance box is the key to using the wand tool effectively. The 'tolerance' relates to the level of difference of tone that adjacent pixels will still be selected at. At its lowest setting (1) if the adjacent pixels are not within one tone unit (black is 0, white is 255) it will only select the single pixel. If the tolerance is set to 255, the maximum, then wherever you click on the image, all adjacent pixels will fall within the tolerance, and the whole image area will be selected.

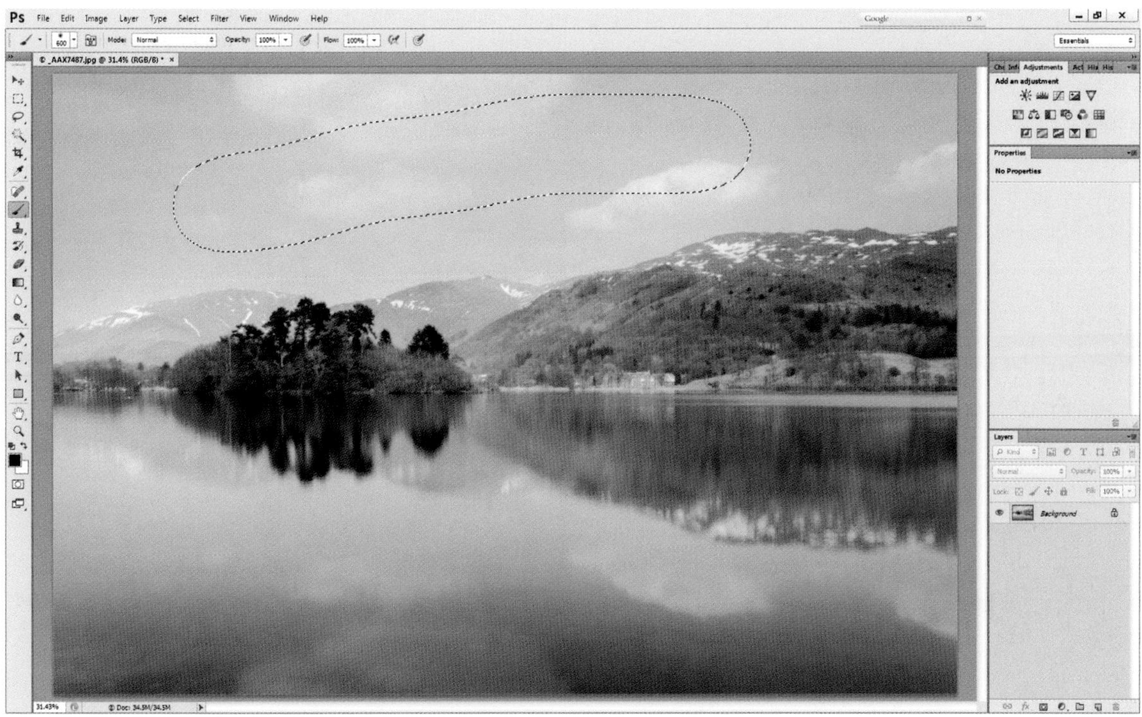

▲ Fig. 3.25
Exit quick mask showing regular selection indicated by marching ants.

only the length of the gradation from 100 per cent to 0 per cent/black to white/red to clear on the quick mask. A short line will give a very hard edge to the gradation, a long line will give a very soft edge to it. If you want the top half of the picture to be selected with a hard-ish gradation, start almost halfway down the picture, click, and drag a short line. Do not start at the top of the picture – it is not the area that the selection covers that you are drawing, it is the length of the gradation.

This seems to be one of the most difficult concepts to get across, as people on my workshops ask me again and again! Just go into quick mask (Q) and practice! Draw countless gradients across the picture – left to right, right to left, top to bottom, bottom to top, diagonally. (Make sure the blending mode of the gradient tool [G] is set to normal, or you'll get a surprise.)

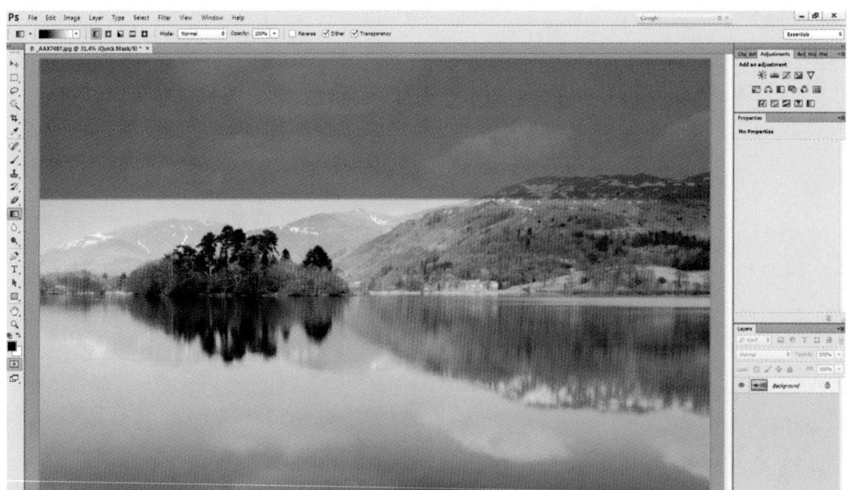

Fig. 3.26
Hard-edged grad (short gradation line) drawn vertically with a very short line to give a horizontal gradient.

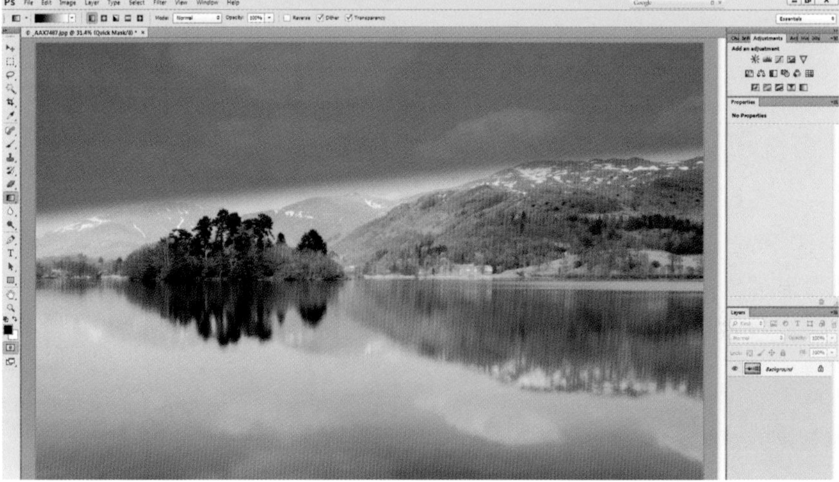

Fig. 3.27
Hard-edged grad (short gradation line) drawn angled to give an angled mask.

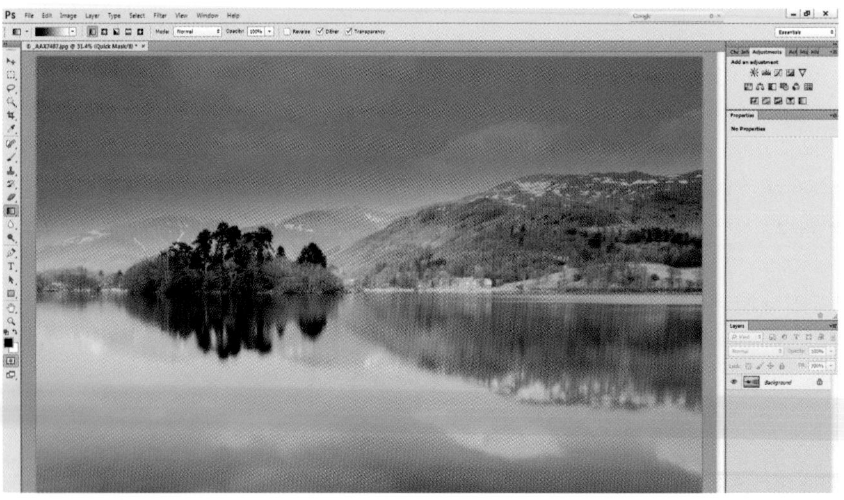

Fig. 3.28
Soft-edged grad (longer gradation line) drawn angled.

Chapter 4

Basic workflow

Knowing the tools in Photoshop is one thing, but applying them in a sensible and logical order that will enable a repeatable approach to each photograph, not simply by following a list of instructions, but by analysing the photograph and planning a logical work order is quite another. Start with the (optional) importation of the RAW file, or the simple opening of the JPEG, then move on to layers and selections to the final result.

OPENING RAW FILES

Lightroom is excellent for storing, cataloguing and cross-referencing files – so you can simply open files directly into Photoshop from Lightroom.

Opening a RAW file directly into Photoshop requires the use of a RAW converter – usually Adobe Camera RAW, within *Preferences>File handling*, one of the tick boxes we didn't alter was 'Prefer Adobe Camera RAW for supported RAW files'.

Either click on *File>Open*, or use the shortcut Ctrl-O, or simply double-click in the grey area in the middle of the screen and you get the open dialogue box. Select an appropriate file to open – with RAW files, all you see is the file logo – NEF for Nikon, CR2 for Canon, ORF for Olympus and so on. Not as helpful as it might be – though most people who don't use Lightroom use Adobe Bridge, which will allow you to view the file picture.

The Adobe Camera RAW box will appear with the picture within it.

As you see, all the sliders on the right of the panel are set to 0 as the Photoshop default. Many users like to do as much work in Camera RAW as possible. Remember that adjustments made on separate adjustment layers can be reviewed and re-edited, whereas adjustments to the RAW image cannot be altered apart from reopening the RAW file. For that reason, do relatively little work in Camera RAW – just making those changes that either cannot easily be made in Photoshop or that will make it easier to use Photoshop.

In this example, the shadows in the copse of trees look a touch heavy – so by moving the 'shadow' slider to the right, it lifts the brightness of the shadow areas in the photo. The clarity slider is unique to Camera RAW, and may best be described as 'micro -contrast'. Whereas simple 'contrast' lightens anything brighter than mid-grey, anything darker than mid-grey will become darker; clarity will – in this example – increase the contrast within the light sky area, whilst simultaneously increasing the contrast across the mid-toned grasses and even the darker copse of trees. As there is no equivalent filter within Photoshop, you could add a fair bit of clarity, as the original file was taken under pretty hazy conditions and just needed picking up a bit.

Camera RAW, with added clarity and boosted shadows.

That gets the file open, and into Photoshop, as a 16-bit ProPhoto RGB file with the basics done.

The next thing to do – and you should do this with every picture – is look closely at the photo. So many people don't, and just press on with 'processing'. In darkroom days, this is the time you would draw a printing plan – detailing the areas that would need lightening, and those that would

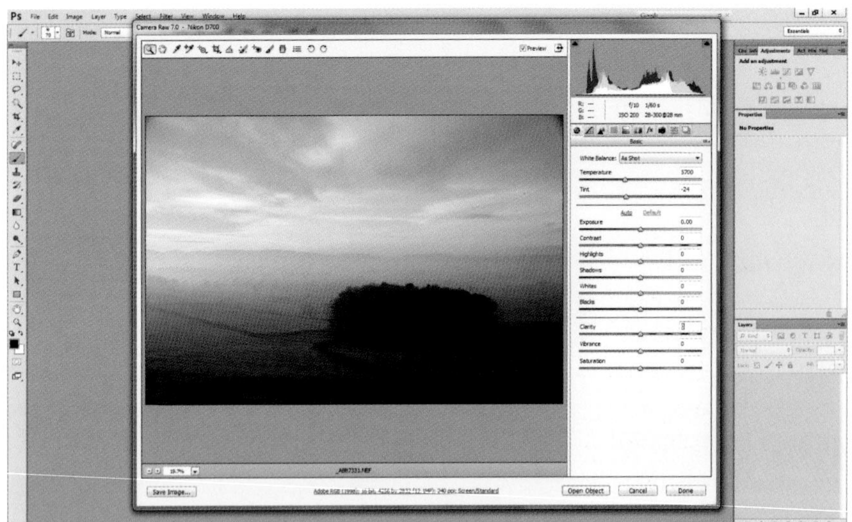

Fig. 4.1
Adobe Camera RAW with all sliders set to 0 (default) showing unadjusted RAW file.

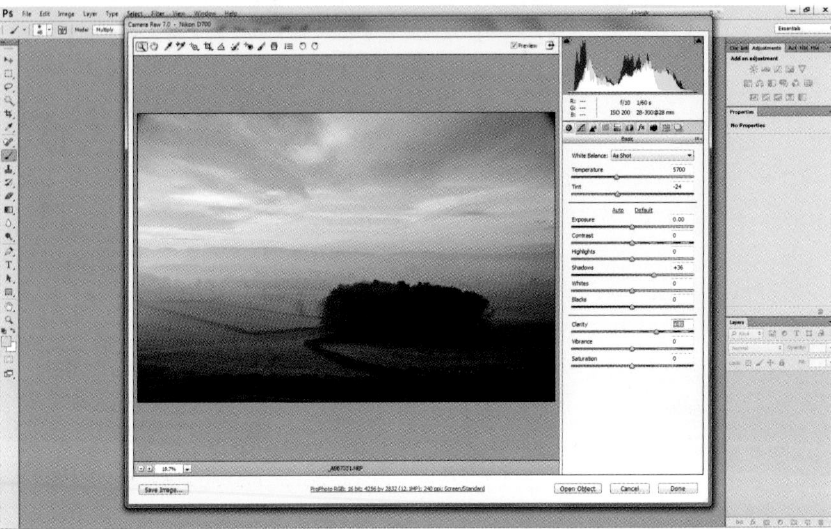

Fig. 4.2
Adobe Camera RAW converter with alterations made to *shadows* and *clarity* in order to improve shadow detail and improve the textures (clarity) in the image.

need darkening. Digitally, it's no different; look at the picture in a similar way, but also mentally consider areas that might need contrast enhancement as well (which was never possible printing colour in the darkroom).

Firstly, look for those little bits that most people overlook that need 'tidying up' – not major cloning, removing trees, adding sheep, or anything to change the nature of the photograph. No more than blemishes and the odd thing that we have no control over.

In the usual viewing mode, or by pressing Ctrl-0, the entire image fills the central area of the Photoshop screen, offering you as large a picture area as possible whilst still seeing the whole image. A typical high definition computer screen however has a resolution of 1920 × 1080 pixels (normal HD). The camera used for this picture (D700) has a resolution of 4256 × 2832 pixels, so to show them on a part of the 1920 × 1080 screen (remember the palettes, borders and so on that take up the outside of the screen) the picture has to be shown in a reduced size – in this case, the image is shown 31.4 per cent of its actual pixel size, meaning that each pixel on the screen is showing about 3 pixels in each direction of the actual picture.

By pressing Ctrl-1, zoom into 100 per cent magnification of the image – actual pixel size, where one pixel on the screen represents one pixel on the image. Almost always this will involve only seeing a very small part of the image on the screen at any one time. It does, however, show the sharpest possible image and reveal the greatest detail on the screen. You can navigate around the picture either by selecting the hand tool (H) or by simply holding the space bar down; the hand tool is temporarily invoked, enabling you to navigate around the screen, and by releasing the spacebar, you immediately return to your previously selected tool.

On this image there are a couple of sensor spots (never easy to keep 100 per cent clean) and a whole heap of tiny vapour trails in the sky to spoil the tranquillity. Getting rid of the spots is a necessity, the vapour trails is personal preference.

There are a number of ways all of this can be dealt with.

Content-aware fill often works faultlessly, sometimes gets it tragically wrong. Tracing a ring around the spot with a lasso tool (or making a selection around it any other way) will leave a ring of marching ants. Hit the delete key and a small dialogue box appears.

The dialogue box should have *'Content-aware'* under *'Contents>use'*. Hit enter and the spot will go, cloned effectively by sampling areas around the spot and interpolating brightness. The only thing questionable about content-aware fill is that it works directly on the background layer, and it's often preferable to keep the background layer untouched.

An alternative way is to add a transparent (new)

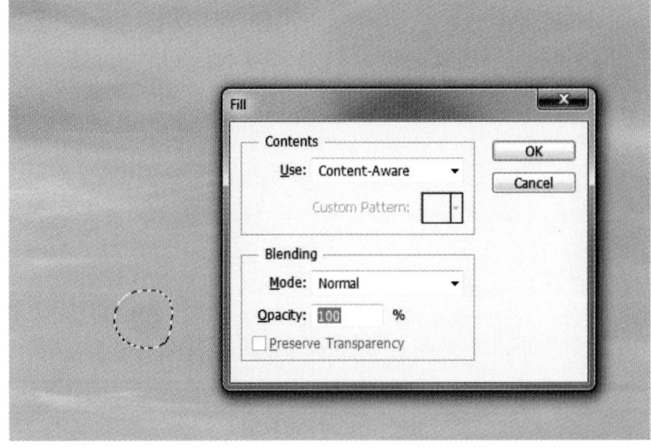

▲ Fig. 4.3
Fill dialogue box set to use Content-aware fill, showing blending mode set to normal and 100% opacity (default settings).

layer – it adds nothing to the file size and the best analogy is that it's like laying a clear gel over an overhead projection slide. You can write on it, mark it, and it has no effect on the background layer. Using the spot healing brush tool (J) – make sure the right tool is selected, there are five options under the healing brush – Shift-J will let you scroll through the options. Make sure on the tool options at the top of the screen that the box to 'sample all layers' is ticked, and simply adjust the tool's size (by using the square brackets) – the left bracket ([) makes the tool smaller, the right bracket (]) makes the tool larger – and simply click over the spot. On a subject like a dust spot, there will be no perceptible difference between content-aware fill or a healing brush. The covering to the spot sits on a separate layer (Layer 1) and you retain the ability to change or delete the repair right up until you flatten the image. It would be easy to remove the four vapour trails just below and to the left of the blue sky. Select them using a small brush in quick mask; on exiting quick mask, they simply become a marching ants selection, and with the background layer active, *Delete>Enter* performs a content-aware fill on the trails perfectly.

It's important to perform cloning/repairs/

▲ Fig. 4.4
Vapour trails visible within the sky.

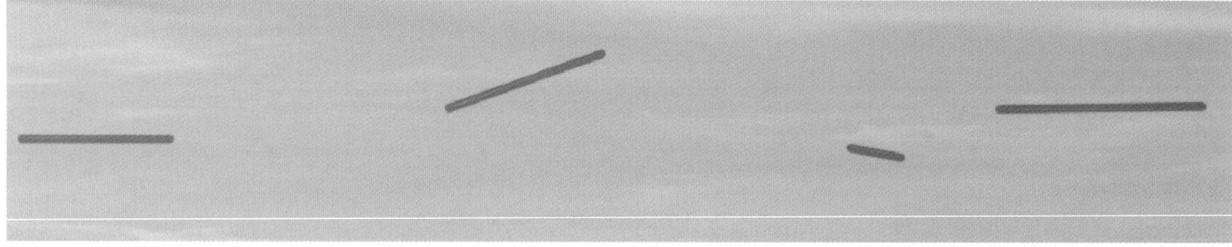

▲ Fig. 4.5
Quick mask/brush tool used to select trails quickly and easily.

▲ Fig. 4.6
Repaired sky showing no visible vapour trails.

content-aware fill at pixel size on the screen (100 per cent) as it lets you see as sharply as possible that your work is accurate.

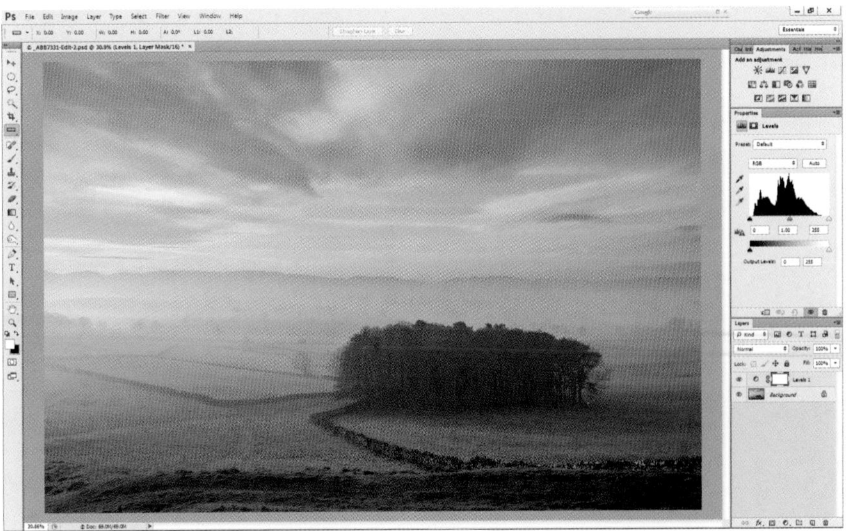

Fig. 4.7
Levels layer added above the background layer, no adjustment made yet.

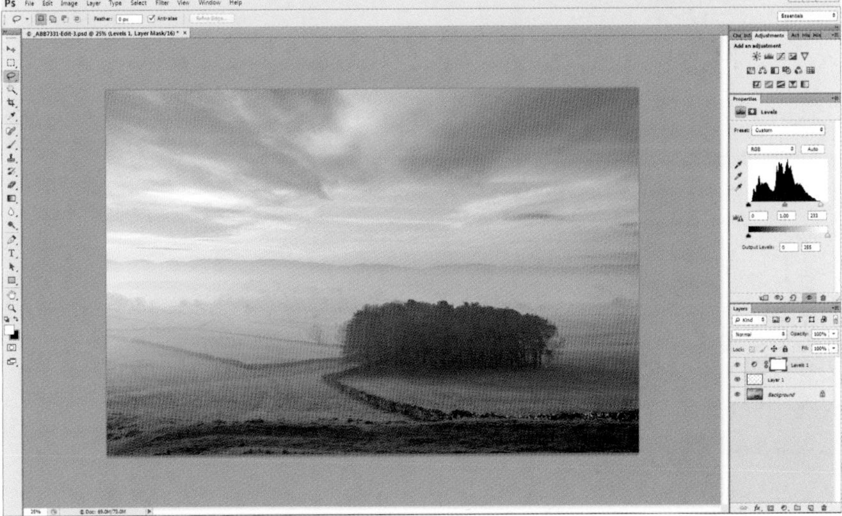

Fig. 4.8
Highlights adjusted by moving the highlight slider from the right-hand end (value 255) to closer to the right end of the histogram (value 233) lightening the white values in the picture.

ADJUSTING THE PICTURE

Initially, take a good look at the histogram and the overall contrast range to see if a general levels layer is necessary.

By adding a levels layer you can see that the histogram falls short of the ends of the graph, suggesting that the image could take more contrast. (Effectively, the blacks could be darker, and the whites, whiter.)

On this image, it would be good to pull out a little more from the woodland so don't change the dark tones yet, but instead just slightly brighten the highlights. On this image, the early morning tones are possibly slightly too warm. That can be adjusted at the same time.

Firstly, slide the highlight slider to the left just to the edge of the histogram (Fig 4.8) – do not slide

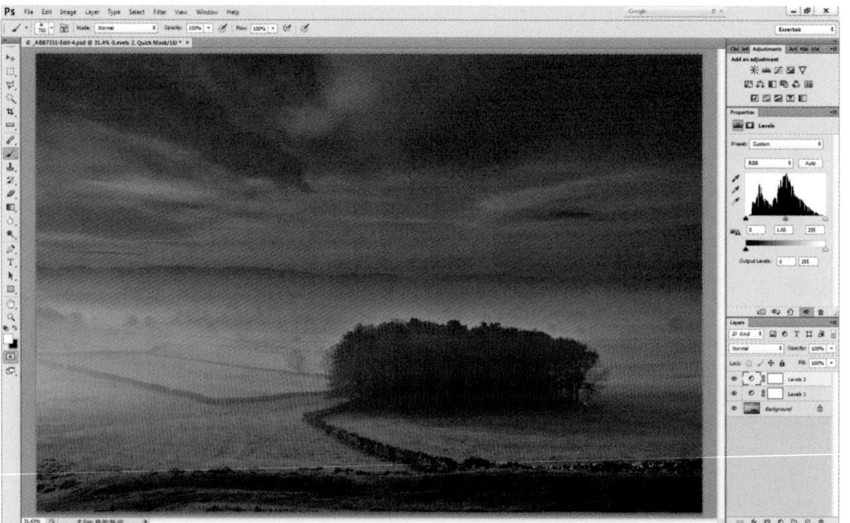

Fig. 4.9
Grey adjustment, set by using the mid-tone pipette to the left of the levels histogram, and clicking on a neutral grey tone within the image to set the white balance

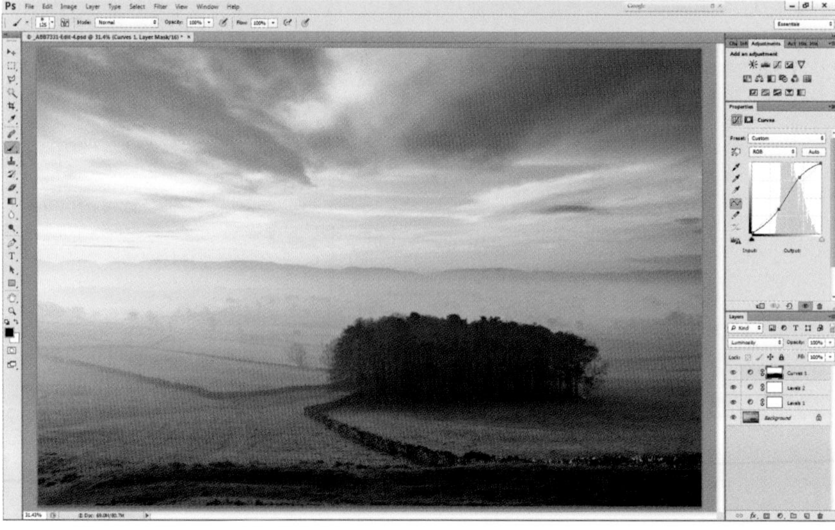

Fig. 4.10
Quick mask over sky by using the gradient tool (G) within quick mask (Q) to select the sky, with a soft edge at the horizon.

further than the end of the histogram, or you'll clip highlight details. A good way of checking this is to hold down the Alt key as you move the highlight slider towards the histogram – as you depress the Alt key, the whole screen goes black, but as you pass the end of the histogram, those parts of the image that are being clipped show as bright tones. Just back the slider off until the screen is black, and you will have brightened the image as far as possible, whilst still retaining full highlight detail.

The next stage is to correct the tones, which is a simple click if the picture has a neutral grey. Just to the left of the levels histogram are three pipettes – the top one black, the bottom white and the centre one grey. The top and bottom ones allow you to set a black or white point in the image (similar to moving in the end of the highlight/shadow sliders). The centre pipette allows you to select any point on the picture that should be a mid-grey. Click on the grey pipette and select part of the image that you

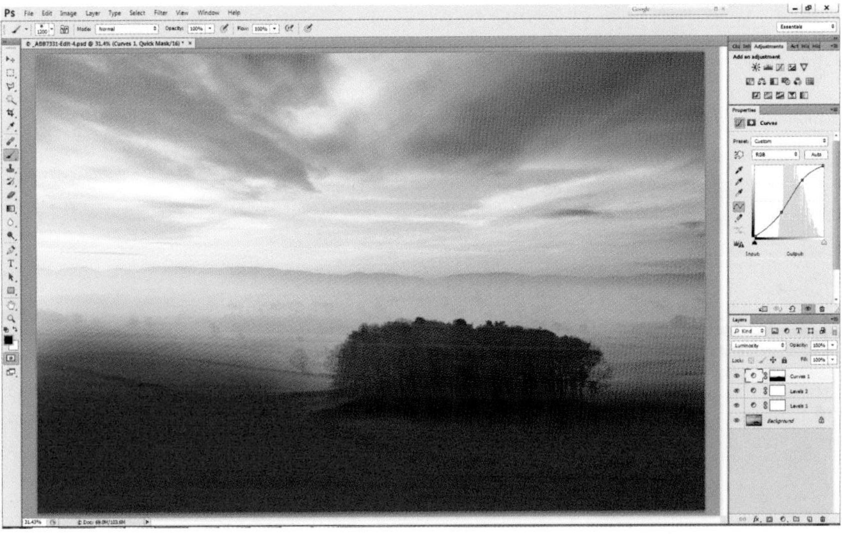

Fig. 4.11
Curves layer added to sky (AFTER exiting quick mask), increasing contrast to the sky tones.

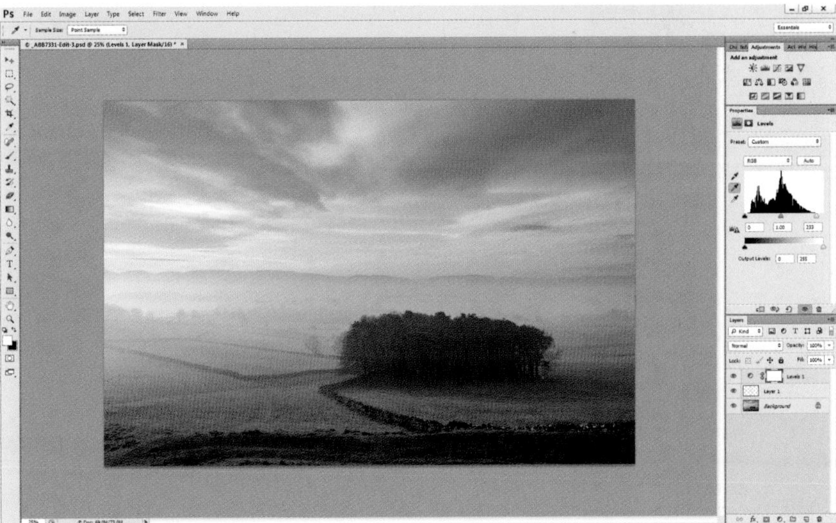

Fig. 4.12
Quick mask gradient selection added to foreground grass.

see as a mid-grey – in this case, the distant hills on the extreme right of the picture. Click on that, and the colours right across the picture will change (Figure 4.9). If you clicked on a spot that changed the colours too far Ctrl-Z will undo the last action, and try again. Go on until you're happy with the result.

A sensible next step would be to add a touch more contrast to the sky – without adding any extra saturation. A quick mask (Q) and gradient tool (G) can select a good chunk of the sky, perhaps using a large white brush (B) (very soft edge) to exclude the area around the copse.

Exit quick mask (Q) to leave a selection, add a curves layer and add a touch more contrast to the sky – if you look at the histogram on the curves chart, you'll see that by steepening it across the histogram that relates to the sky brightness, the contrast in the sky increases, making it stand out more in the picture.

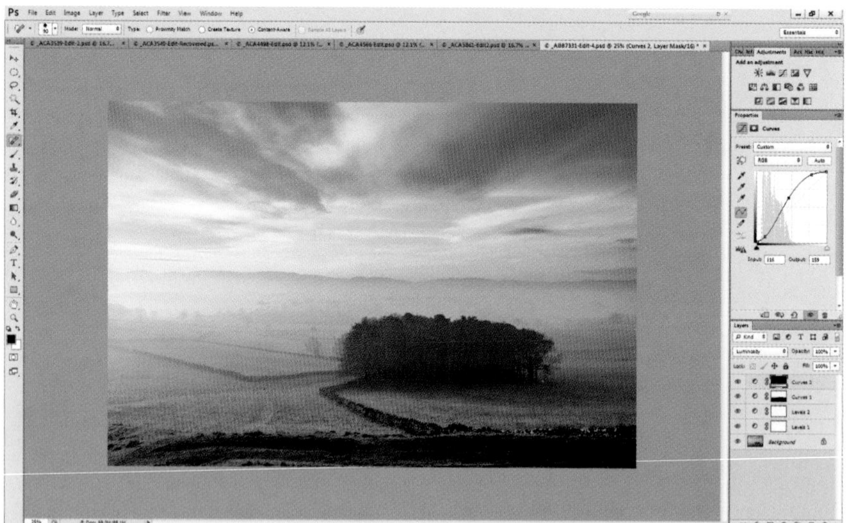

Fig. 4.13
Curves layer added to grasses to brighten the ground and emphasize the feel of frost on the surface, and to increase contrast.

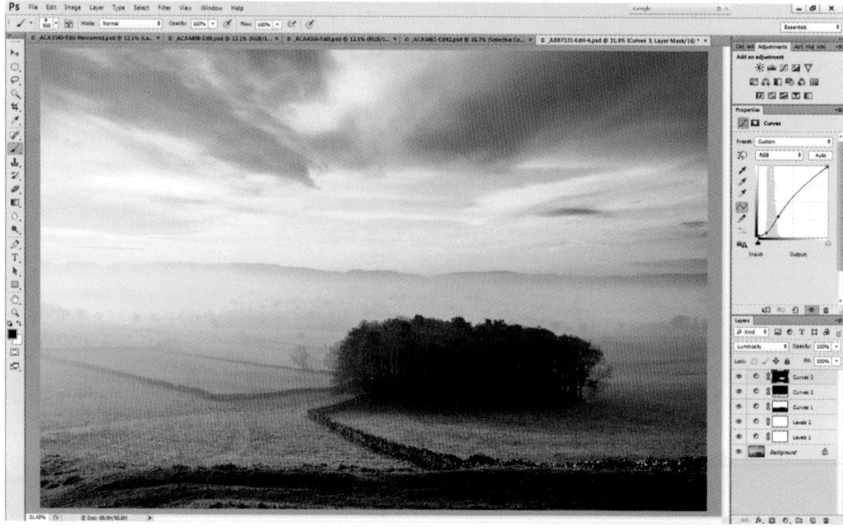

Fig. 4.14
Curves layer added to copse to lighten the tones of the trees and increase the separation of tones therein.

Next, select the ground (excluding the copse), in a similar manner.

And again using curves, add a little localized contrast to this area – how you change the contrast is up to personal interpretation. In this case, by steepening the curve through the histogram, but keeping the darker tones unchanged, the feeling of frost on the ground has been emphasized.

Next, select the trees in a similar manner, using quick mask (Q) and a brush tool (B) – black brush – to select the area with a very soft edge. Without blocking the shadow details too much in the dark areas, give the copse a touch more 'bite' by adding (another) curves layer and carefully increasing the steepness of the curve. Remember, with all these adjustments it's important to make the changes subtly, so they are imperceptible to the viewer.

Equally important at every stage is to stand back and look at the photograph, to see if the balance of the picture remains in harmony, or if it has become

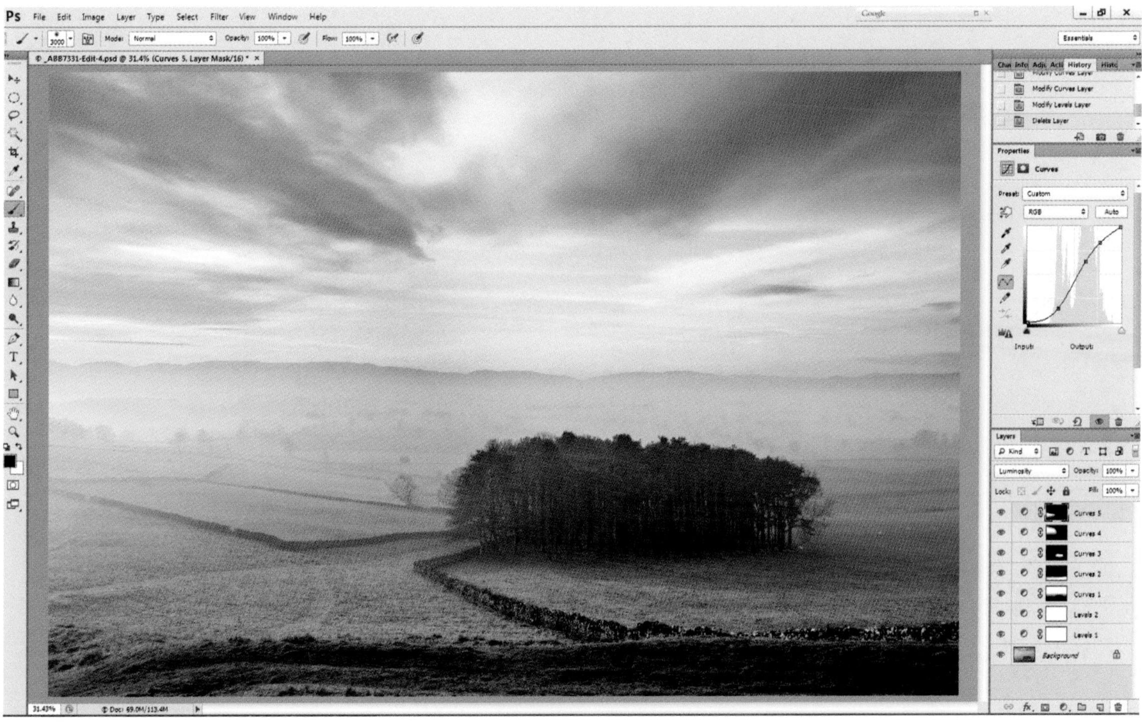

▲ Fig. 4.15
Changes to the sky and land (Curves layers 4 and 5) to the left of the picture, layer 4 to increase definition within the clouds by increasing contrast slightly without unduly lightening the tones, layer 5 on the ground to again increase depth and separation, but lightening the tones slightly to emphasize the early-morning feel.

imbalanced. In this instance, the left-hand edge is looking a little over-bright, so further work is needed there. A selection of the left side (you can use a gradient tool, or a very large brush, or a combination of the two; maybe by taking a gradient of the left side of the image, then removing part of the selection by using a white brush), possibly taken in two selections – the sky and the land. Add separate curves layers to these and work them individually. The sky selection can take some darkening, just to bring those bright areas of sky down to a similar tonality to the rest of the sky and stop the viewer's eye from being drawn to the light areas at the corner of the print. Try changing the blending mode to luminosity to avoid increasing the saturation in those areas as well.

The ground area needs a touch more contrast – focused on the tones of the walls, to make them stand out more from the field; the adjustment can be almost imperceptible, but all these little stages make a huge difference to the final picture.

The left-hand side of the photo now balances the rest, but the strong yellow tones still present might not be to everyone's taste. Using the brush tool in quick mask (Q) make a very soft-edged selection of the predominantly yellow areas. As the larger soft-edged brushes give a softer edge than the smaller brush sizes, try using a brush diameter of about 2,000 pixels. Remember, the brush size can be adjusted using the square brackets, and the brush hardness by using Shift>square brackets. .

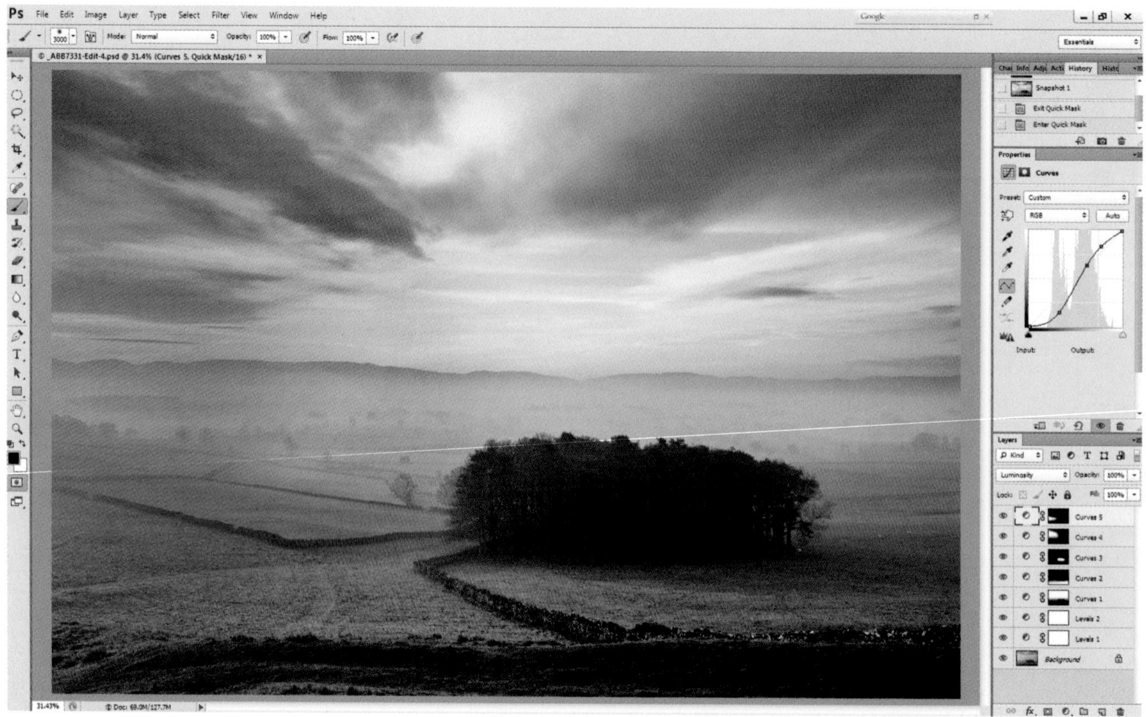

Fig. 4.16
Selection of yellow areas of sky and land with quick mask/brush tool, using a very soft-edged and large brush (3000 pixels wide).

Exit quick mask (Q) and based on this selection, add a vibrancy layer. Try reducing the vibrancy until the vivid yellow becomes more in keeping with the frosty, misty feel of the morning. This example took it down to 40 (Figure 4.17). Vibrance is better for this type of adjustment than hue and saturation, as it preserves the saturation of the less dominant tones, just subduing the brighter colours. For those on Elements rather than Photoshop, you don't have the advantage of the vibrance layer, so might have to use a hue and saturation layer. If this is the case, select from the hue and saturation options; the 'master' drop-down menu allows you to select primary (red, green and blue) or secondary (cyan, magenta or yellow) colours. Choose yellow, and reduce the saturation – in this case, −25 seemed about right, but the adjustment is subjective – it's all a matter of personal taste, the important thing is not to overdo it at any stage and just to move things forward a bit at a time.

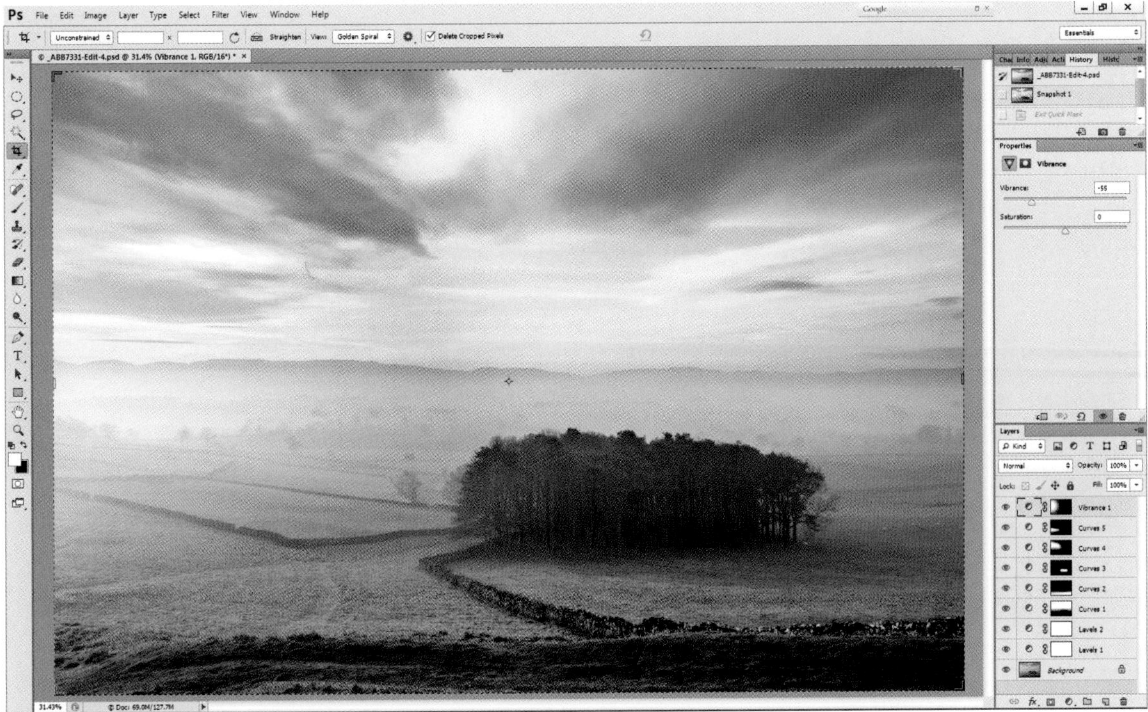

▲ Fig. 4.17
Vibrance reduced to the yellow tones on the left of the picture to portray the frosty cold feel across the image.

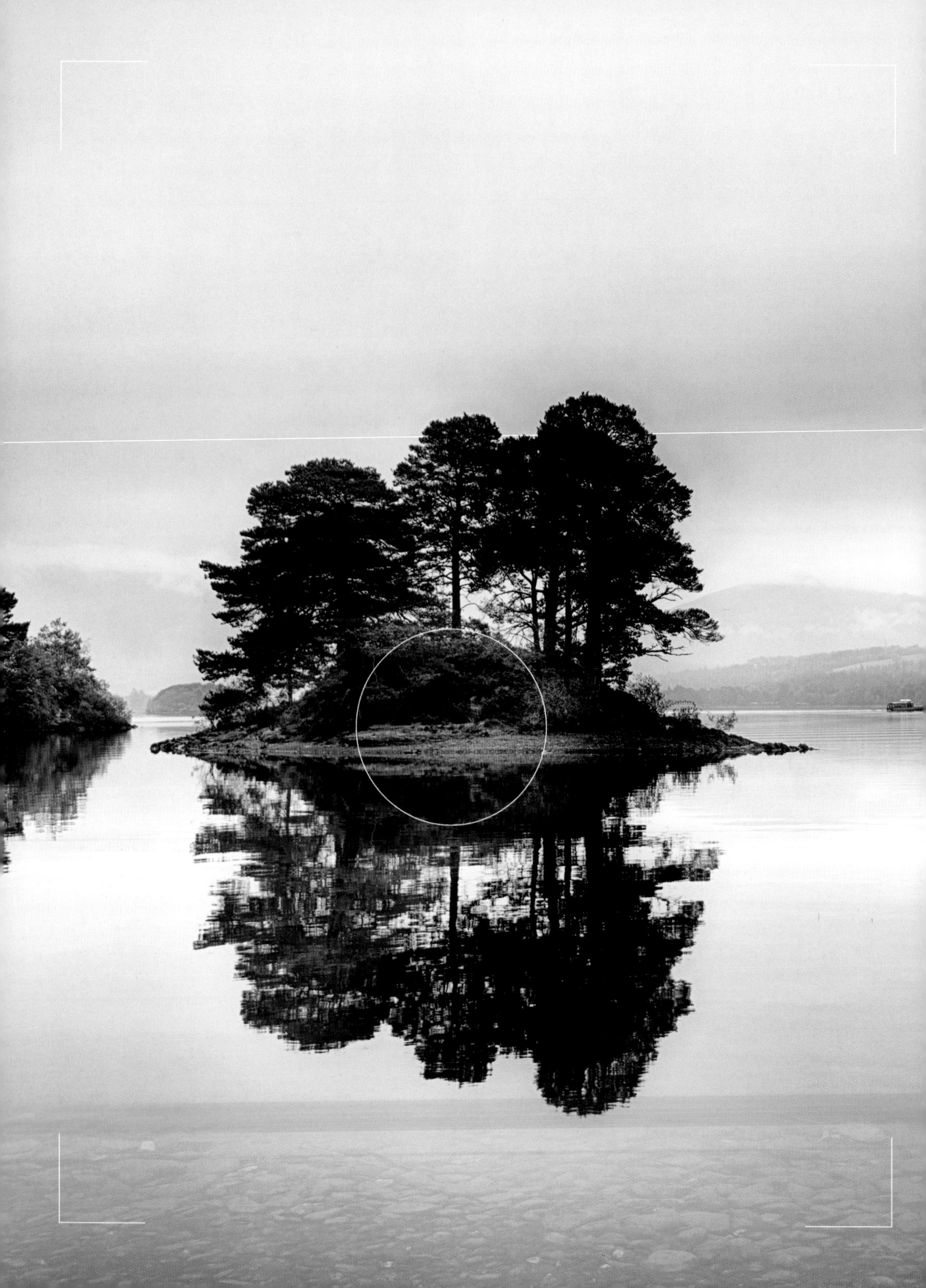

Chapter 5

Local adjustments

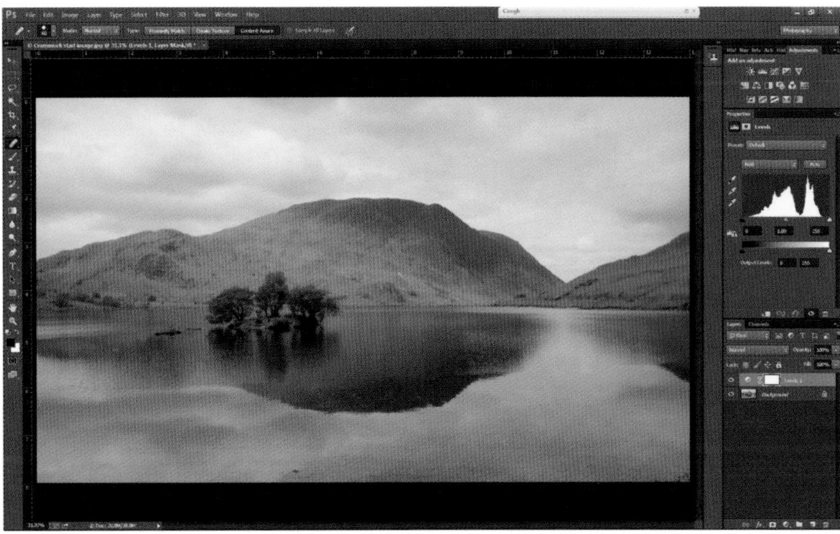

Fig. 5.1
Basic levels layer added above Background layer.

In this chapter we look at ways of working on selective parts of the picture, possibly to darken an over-bright sky and make it more dramatic, or to lighten dark patches within an image that don't quite have enough detail.

USING THE LEVELS ADJUSTMENT LAYER

Add a levels layer (as described above) to a fairly low-contrast image, like the one here.

The histogram that you see in the properties window falls short of each end of the available axis, therefore there is no real black, nor any pure white – the photo generally looks flat, and low in contrast. Surprisingly, this is not a bad thing, and gives us a spread of data that we can really work with. A good standard workflow might almost always start with a basic levels layer.

Starting at the left side of the histogram, grab the small black triangle (known as the shadow slider) with the cursor, and slide it to the right until it reaches the edge of the histogram, but be careful not to go too far, or you will lose all shadow detail. A good way of checking this is – as you move the shadow slider – hold down the Alt key – the whole image will go white, until you reach the edge of the histogram, when the clipped areas will show. It's important not to clip the shadows – so back it off a little. (Figure 5.2)

Now do the same with the highlight slider; in this case, holding down the Alt key makes the screen go black, clipped areas show as white, with clipped channels showing as yellow/green/red and so on. Do be careful to avoid clipped details – you take great care in the field ensuring that detail is kept by

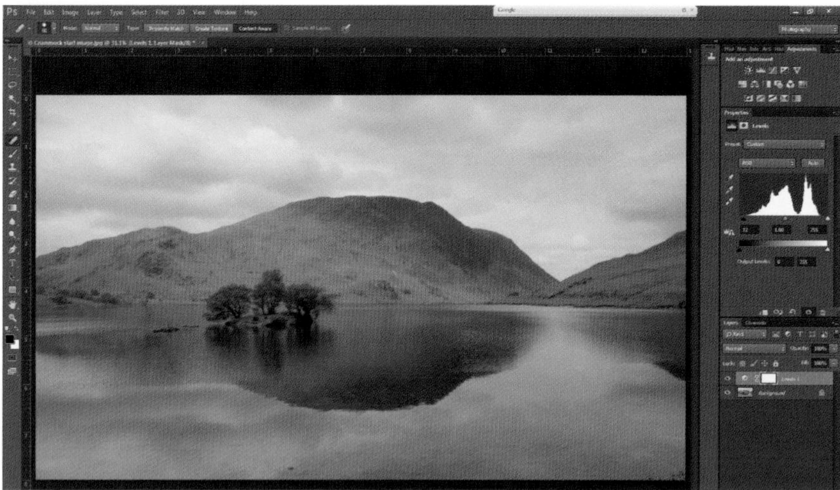

Fig. 5.2
Shadow slider moved into the end of the left side of the histogram.

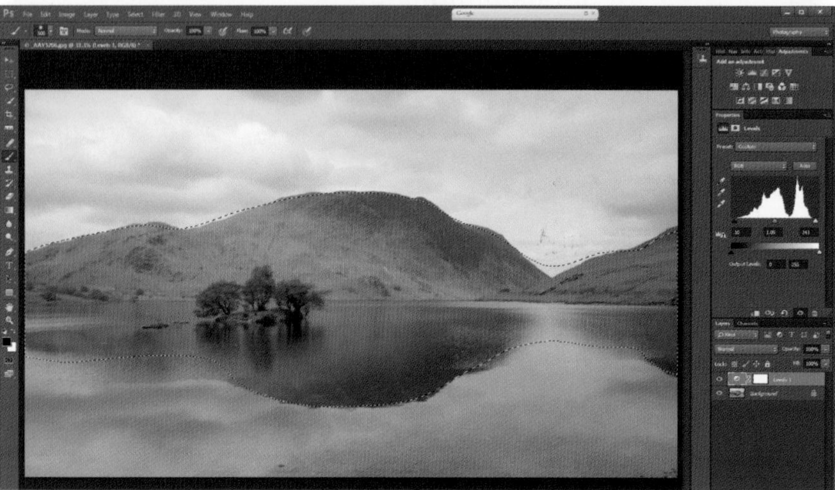

Fig. 5.3
Highlight slider moved into the end of the right side of the histogram.

careful exposure, don't mess it up in processing. These adjustments have ensured that you have a range of tones from black through white across the image, rather than a set of dreary greys. (Figure 5.3)

SELECTING WITH QUICK MASK

Rather than trying to increase the contrast on the whole picture, treat each area separately, in this instance the sky, the land and the water. As the land itself looks pretty flat and dull, try a selection of the land (and its corresponding reflection) using quick mask (Q) in conjunction with a brush tool. With quick mask selected and using a large, soft brush, with the foreground colour set to black, paint over the land until it has turned red. Exit quick mask (Q) to leave you with a selection.

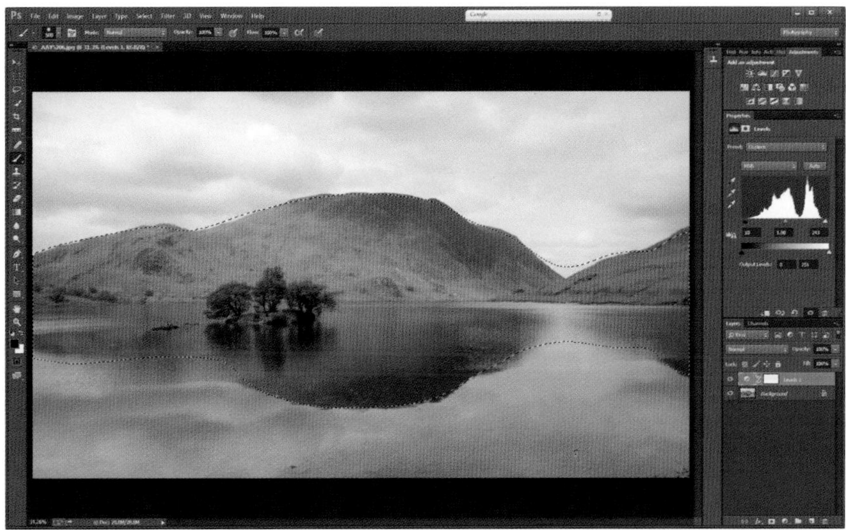

Fig. 5.4
The selection in place over the land – with a soft edge to the selected area.

USING CURVES TO INCREASE CONTRAST

Example 1

With this selection in place, add a curves layer, and steepen the 'curve' to increase contrast over the unmasked area (the white area [land] on the layer mask). In this instance you might find the slight increase in saturation caused by leaving the blending mode at 'normal' benefits this picture.

Whilst the increase of contrast over the land as a whole improves the feel of the picture, the island in the foreground seems to have lost detail within the shadow areas, where the increase in contrast over the whole land area has 'overcooked' the island. The benefit of working on separate layers and corresponding layer masks is that this can be further modified.

Selecting a black brush and setting the opacity low (around 20–30 per cent) with a soft edge, will let you paint over the island, gradually building up the density – and by gradually erasing the effect of the curves layer, takes the island back to the lower-contrast original state, whilst still preserving a slight increase in contrast.

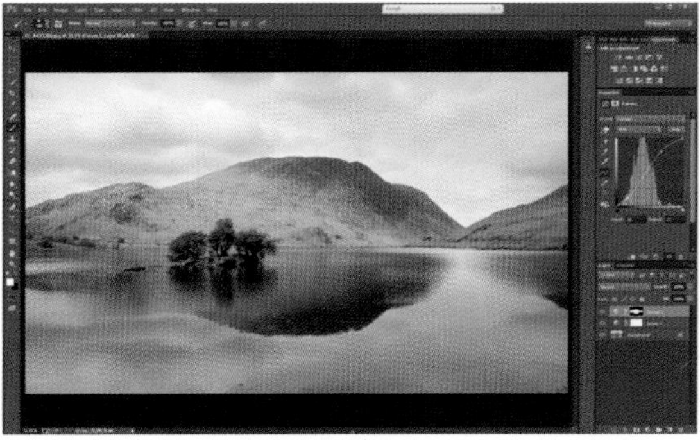

Fig. 5.5
Curves layer 1 added showing the layer mask in place to restrict adjustments to adjust the contrast of the land only.

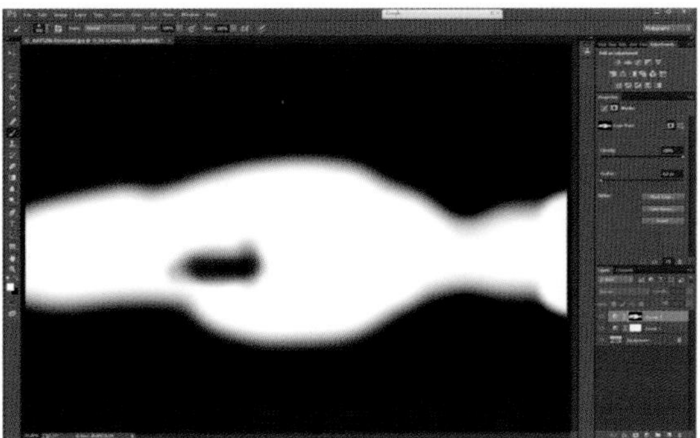

Fig. 5.6
The layer mask, showing the brush applied to the area of the island to prevent too much contrast from affecting the darker shadows within. (Layer masks can be viewed by holding down the Alt key and clicking with the mouse on the mask in the layers palette).

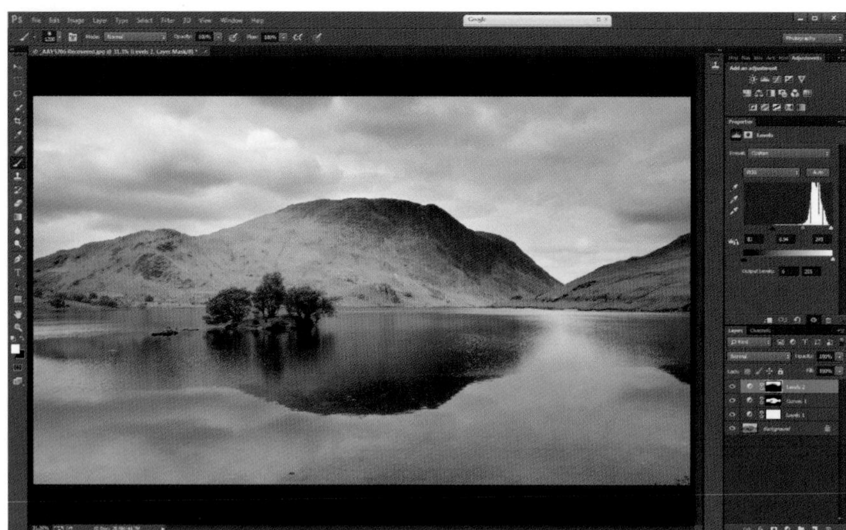

Fig. 5.7
Levels layer added to adjust the sky – the layer mask on the levels 2 layer indicates the area that will be affected by the adjustments.

The layer mask (Figure 5.6) shows the brush applied to the area of the island to prevent too much contrast from affecting the darker shadows within. (Layer masks can be viewed by holding down the Alt key and clicking with the mouse on the mask in the layers palette.)

Next, take the sky – again, select simply by using the quick mask and either a gradient tool or the brush tool set to a soft edge and a very large brush. Remember, after you have painted the selection mask, exit quick mask (Q) to give you a marching ant-bounded selection, before adding an adjustment layer.

Add a levels layer, and pull the shadow and highlight sliders up towards the edge of the histogram. This ensures the full range of tones through the sky (Figure 5.7) – make sure not to make it look too artificial, and consider changing the blending mode to luminosity, as the sky will not benefit from increased colour saturation. Remember, Photoshop is there to enhance photos, not to make them look unnatural. In this example, just the levels on the sky has not given quite as much contrast, so the selection from the levels layer can be reselected by positioning the cursor over the layer mask, holding down the Ctrl key and left-clicking the mouse. You will see the marching ants appear on the image corresponding with the clear (white) area of the mask. This is a very useful shortcut when using a range of layers incorporating the same mask on the image.

In this case – add a curves layer (Figure 5.8) (you will see the layer mask attached is identical to that of the levels layer below), and increase the steepness of the curve through the area of the histogram, by adding two points at the appropriate points on the curve.

Finally, the sky still looks paler and less dramatic than its reflection in the lake – select just the sky area, which can be done by Ctrl-clicking on the levels 2 layer, which reselects the sky and the lake; hit Q to re-enter quick mask, and using a white brush of 100 per cent opacity, brush out the lake selection. 'Q' will exit quick mask, leaving a marching ants selection over the sky area only. Add another curves layer (curves 2) and by pulling down the left side of the curve, the sky will darken and contrast will increase. Remember: to prevent colour changes, alter the blending mode of this layer to luminosity.

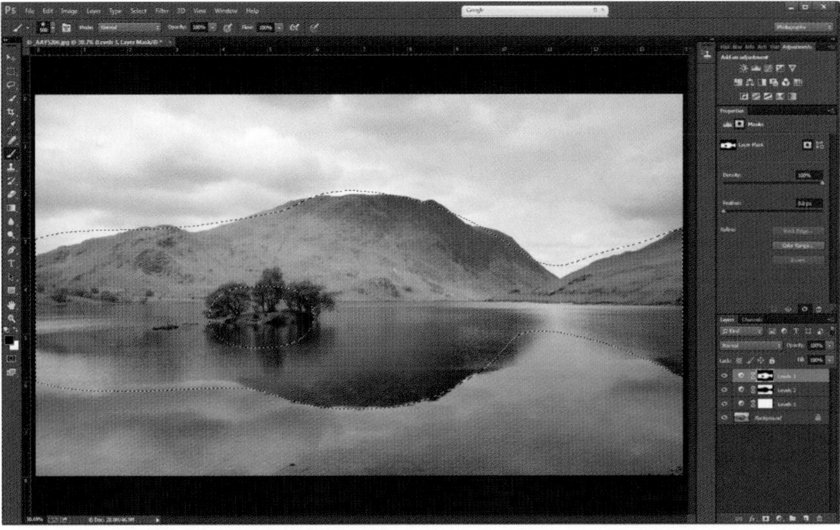

Fig. 5.8
Marching ant selection of the levels layer mask – achieved by holding the Alt key and left-clicking the mouse on the levels 3 layer mask.

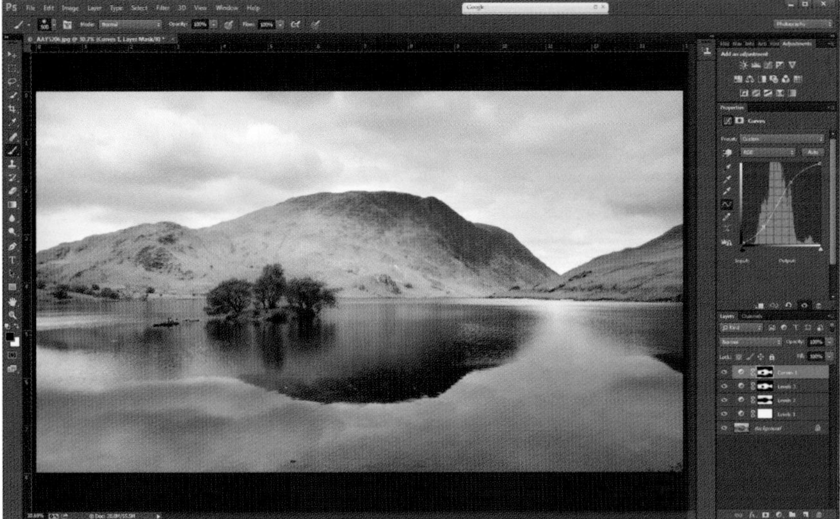

Fig. 5.9
Curves 1 layer created from the selection in the previous picture – curves layer adjusted by increasing the steepness of the curve over the width of the histogram.

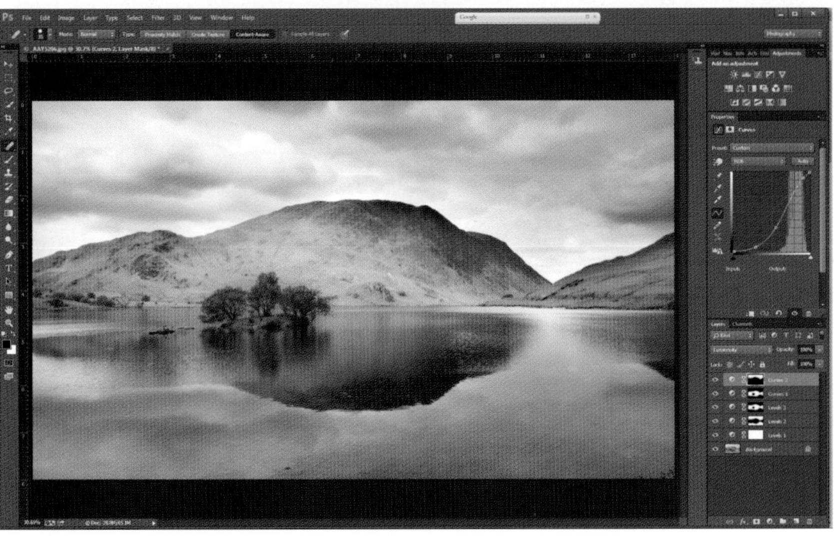

Fig. 5.10
Curves 2 layer.

Example 2

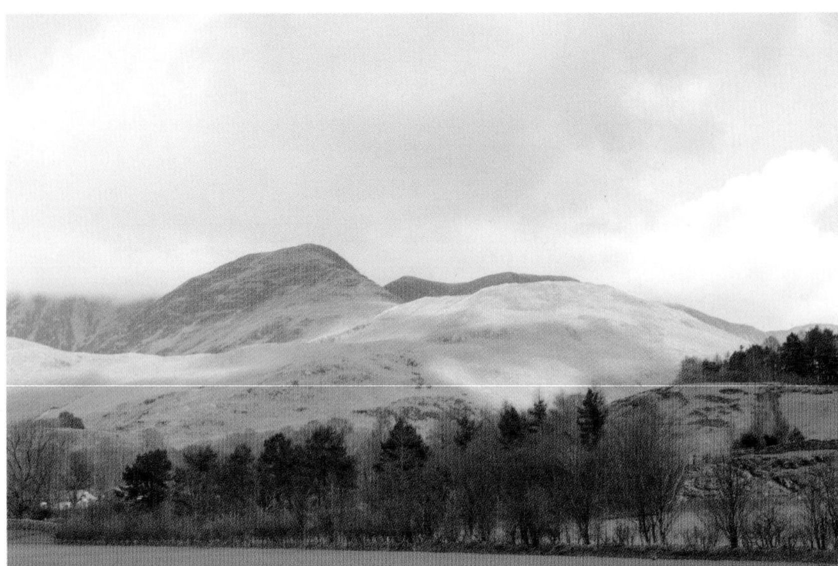

Fig. 5.11
A straight RAW file of the fells above Buttermere.

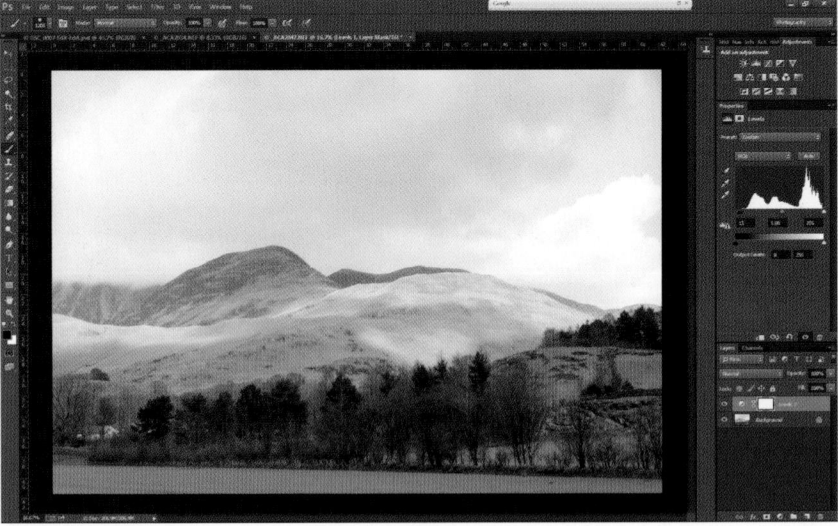

Fig. 5.12
A basic levels adjustment to give a full range of tones through the histogram. Figs 5.13 to 5.19 show the various stages of local adjustments that process the image to completion.

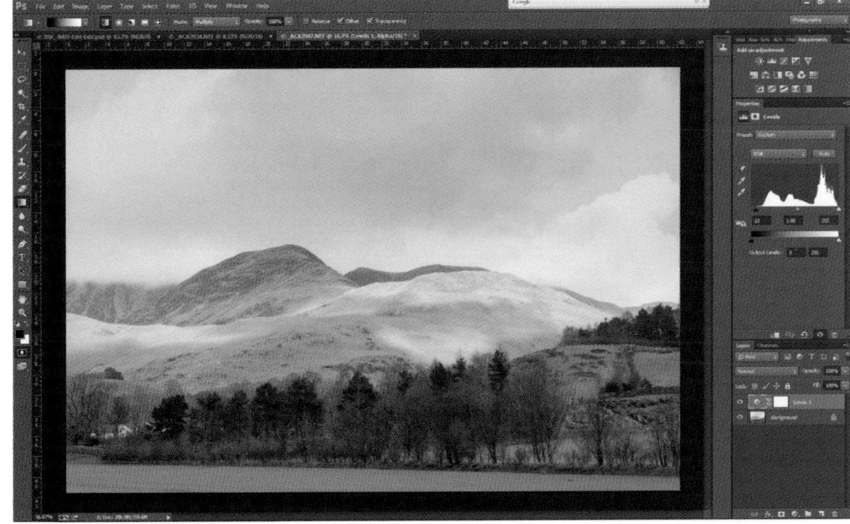

Fig. 5.13
A selection mask over the sky using the gradient tool (G) in conjunction with the quick mask (Q). By changing the blending mode of the gradient tool to *multiply*, gradients can be added together to form a concave gradient, in this case, over the central fell.

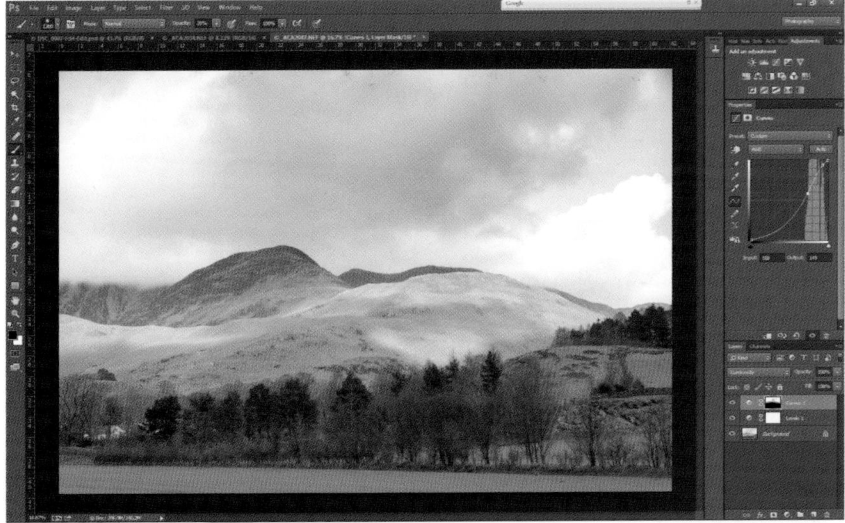

Fig. 5.14
A curves layer of the sky selection, with the curve line steepened through the area of the histogram to increase the contrast of the clouds generally. Adjustment layer blending mode altered from *Normal* to *Luminosity*, to avoid any change to the saturation of the colours.

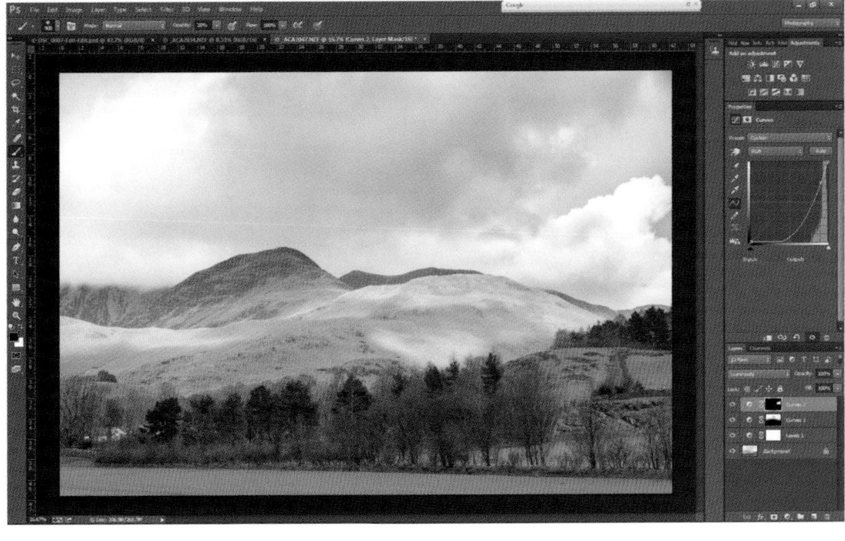

Fig. 5.15
A second curves layer (Curves 2) with a selection made with a very soft brush in Quick mask of the white cloud on the right of the picture. The Curves 3 layer has had the central part of the curve pulled down to darken the mid-tones within bright cloud and bring out the detail. Blending mode to *Luminosity*.

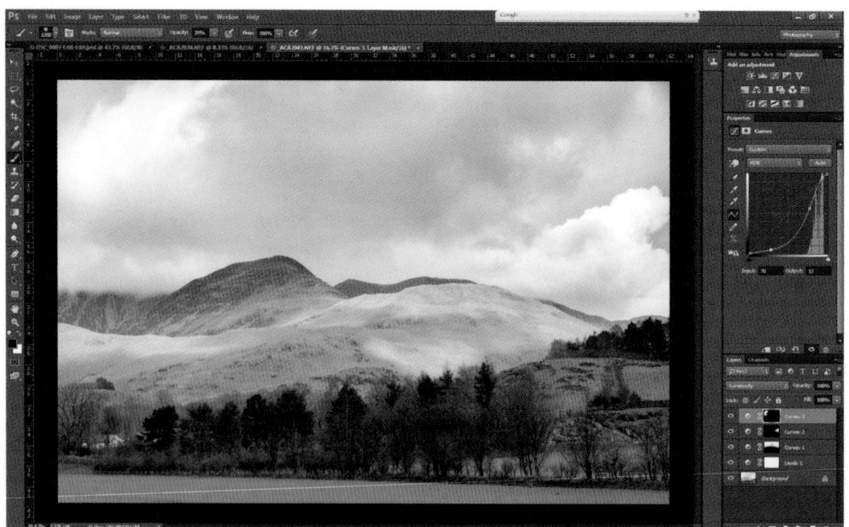

Fig. 5.16
A selection made in the same way as the last, but of the very flat left-hand cloud. Curves 3 adjustment layer created to increase the contrast through the cloud. Blending mode to *Luminosity*.

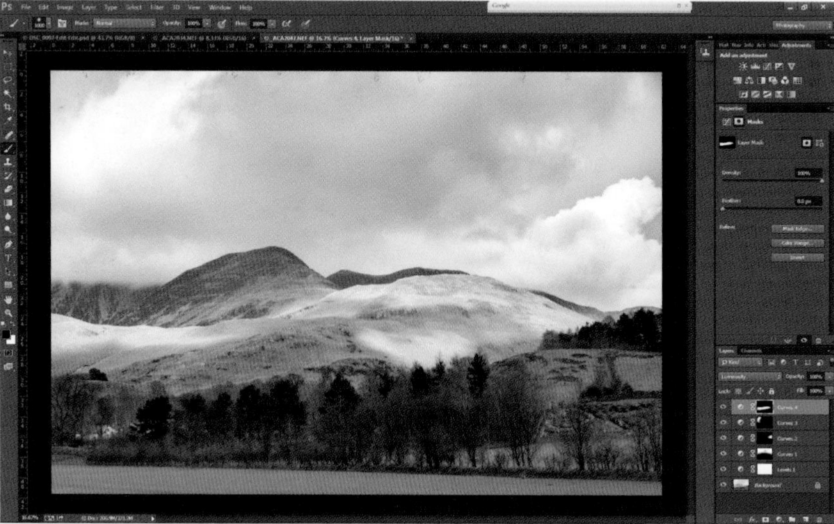

Fig. 5.17
Curves 4 adjustment layer, a selection of the central fells above the dark tree line. This selection was made using a large soft-edged brush (B) in quick mask (Q) to select a swathe through the centre of the picture, then tidied up over areas where it had overlapped into trees by painting over them with a white brush, which takes away from the mask. The selection created a curves layer, to add contrast locally to the hills.

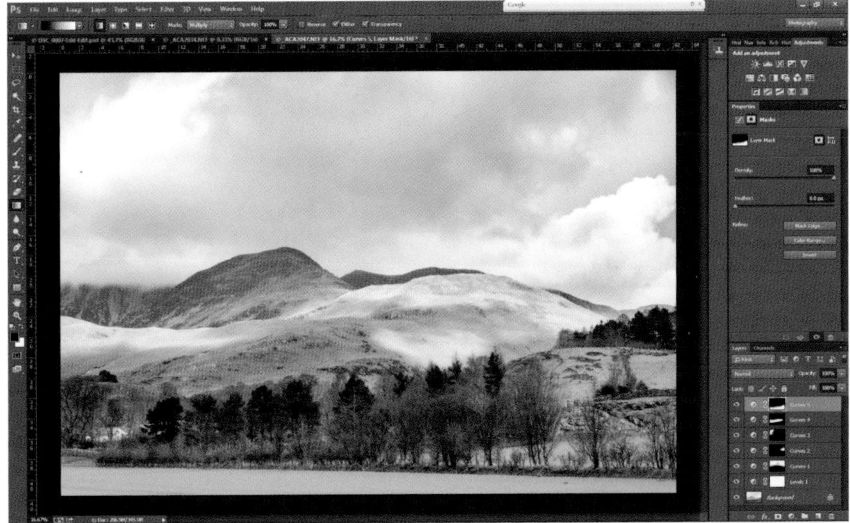

Fig. 5.18
Gradient tool (G) used in quick mask (Q) to select the base of the picture up to the tops of the dark trees. The gradient tool line was drawn at a slight angle to allow the gradient line to follow the trees perfectly. If it doesn't work at the first attempt, keep going until you are happy with the gradient. (although do ensure the gradient tool's blending mode is set to *Normal*, rather than *Multiply*, as it was earlier, or you will keep adding gradients to each other).

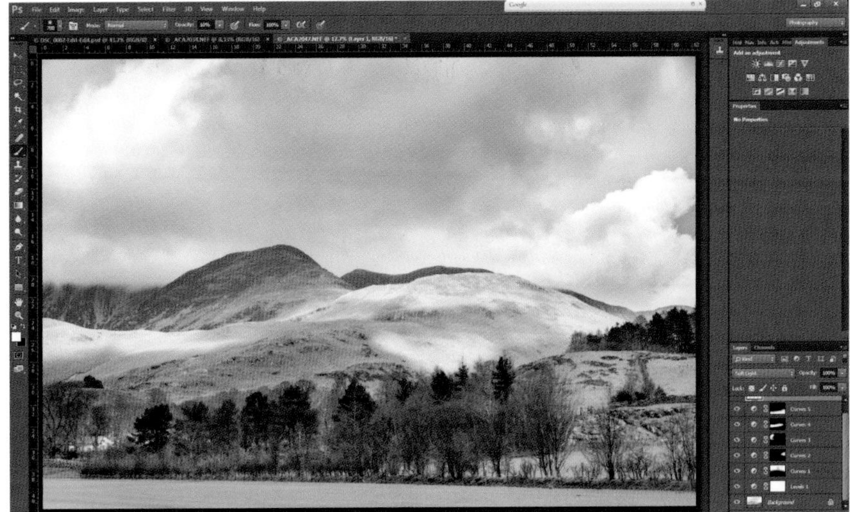

Fig. 5.19
A new layer added to the stack of layers, and the blending mode altered to soft light. Then using a soft-edged brush at a very low opacity, painting on that layer with black colour of 10 – 30% opacity darkens those areas, whereas painting with a white brush of low opacity lightens those areas. Perimeters of the light clouds in the sky have been slightly darkened, whereas a few of the darker foreground trees have been individually lightened.

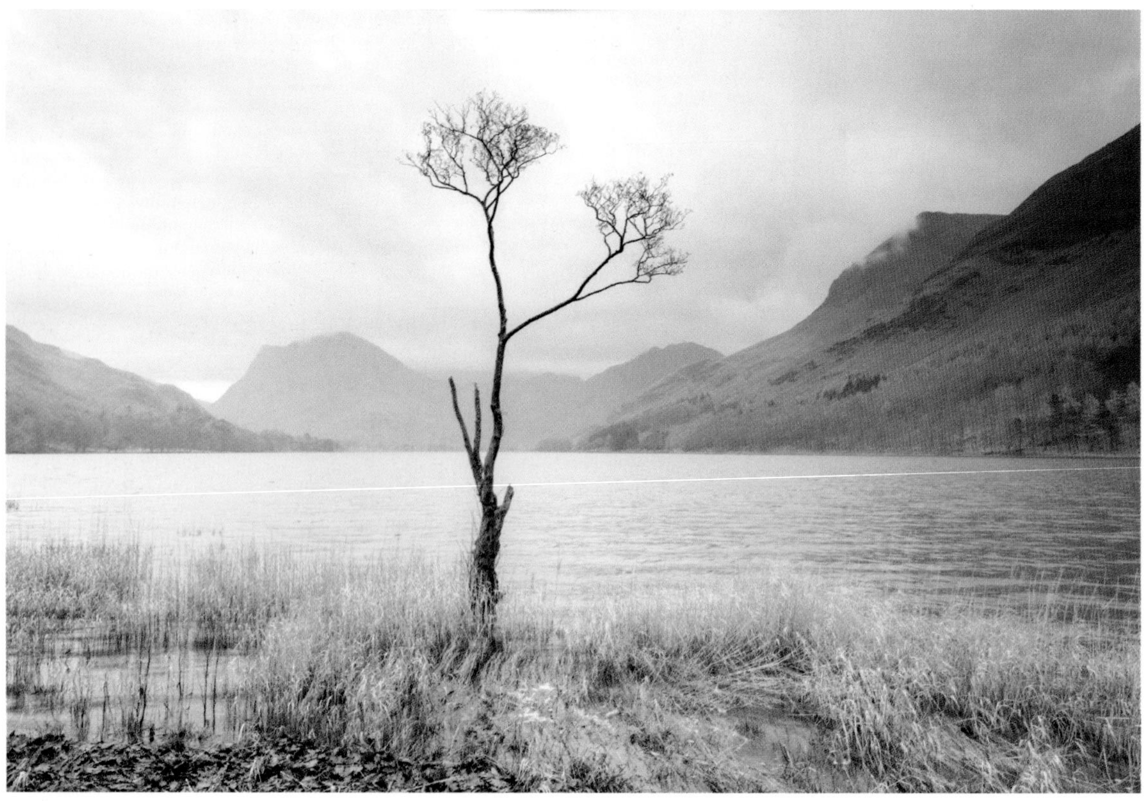

▲ Fig. 5.20
An image of Buttermere processed, but unsharpened. Fig. 5.21 shows a 100% area of the tree. Although the image is in sharp focus, shot with a decent lens and on a tripod, sharpening will just enhance the finest details in the picture.

IMAGE SHARPENING

An area within Photoshop that is so often overused, the term 'over-sharpened' is heard so often when looking at printed photographs, almost as much as comments like 'can a picture be too sharp?' It is important to realize that the sharpening of a digital image is different to making an 'unsharp' picture sharp. It serves to crisp up the image, as digital cameras and sensors blur an image to some degree and therefore need sharpening prior to displaying (whether digitally or as a print).

There are a number of useful sharpening tools within Photoshop; most of the sharpening tools can be found under *Filter>Sharpen*, although the obvious ones are not the best to use. Sharpen, sharpen more and sharpen edges are old filters designed to work with very small file sizes, and are not suited to today's large files. The most useful of the sharpening filters are unsharp mask and smart sharpen.

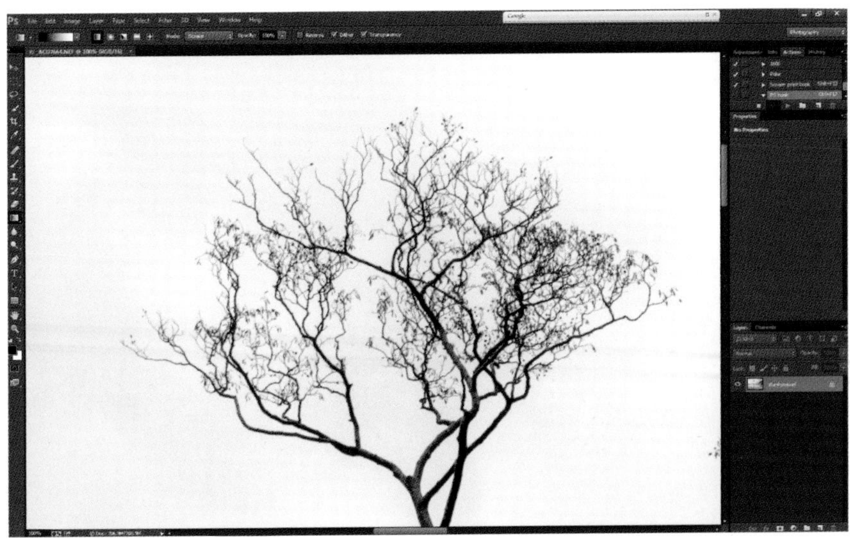

Fig. 5.21
100% (pixel view) area – unsharpened.

Unsharp mask

For many years the sharpening tool of choice, unsharp mask is a controllable sharpening tool. It is based around three adjustable sliders: amount; radius and threshold. To take them in reverse order:

Threshold

Adjustable from 0 to 255. When the filter is applied, threshold can determine how much of the image is sharpened. It effectively looks at adjacent pixels, and determines the difference in brightness between them and applies (or doesn't apply) sharpening to them. At a threshold of 0, the sharpening filter will be applied to every pixel; at a threshold of say, 10, if there are 10 or fewer units of brightness difference between adjacent pixels, no sharpening will take place on those pixels, but more than 10 units of brightness difference will be sharpened. This can be useful for areas of smooth tone, where sharpening might not enhance the image; skies, for example, rarely need sharpening. In fact sharpening a sky can create noise in the otherwise smooth tonal areas. If a threshold of 255 is selected, no sharpening will be applied at all. Typically a very low threshold should give the best results.

Radius

Adjustable from 0.0 to 1000.0 pixels. Affects the radius of sharpening around each pixel. High levels look awful – and are the main cause of over-sharpening. Ideal value of radius is 1.0.

Amount

As a percentage, from 1 per cent to 500 per cent. The amount of sharpening depends entirely on the file size; a large file will take more sharpening than a small file. A picture for the web of only 1,200 pixels wide might only need 20–30 per cent sharpening, whereas a 36Gb file from a modern DSLR might require over 100 per cent. The simplest way is to judge it by eye, then back the filter off a bit (as typically we push the filter slightly too far).

Figure 5.22 shows a 100 per cent enlargement of the same image with recommended levels of unsharp mask applied. Figure 5.23 shows unsharp mask with too high an amount, and too great a radius; the oversharpening is clear on the tree branches, which have now developed a glowing line around them.

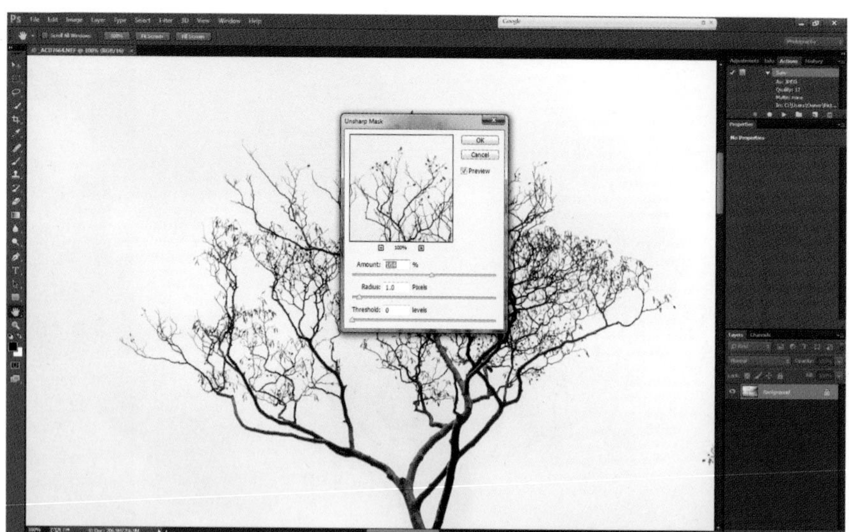

Fig. 5.22
Unsharp mask applied to image with sharpening set to 104%, at a radius of 1.0, and threshold of 0.

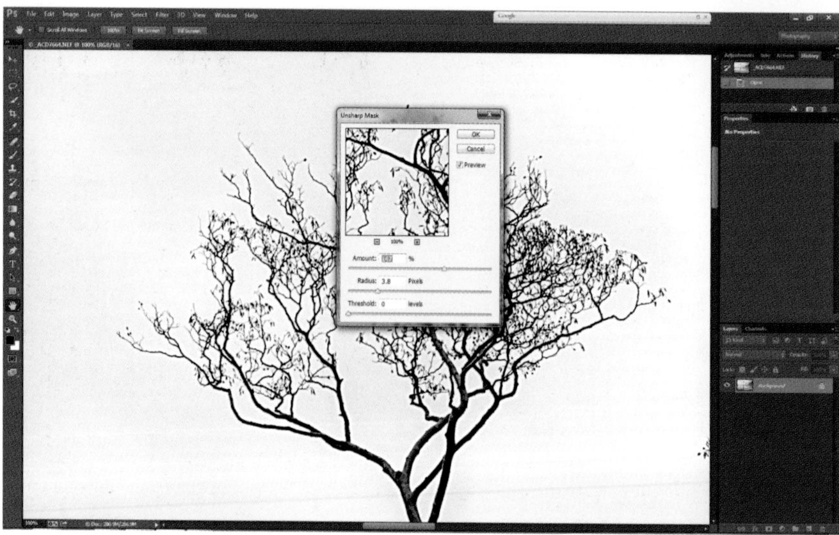

Fig. 5.23
Unsharp mask with excessive radius and amount, showing the glow caused by oversharpening.

Smart sharpen

A newer addition to Photoshop than unsharp mask is the smart sharpen filter. Oddly, it has dropped threshold, but retains radius. Recommended setting is to keep radius around 1.0. It also offers noise reduction alongside the sharpening filter, which can be useful where high ISOs have been used. Figure 5.24 illustrates a 100 per cent enlargement of the smart sharpen filter.

If your image has a large area of featureless smooth tone (a plain sky, for example), try selecting the area to be sharpened (excluding the sky area), prior to applying the filter. The selection can be very approximate, but excluding the sky from being sharpened can reduce noise if the original has some noise present.

Outside the *Filter>Sharpen* section there is another popularly used sharpening technique. Known

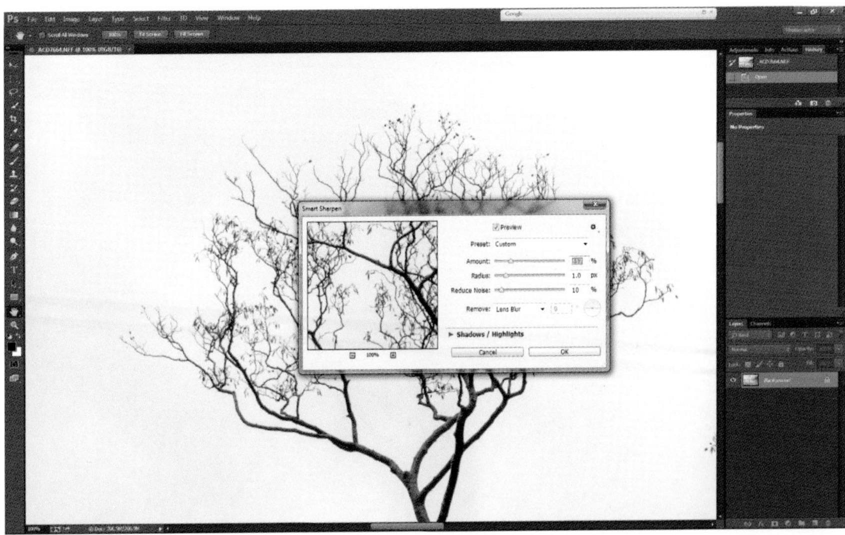

Fig. 5.24
Smart Sharpen filter set to 117%, radius of 1.0 and 10% reduce noise.

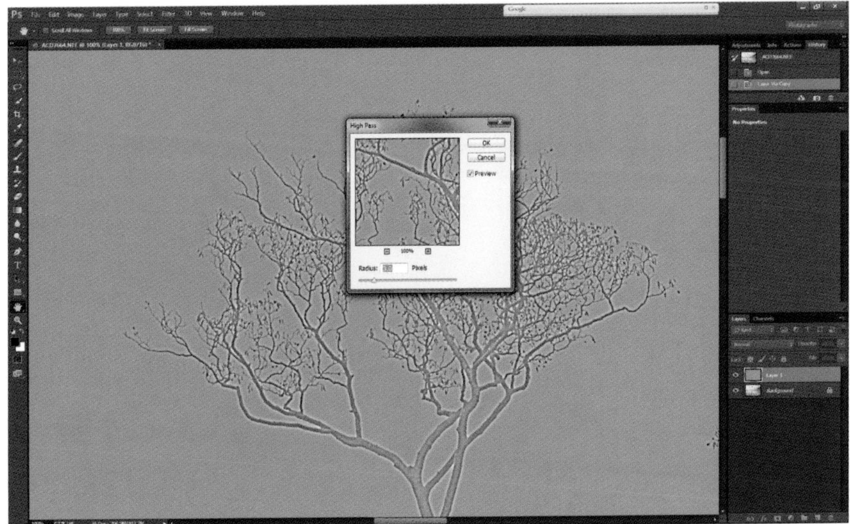

Fig. 5.25
High-pass filter applied to duplicate layer with radius set to 8%.

simply as the high-pass sharpening method, it is a very good, adjustable filter for edge sharpening of areas with fine detail, such as patterns of tree bark, log ends etc. Working on the same picture as before, start by *duplicating* the background layer (*Ctrl-J*). Under *Filter>Other*, there is a filter called high pass. (Figure 5.25)

This filter turns the picture almost totally mid-grey, apart from around edge details, where it forms almost bas-relief style light and dark tones, picking out the edge details of the image. The radius is adjustable from 0 to 1,000 pixels, and again, lower values are more effective. On this image, a value of between 3 and 5 seems to work well against the sky, but at 5.0 there appears to be a strong glow around the bare branches. Applying the filter leaves a predominantly grey layer, looking somewhat odd.

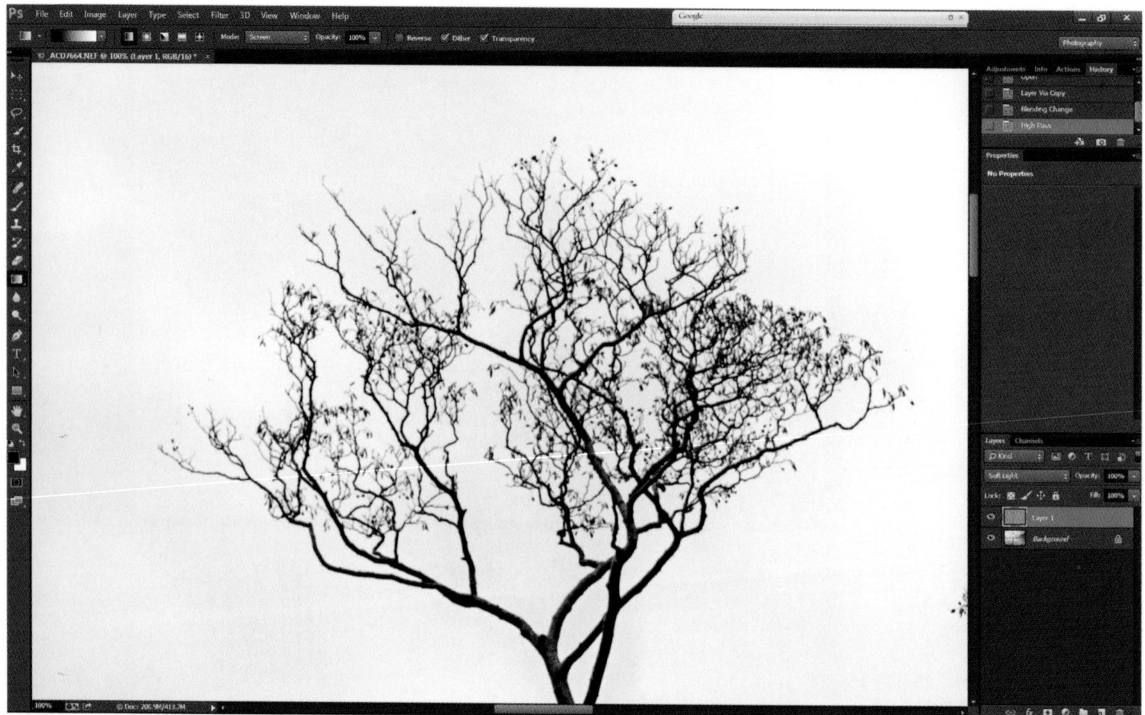

▲ Fig. 5.26
Blending mode of high-pass layer changed to soft light.

From the previous session, where we dealt with darkening and lightening on a soft light background, the same logic applies here. By changing the blending mode of the background copy (the high-pass layer) to soft light, the grey areas become transparent, allowing the light and dark areas to have an effect on edge details through the picture, hence performing a very effective edge-sharpen.

Once you have tried this technique and understand how it works, try changing the blending mode of the background copy layer before you apply the high-pass filter. This way you will not see the full-screen grey filter, rather you will see the sharpening effect on the whole image, with only the pop-up dialogue box showing the grey high-pass effect. It is a much easier way of judging the strength of the filter on the image.

Whatever you choose, the key to sharpening is, don't overdo it – if in doubt, back it off a bit. It is common to hear people refer to a picture as 'over-sharpened' but remarkably rare to hear anyone call a picture 'under-sharpened'. So be careful.

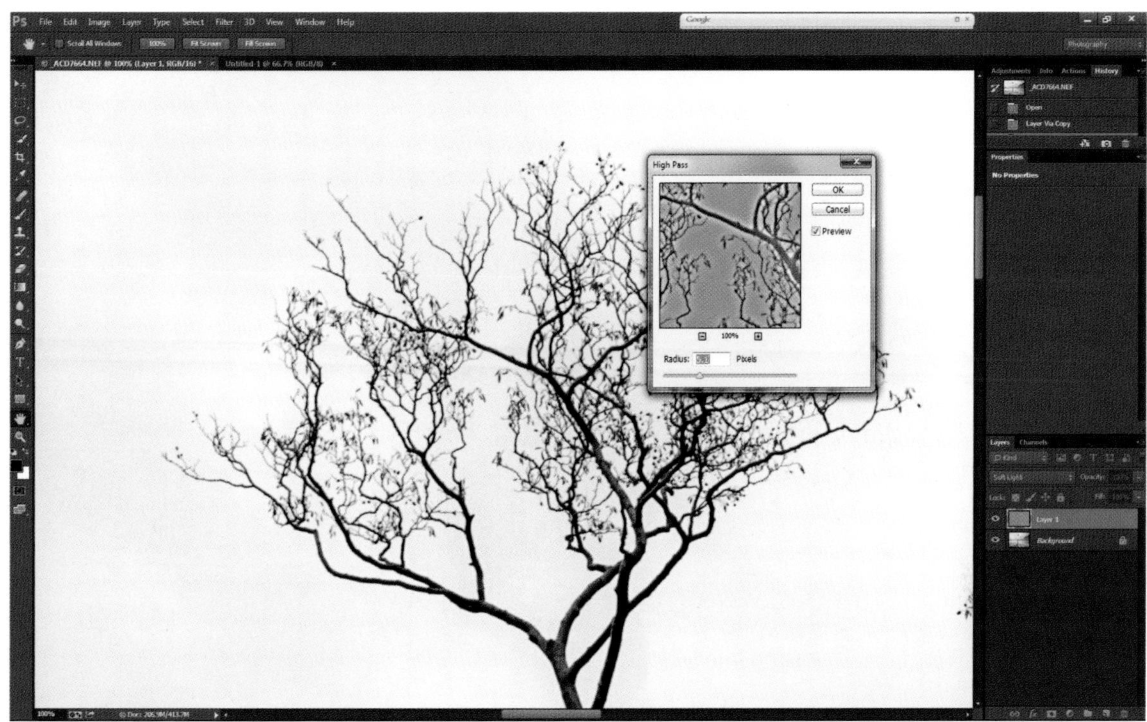

▲ Fig. 5.27
Adjustment to high-pass layer carried out in soft light blending mode, where it is easier to see the sharpening effect.

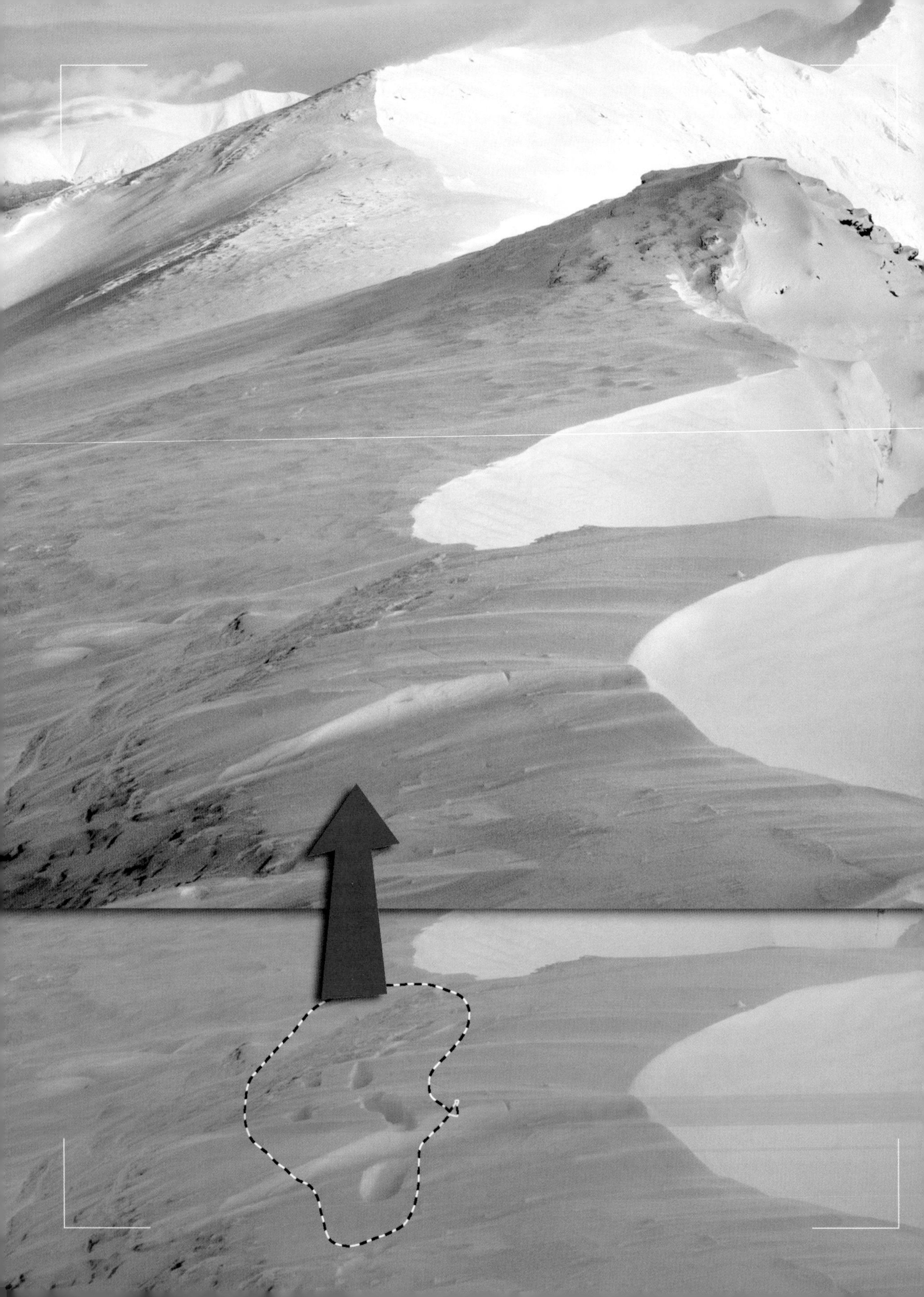

Chapter 6

Further techniques

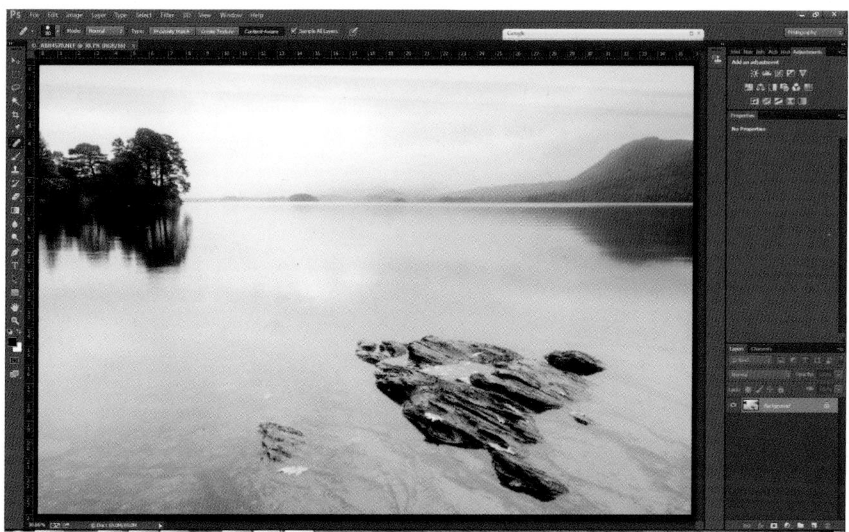

Fig. 6.1
Original file of a shot of Derwentwater showing blemishes on both the sky and the land that need tidying up.

In this chapter we are going to look at those techniques that might not form part of the basic workflow, or indeed be necessary on all images. These will include cloning, healing, and use of content-aware fill. Warping, rotating, and ways of transforming the shapes of images to eradicate problems, and lesser-used, but invaluable adjustment layers.

One of the most significant tools within Photoshop is the ability to remove unwanted elements from photographs; recent versions of Photoshop have increased the arsenal of tools available beyond the original clone stamp tool (S) to include a healing brush tool and spot healing brush tool (J), and the content-aware fill option.

Despite developments in Photoshop over the years, none of these 'eradication' tools are surplus to requirements, all have their uses, and whilst there is room for overlap between the tools, they still have their ideal purposes.

HEALING BRUSH (J)

Starting with the healing brush, and the spot healing brush (J). One of the best uses for the spot healing brush is for cleaning up marks on the image – dust spots on the sensor (yes, they do happen – especially at small apertures), odd bits of litter/light stones and so on in the foreground that you overlooked at the taking stage.

As with all work in Photoshop, try to leave the background layer relatively untouched. This goes for using the healing brush too. Looking at the image (Figure 6.1) of Derwentwater, there are a number of minor blemishes on both the sky and the area of land above the horizon on the right. The healing brush tool is ideal for quickly getting rid of these.

First, add a layer using the new layer button at the bottom of the layer palette.

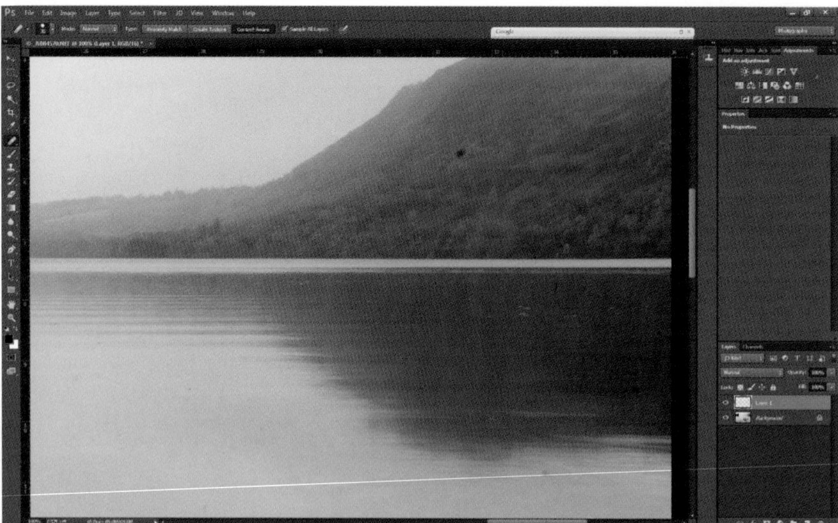

Fig. 6.2
Close-up of part of image at pixel size (100% magnification) to show sensor dust and the addition of a new layer (Layer 1).

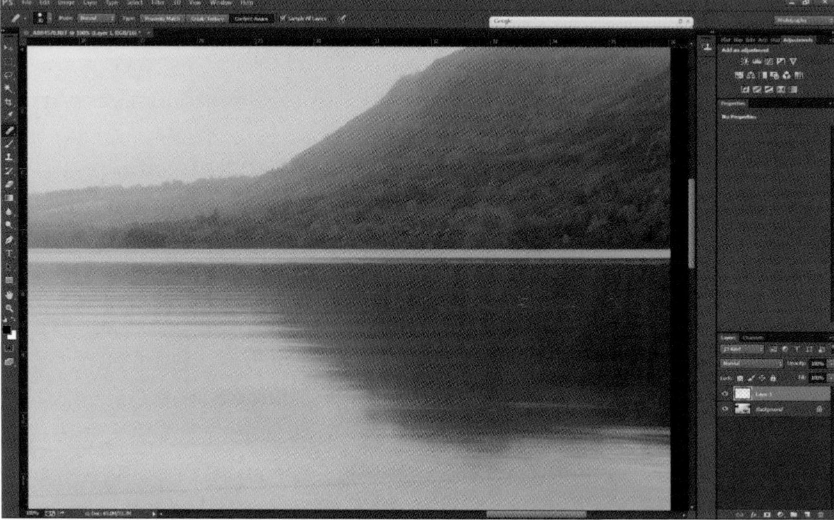

Fig. 6.3
Content-aware healing brush used on Layer 1 with tool options set to 'sample all layers' and *Type* set as 'content-aware' to repair blemished areas.

This will form an active (blue bar) layer 1 above the background layer. Ensure the spot healing brush is selected (J) or Shift-J if one of the other tool selections are present.

In the tool options along the top of the screen, under 'type' there are three options:

- Proximity match
- Create texture
- Content-aware

Generally, content-aware will give the best results for spot removal, but occasionally, proximity match can be used as an alternative. Ensure the healing brush is set to a hard edge (Shift + right-hand square bracket until you get a hard brush) and using the square brackets select the brush size that neatly covers the blemish on your picture.

As you are working on a transparent layer, not the background layer, ensure that the 'Sample all layers' box is ticked on the tool options. As you paint over the blemishes, this will copy pixels (using content-aware fill technology) from the background

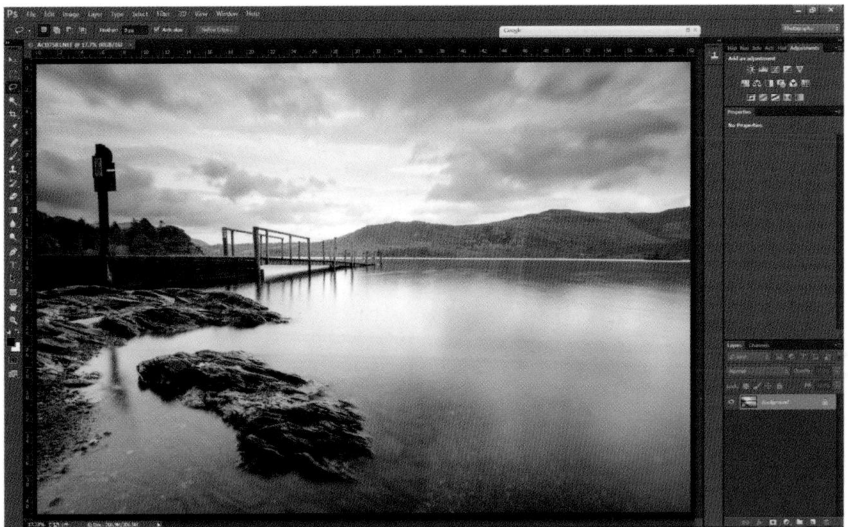

Fig. 6.4
Original file of picture of Hawes End Jetty showing a distracting handrail sign.

layer to the transparent layer, covering up the blemishes, but not making any changes to the background layer below.

Should the healing brush give any 'odd' results, these will only be on the layer of transparency and by using the eraser tool (E) any less than perfect healed areas can be erased from Layer 1 and you can try again.

The reason for the healing brush to have a hard edge is that with a soft edge to the brush, it tends to cover up the blemish only partly; it has an almost translucent effect.

CLONE STAMP TOOL (S)

One of the most talked about, most used tools in Photoshop, and so often misunderstood, the clone stamp tool is a great way of covering larger elements that might obtrude in a photograph. Whereas the content-aware fill tool can work really quickly, and will often create the perfect fill, the clone stamp tool can sometimes add that touch of precision.

There are two modes for the clone stamp tool – aligned and non-aligned. Aligned measures the offset from the sampled position to the clone position; when you move your mouse to a different location in the picture, it measures the same offset from which to take its start point. Whilst this can be very useful if you are working on small blemishes around a picture, if you are sampling from a very small source point, the unaligned option can be best, as each time you relocate the mouse, the source point stays at its original position.

In the picture of the jetty, the sign on the handrail 'Slippery when wet' adds nothing to the image. Again, add a new layer, and select the clone stamp tool (S). Ensure the aligned box is ticked, and the sample box is set to 'Current and below'. (If you leave it set at the default 'Current layer', when working on the blank new layer you will simply be cloning transparency.)

Hold the Alt key down and click with the mouse on the start point where you want to sample from (the right-hand jetty post). Reposition the cursor to over the left post and click and drag the mouse to clone the right post over the left. Don't worry about the extra bit of handrail that clones with the post.

One of the great advantages of cloning onto a new blank layer is if the clone isn't perfectly lined up, as it is on a totally independent layer, by selecting the move tool (V – or hold down the Ctrl key to temporarily invoke the move tool), reposition the

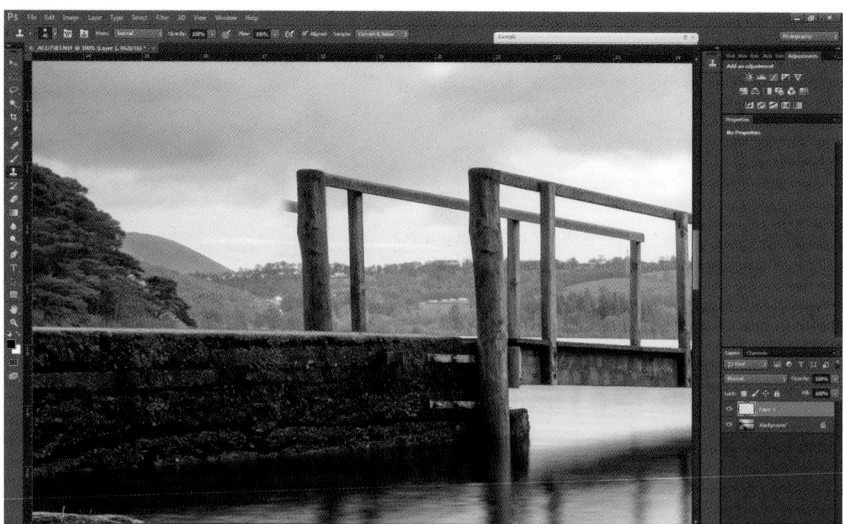

Fig. 6.5
Sign removed with clone tool, although the small section of additional fence on the clone layer remains.

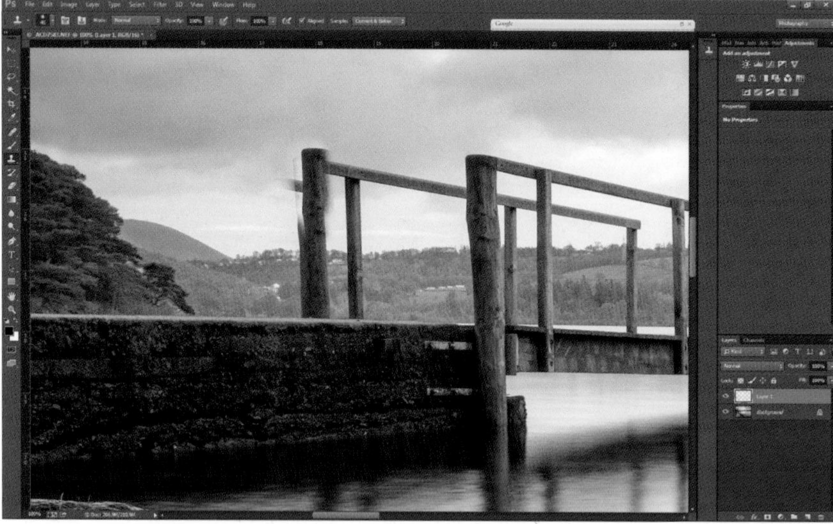

Fig. 6.6
Misaligned clone, but being on a separate layer it is easy to reposition.

clone layer to line it up perfectly. If the source from which you clone is at a slightly different angle, the clone layer can be rotated or scaled to suit. A slight CCW rotation helped align this perfectly.

To remove the excess cloning (the handrail) either: carefully erase it using the eraser tool (E), with a hard edge or add a layer mask (by clicking on the layer mask icon at the bottom of the layers palette), and erasing the unwanted handrail by painting on the layer mask with a (hard-edged) black brush. This method has the advantage that if you erase or mask too much, by painting back with a white brush you restore the cloned element.

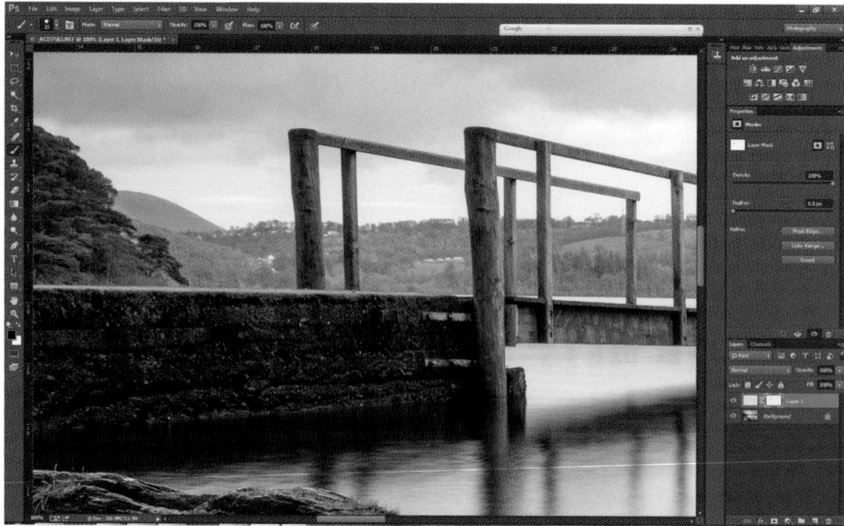

▶ Fig. 6.7
Realigned clone with excess cloning of fence removed on a layer mask.

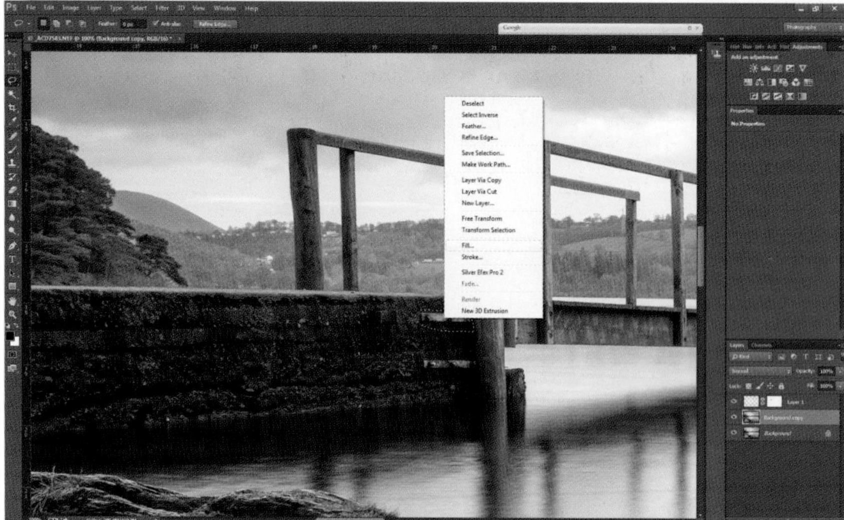

▶ Fig. 6.8
Selection of metal bracket and fill option to perform content-aware fill.

CONTENT-AWARE FILL (NO SHORTCUT KEY)

The most recent introduction in the Photoshop stable, content-aware fill was introduced with CS5, and was hailed as the answer to all our cloning prayers. To some extent it is – being a truly powerful tool – but it can get it wrong, and it is best to use it in conjunction with the healing brushes and the clone stamp tools at the most appropriate times.

The two brackets fixing the end post of the jetty to the concrete of the walkway are pretty unsightly, and removing them would improve the appearance. They are too large to use the healing brush/ spot healing brush, and to use the clone stamp tool would replicate the textures of the concrete too obviously. Content-aware fill is the ideal tool for this. The main difference between content-aware and the other 'cloning' tools, is that it cannot work on a transparent layer. It can therefore be used directly on the background layer, or if you are worried about

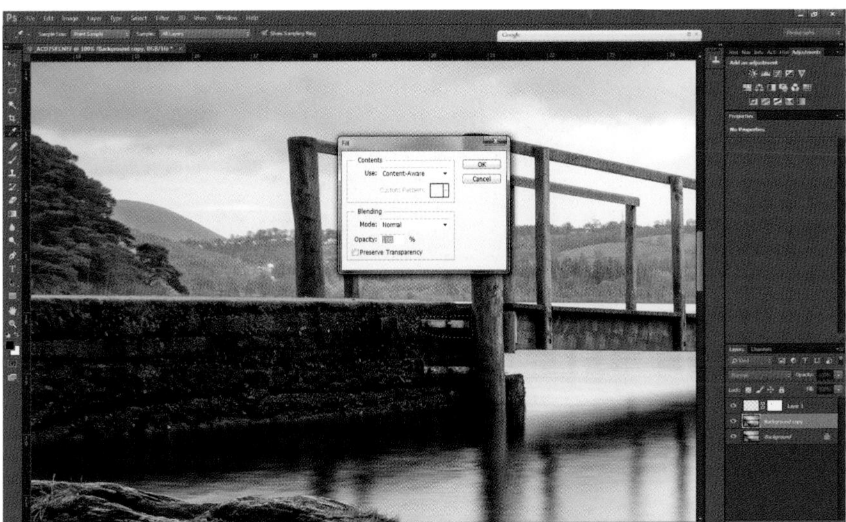

◀ Fig. 6.9
Content-aware fill selected (blending mode at normal and opacity at 100%).

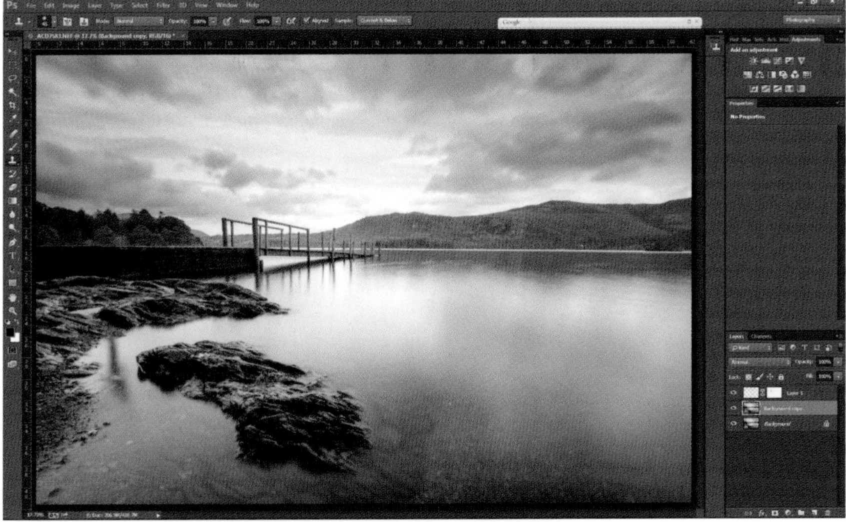

◀ Fig. 6.10
Entire image showing completed cloning.

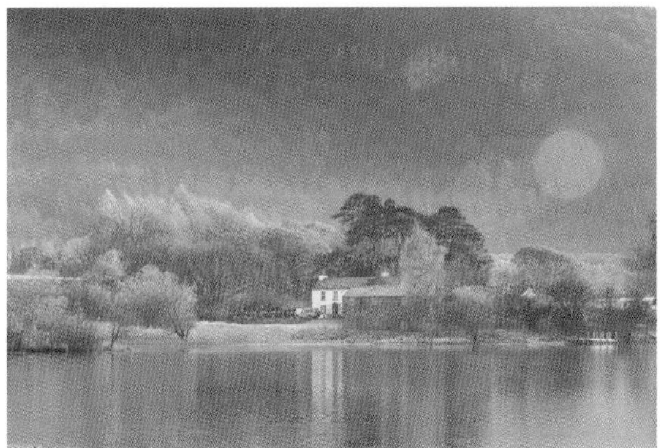

▲ Fig. 6.11
Original image of early morning picture at Calfclose bay with flare spots.

making a mistake (remember – there is always the history undo facility), you can duplicate the background layer. (Click on the background layer on the layers palette, and hit Ctrl-J or Command-J on a Mac to duplicate the layer.)

For something as simple as these brackets, select around them roughly using a lasso tool, right-click within the selection and a dialogue box will appear with a 'Fill' option about halfway down the list.

Select fill, and under 'content' make sure 'content-aware' is selected.

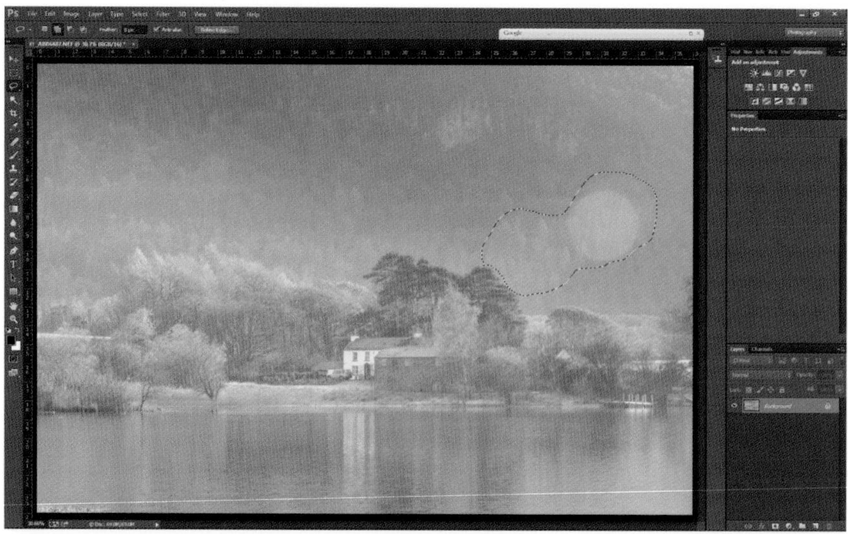

Fig. 6.12
Selection of flare spots.

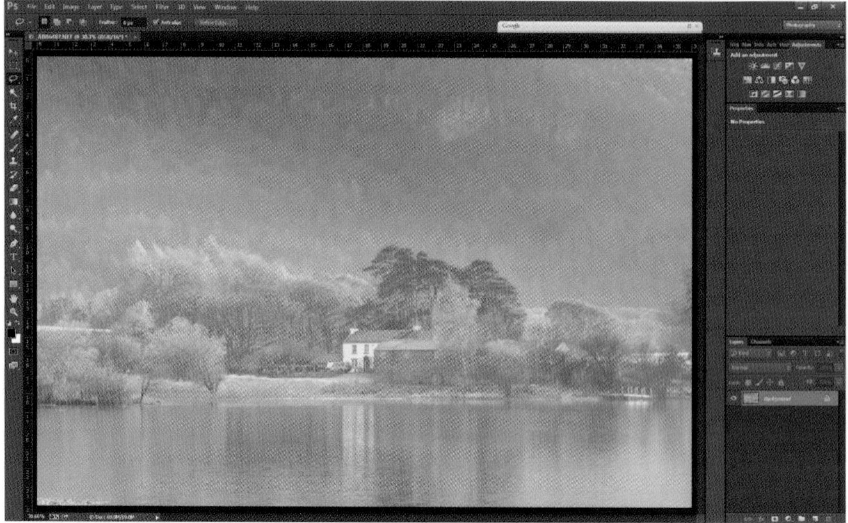

Fig. 6.13
Flare spots removed using content-aware fill.

If the result isn't to your liking, undo the fill and the selection and start again. Repeat the action for the second bracket. The large post to the left of the jetty could also be removed using content-aware fill in the same manner. If the top edge of the concrete doesn't perfectly line up, a slight repair using the clone stamp tool can line it up quickly and easily.

The final result looks tidier and natural, allowing the viewer's attention to be taken to the important parts of the picture.

Another use of the content-aware fill tool can be seen on Figure 6.11.

A photograph taken towards the sun, where even with a lens-hood, the low level of the sun gave rise to a couple of large flare spots. Select the flare spots using a lasso tool

On a first attempt, the large selected area might partly fill with unwanted parts from the picture, like the less hazy foreground trees. Simply reselect the small area of unwanted fill and refill it – a few attempts should give a perfect result.

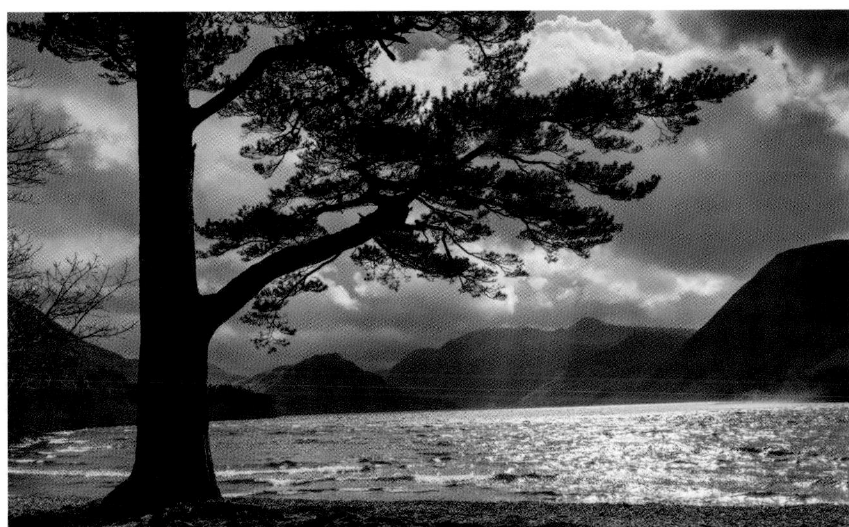

Fig. 6.14
Original image looking down Crummock Water showing crooked horizon.

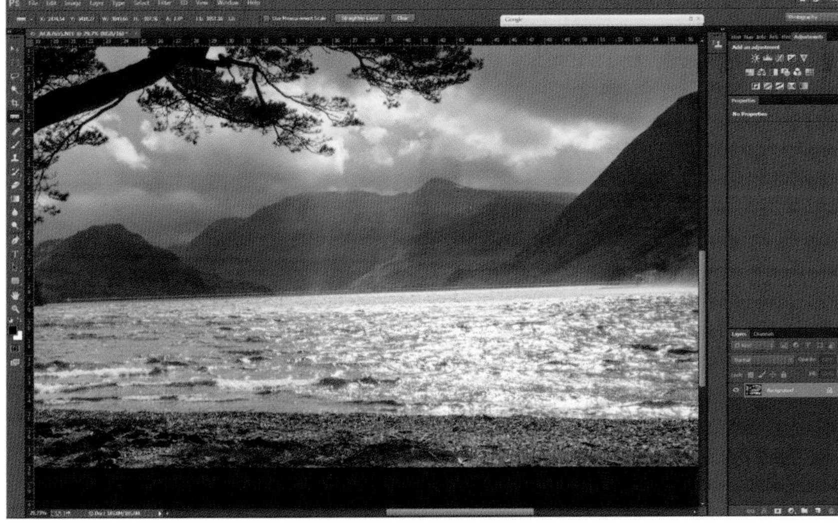

Fig. 6.15
Ruler tool set along far shoreline, which should be a horizontal line.

USING TRANSFORM TOOLS

There are a wealth of options under the *Edit>Transform* or *Image>Rotate* tools within Photoshop, many of which are of great use to the landscape photographer.

There can be the odd occasion that, despite using tripods and spirit levels for every landscape photograph, one escapes the net and still looks a touch crooked on the picture.

Straightening the picture couldn't be easier. Under the eyedropper tool (I) on the tools palette is the ruler tool. Click on the end of a known horizontal (or vertical) line, and drag to a corresponding point. Remember, looking across a lake, such as in this photograph, whilst we usually visualize the far shoreline as horizontal, if you are looking at an angle across the lake, it can actually *be* at an angle. If there

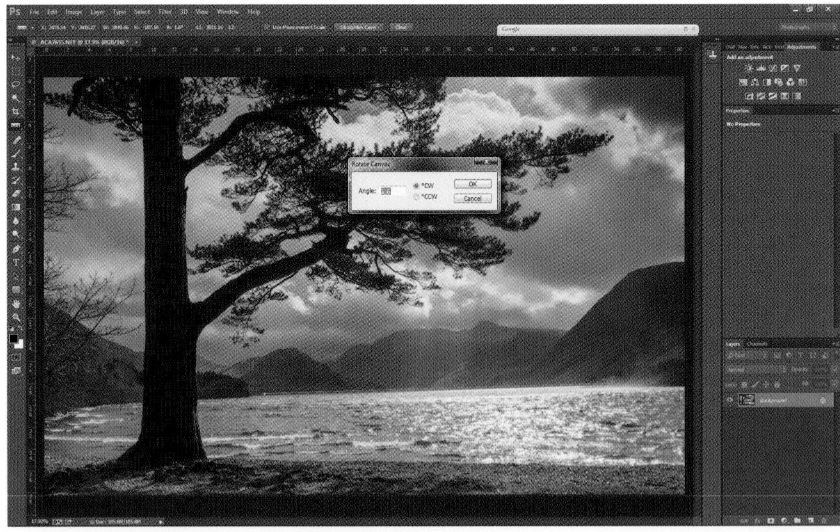

Fig. 6.16
Rotate arbitrary selected, showing a 1.6 degree clockwise rotation needed to level the line to horizontal.

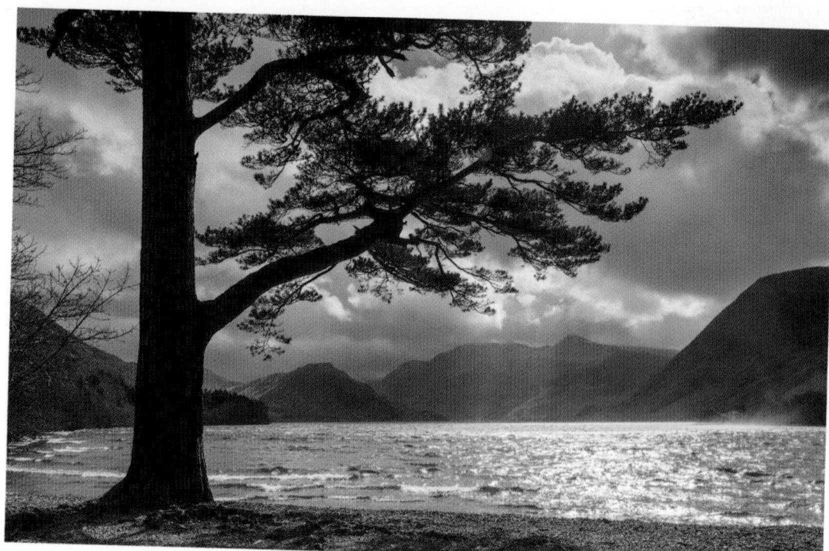

Fig. 6.17
Rotated image levelling the horizon.

is a tree or something similar reflected in the lake, remember any part of the tree will be vertically above its reflection. On this image, however, the far shore of Crummock Water is a horizontal line, so click (and hold) the ruler tool on one end of the crooked shoreline, and move the cursor to the other end of the shoreline.

The line is clearly at a slight angle, Under *Image>Image rotation>Arbitrary*, Photoshop measures the horizontal and vertical offsets of the line and inserts the CW or CCW rotation required.

All that is needed after that is to crop the image to suit. However, in this particular image, the tree to the left of the photograph appears to lean in to the picture slightly. Using other transform tools can rectify that. Remember, this adjustment is personal choice only, although the lean on the tree is a correction of converging verticals.

In order to compare before and after results, it's worth making a duplicate layer (Ctrl-J). To ensure

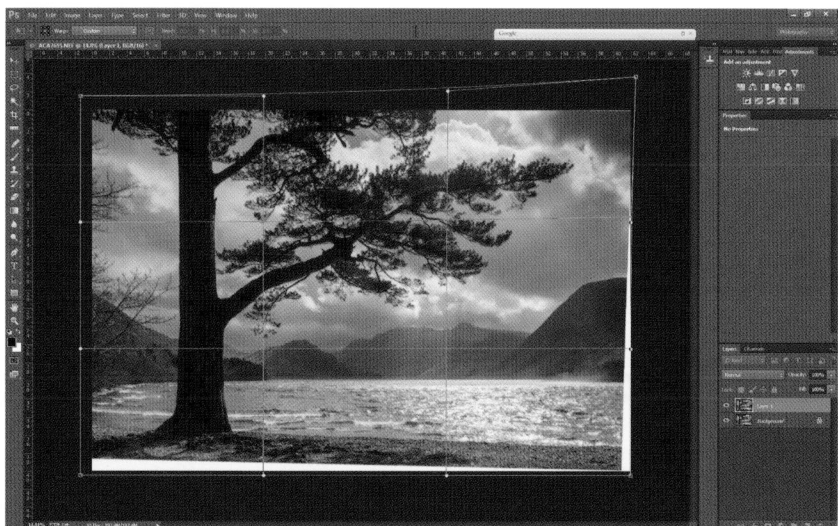

Fig. 6.18
Use of the skew tool to straighten the tree and the warp tool to adjust the top right-hand corner.

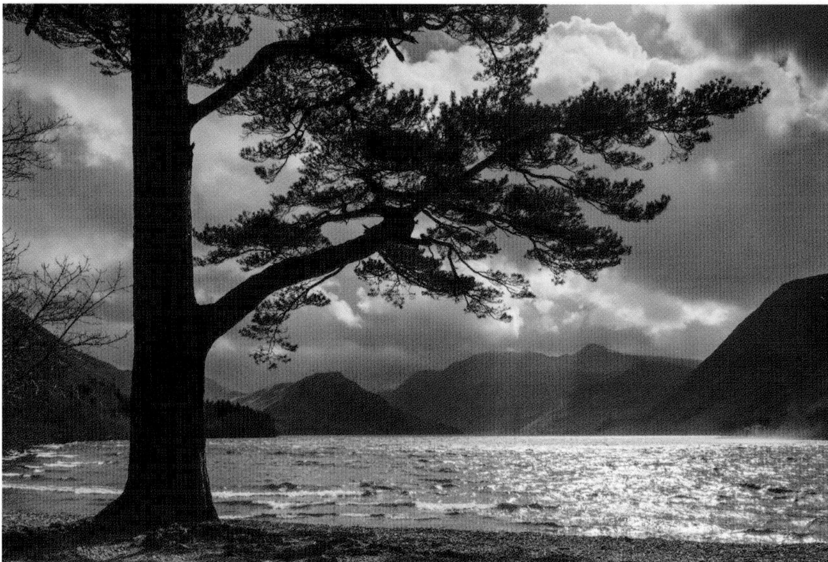

Fig. 6.19
Completed photo cropped to size.

your lines are square, switch on the grid (Ctrl-') or *View>Extras*. Select *Edit>Transform>Skew* and clicking on the top left-hand corner of the picture, drag the point out to the left until the tree is as vertical as looks correct.

Turning the layer on and off by clicking on the 'eye' icon will show the before and after versions.

In this image, cropping off the white borders caused by the image rotation to straighten the picture works on the sides and the bottom of the picture, but would be a touch tight on the top branch of the tree, setting it slightly too close to the edge of the picture. There are a few techniques that can be used to fill the top right white section – content-aware fill might work, but in this case, as the tree is of a non-specific shape (unlike, say, a building), try *Edit>Transform>Warp*, and drag the top corner up a little (Figure 6.18). Finish off with a crop to tidy the edges and you have your completed picture.

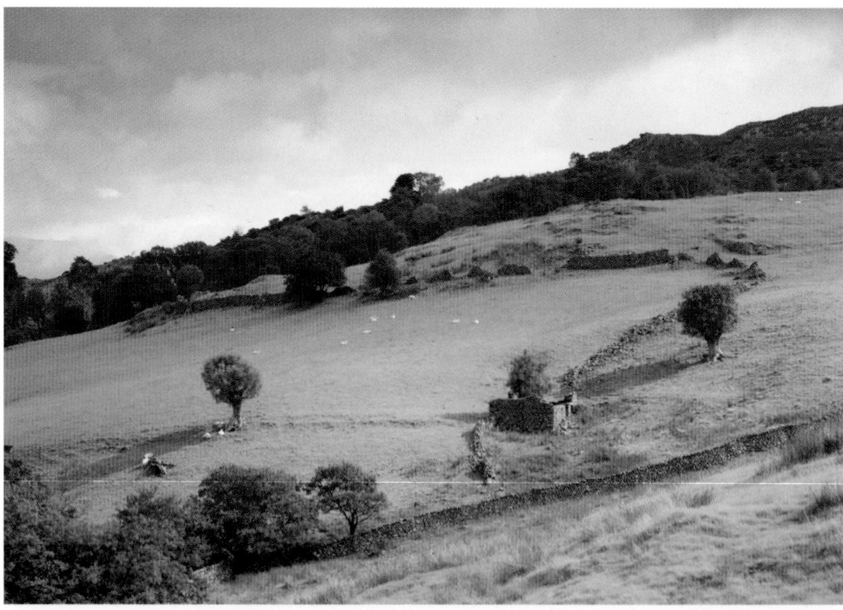

Fig. 6.20
Original landscape image showing very strong green tones.

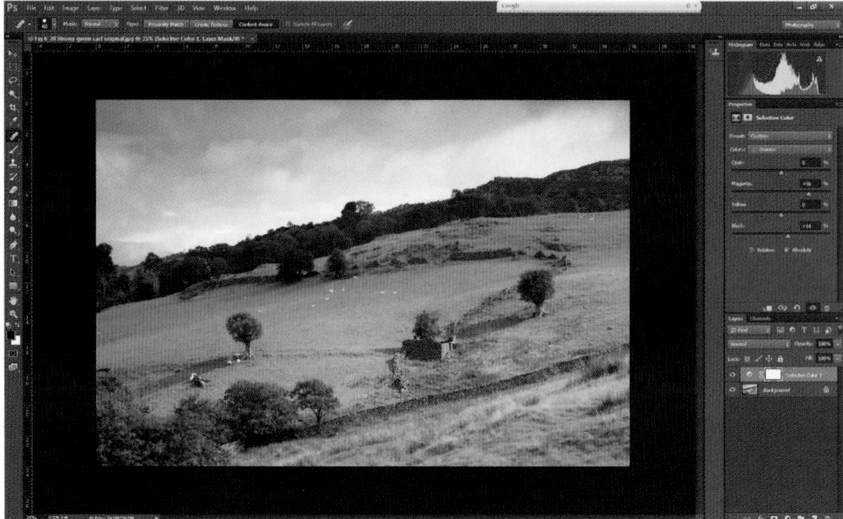

Fig. 6.21
Selective colour adjustment layer inserted, adding magenta to the greens, resulting in more natural tones.

SELECTIVE COLOUR CORRECTION/CONTROLLING COLOUR

Despite the sophistication of the RAW image and the ability to change white balance easily in processing, occasionally colours within a scene do not always record as you visualize them. Greens in particular can have a habit of appearing too vivid when they are a lush green in a scene – however accurately the camera might record them. Photography, like all art forms, is about interpretation and perception, and colours in photos often need to be how you perceive them, rather than their precise colour. Summer greens are so often one such colour; they often record so green that they look almost unnaturally lush. The example in Figure 6.20 is one such picture.

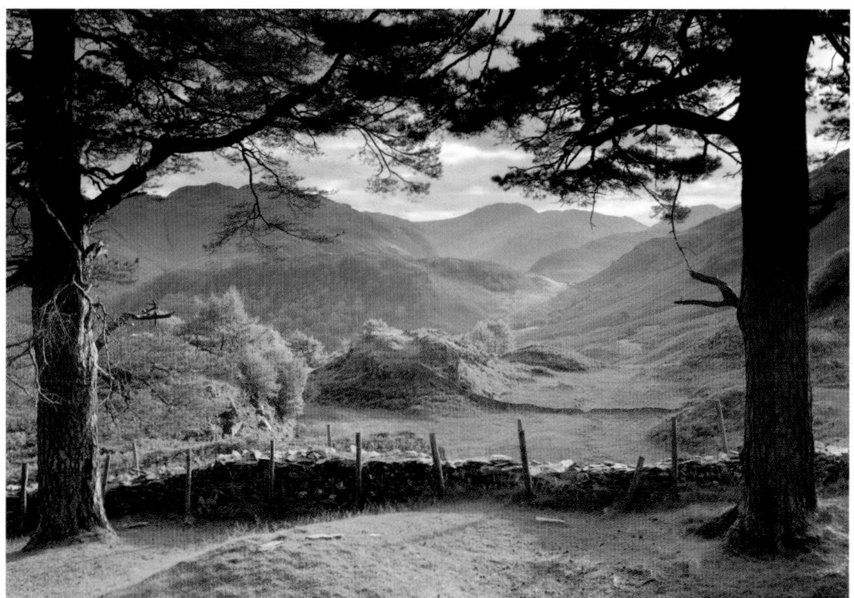

Fig. 6.22
Castle Crag trees original with dark tops to the trees where a graduated filter was used.

Correction of these greens is very straightforward and simple. Many photographers would reach for the 'photo filter' adjustment layer, but before trying this, there is a simple way that often works perfectly and is much more controllable.

Add a selective colour layer and on the colours drop-down on the properties palette, select greens. There are two strengths for selective colour adjustments – relative and absolute. Relative is a very gentle alteration, absolute is much stronger and for this type of adjustment, is the best one to choose. The second of the sliders on the selective colour properties is magenta, which is directly opposite to green on the colour wheel. Adding magenta to the greens mellows them off. There is no set figure for this; simply adjust the magenta slider until the greens look about right.

Although this example is directed at the greens within a landscape, all the other colours (red, yellow, green, cyan, blue and magenta), can be adjusted in similar ways. By adding black to blue, skies can be darkened; by adding black to bright reds, the colour becomes slightly less 'orange' on the resulting print.

CORRECTING FILTERING PROBLEMS

The photograph of trees at Castle Crag shows a problem faced by many landscape photographers. The sky was quite bright, and without the benefit of a graduated filter, would have blown out the high-light detail badly. One solution to this might have been to have bracketed the exposure and created an HDR image, but the wind was blowing the trees around and ghosting of the leaves and branches could have been an issue. Using the graduated filter however, the sky has been rendered well, but the top of the trees have come out semi-silhouetted.

By careful exposure, detail has been retained in the shadow areas of the trees, and therefore can be lightened. Selection of the tops of the tree trunks, branches and dark leaves can fairly readily be done using the magic wand tool (W). Use the wand tool at a fairly low tolerance (8), with the 'add to selection' button selected and contiguous unticked in order to select from the whole area, to speed up selection

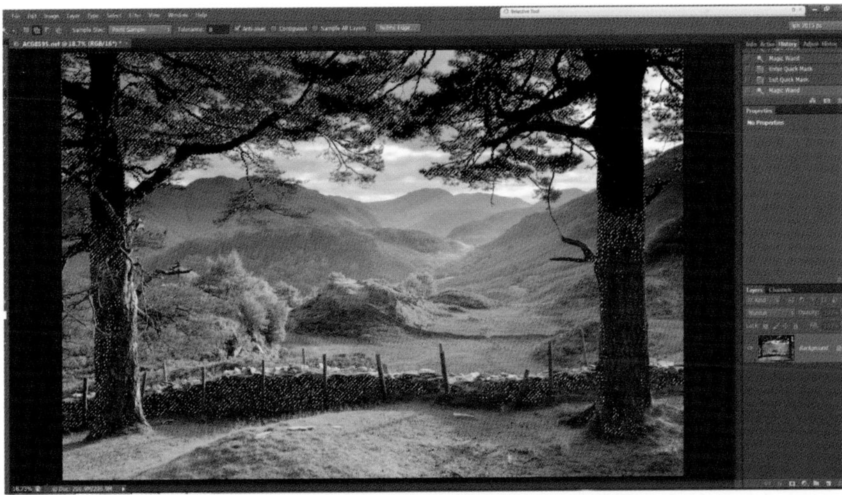

Fig. 6.23
Selection of top of the trees, extending down to parts of the lower trees and the wall.

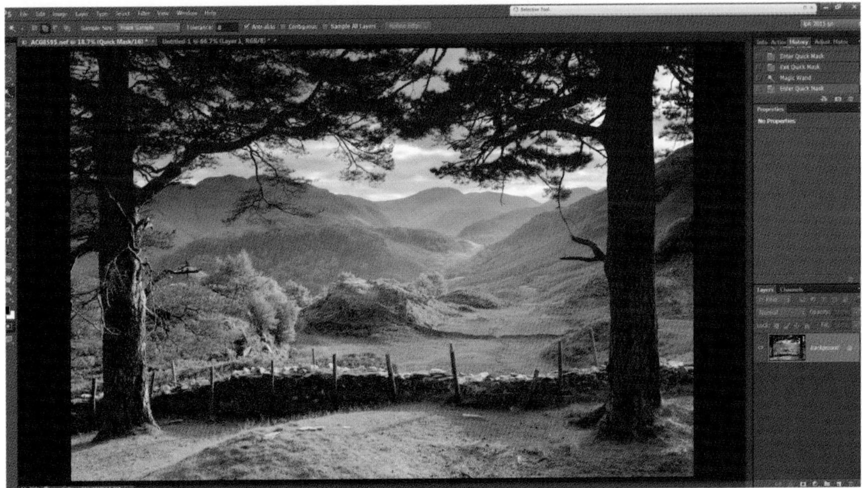

Fig. 6.24
Quick mask mode showing full selected area includes part of the wall.

and to ensure that most of the dark area is selected. (Figure 6.23). In this case, unticking contiguous, whilst giving greater accuracy in picking up stray leaves and the like at the top, has also selected parts of the lower trunks of the tree and some of the dry stone wall.

The full extent of the selection is easier to see by entering quick mask mode (Q) in Fig 6.24.

The next stage is simply to remove the lower areas from the selection. A remarkably easy and straightforward step. Whilst in quick mask, select the gradient tool, and change the blending mode of the gradient tool to 'screen'. Ensure the gradient is set to black to white (or foreground-to-background colour, with default colours set). This, when the gradient is drawn downwards where the original graduated filter would have been positioned, will remove the lower parts of the selection.

The next step is to ensure the edges of the selection are neither too defined nor too feathered, so adjustments carried out on the selection look natural. Firstly exit quick mask (Q) so your selection is again a series of marching ants. Then either by right-clicking within the selection with any selection tool active, or by clicking on *Select>Refine edge/ Select and Mask* or Alt>Ctrl>R, the pop-up menu shown in Figure 6.26 will appear, along with the selection appearing as a mask.

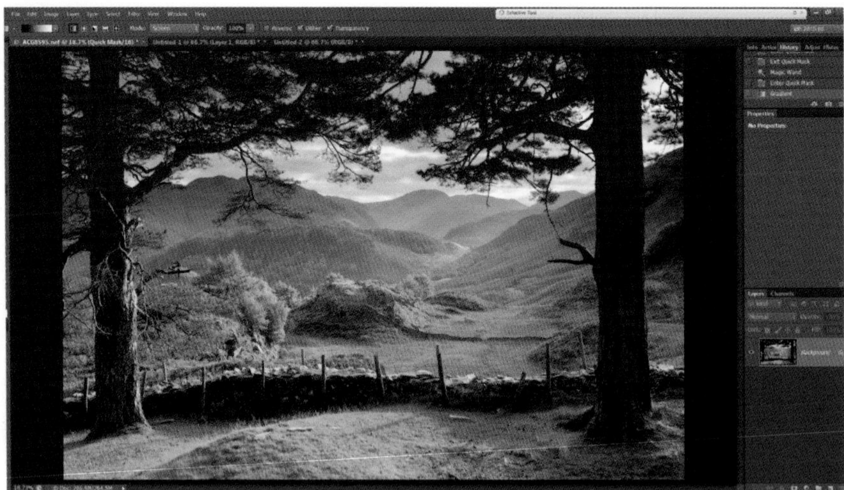

Fig. 6.25
Lower part of the selection removed by gradient tool set to screen blending mode.

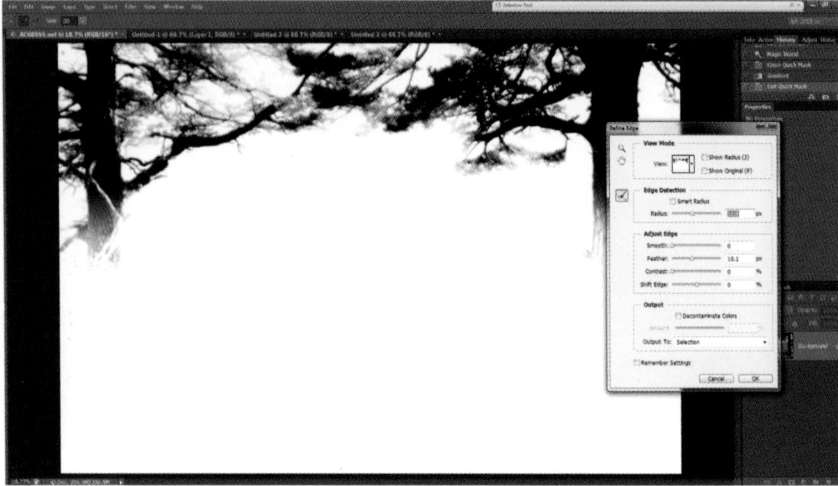

Fig. 6.26
Refine edge/Select and Mask selected to feather the edge of the selection and fit it to the shape of the trees.

In this image, a feather of about 10 pixels works well, but changing the edge detection radius allows the edge of the selection to fit to the contours of the trees really well. A radius of about 11 gives an excellent result. Clicking on OK will return to the main image with the marching ants still visible. The selected area can now be lightened by using either levels, or as in Figure 6.27, curves, just by lifting the centre of the curve.

In this image, the top section of the trees needed a little more lightening. By trying to lift the curves lighter, the lower part of the selection would have become too light. A repeat of the selection stage with the gradient used to select only the top section of the trees and a further curves adjustment layer is shown in Figure 6.28 (check the second curves layer added and the shape of the mask). This two-stage lightening has just lifted the tones in the branches enough to look believable rather than over-worked.

Figure 6.29 shows the final image.

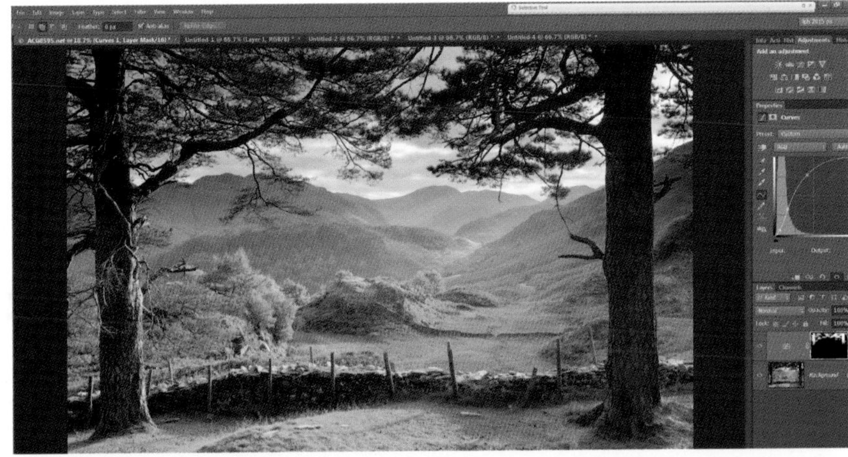

Fig. 6.27
Curves used to lighten the dark tree areas.

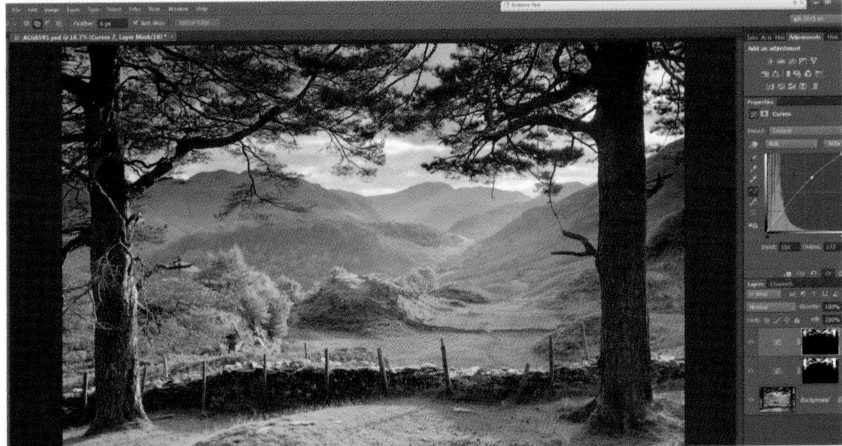

Fig. 6.28
Second curves layer working on a slightly reduced mask area, restricted to the top edge of the image area.

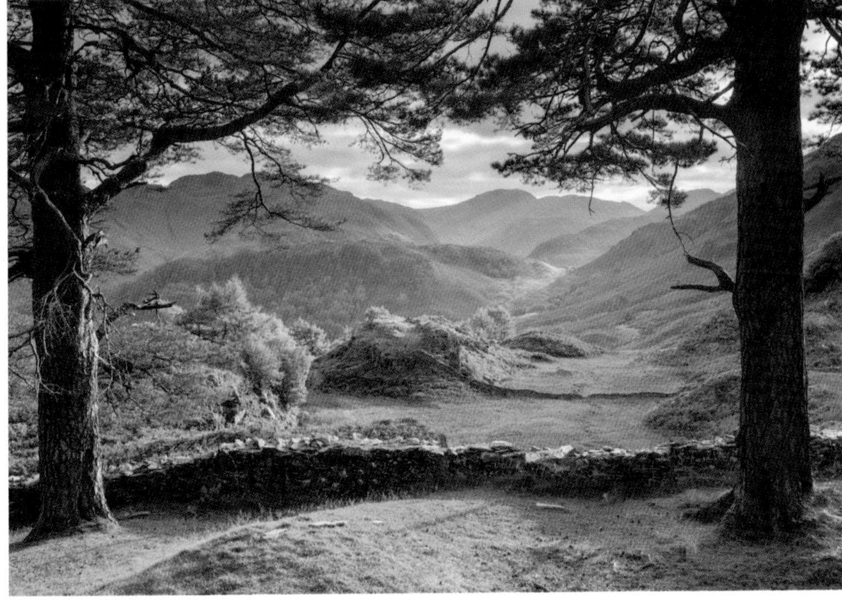

Fig. 6.29
Final image, showing the top areas of the trees much closer in tone to the lower trunks, looking natural in tone, but with detail preserved in the sky beyond by use of the graduated filter at the taking stage.

Chapter 7

Black and white landscapes

Sometimes colour adds too much to the landscape, and the simplicity and tonality of black and white gives a greater feel and atmosphere. Ansel Adams, one of the world's greatest landscape photographers, used the black and white medium to portray the drama and mood of the landscape like no other. That is one thing that black and white is superb at; portraying dramatic light, by just working with tone and contrast, rather than colours. It can also be superb at portraying the subtle, pastel tones of mist or rain in a minimalist style.

Firstly, it is recommended that you always shoot in colour, as the colour data contains a red, green and blue channel, allowing you to subtly alter the various tones within the picture during post processing. The three channels also give you three times the data of a photo shot in black and white, which only contains grey data. Of course, if you shoot a RAW file, although it will appear as a black and white on the LED screen on the camera, when downloaded to your computer, it will revert to a standard colour RAW file.

At first glance through Photoshop, there does seem to be a great number of ways that pictures can be converted to mono, including:

- Desaturate
- Greyscale
- Channel mixer
- Black and white conversion

Given that all colour pictures are made up of a mix of red, green and blue pixels, Figure 7.1 shows three rectangles of pure red, green and blue (together with a reference 50 per cent grey and a white bar at the base).

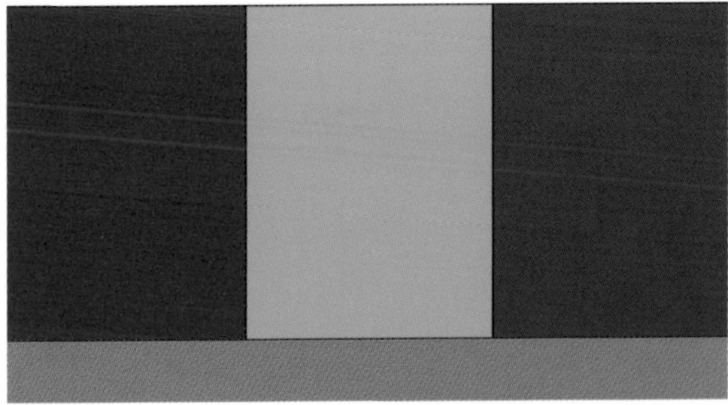

▲ Fig. 7.1
Pure RGB Tones, and a mid-grey band for reference.

▲ Fig. 7.2
RGB tones desaturated, showing red, green, blue and the mid-grey band all the same shade of grey.

We all perceive colours slightly differently, but most people 'see' the blue block as the darkest tonally, usually with the red in the middle and the green as the lightest of the three primary colours. Although the red and green sometimes are perceived the other way round, with the red lighter than the green, rarely are they all seen as equal brightness.

Desaturation

Many people think that black and white is simply colour with the colour taken away, in other words

▲ Fig. 7.3
Gradient map showing red, green and blue as different tones.

desaturated. The result of this is often surprising, but worth looking at.

Taking the RGB file and adding a hue and saturation layer to it, slide the saturation to zero. The red, green and blue panels all turn 50 per cent grey – and match the reference grey bar perfectly.

What desaturation effectively does is to turn the picture black and white, but also to take away the punch and contrast that existed in the original. The result on a normal picture would be to make it look flat and lifeless.

Greyscale

Greyscale seems a logical choice, and it can be found under *Image>Mode>Greyscale*. But as soon as you click on that it comes up with a warning that you are about to discard all colour information. Converting to greyscale actually reduces the file size to 33 per cent of its original size; of course, losing data in the process. There are times when greyscale is the only option, but as we spend all our time trying our best to maximize data, throwing 67 per cent of our data away doesn't seem the best option.

Which leaves two options; channel mixer and black and white conversion. The black and white conversion layer only exists in more recent versions of Photoshop, previously channel mixer was the only real option. They have a lot of similarities, and yet there are times one may be easier to use over the other.

Gradient map

Not often used by Photoshop users, but a really useful conversion for Elements users. Taking the RGB image, add a gradient map layer, and click on the drop-down arrow on the very grey, default gradient on the properties palette. Choose either the foreground to background (if you are set to default colours) or the black to white option and click on the gradient itself. This will open a separate dialogue box with a gradient editor. Click on the white box at the lower right end of the gradient; this allows you to set a colour midpoint for the highlights, click within the gradient and move the new white colour stop until the effect on the green square looks right. In this instance, there is no need to adjust the blacks with a mid-point adjustment, as the blue and red squares are dark enough. There isn't quite as much control as with the channel mixer and black and white conversion layers, but it is a useful alternative to know about.

Channel mixer

As all images are made up of a mix of red, green and blue channels, the channel mixer adjustment layer allows us to combine these various channels together to create different effects on the image. The individual red, green and blue channels can be viewed on the 'Channels' palette – clicking on the individual channels, or using the shortcut keys Ctrl-2, Ctrl-3, Ctrl-4, will show the red, green and blue channels respectively. As they always show in black and white, they help to show the effect of the various channels on the tones within the picture; effectively the same as shooting a black and white picture through a red, green or blue filter.

The theory behind this is that any filter (channel) will allow its own colour to pass through, but block other colours. For example, a red filter/red channel will show a red rose against green leaves as a light rose on dark leaves. Correspondingly, through a green filter/channel, it will appear as a dark rose against light leaves.

▲ Fig. 7.4
Channel mixer default custom setting (Red 40%, green 40%, blue 20%).

▲ Fig. 7.5
Channel mixer set to Red 25%, Green 70%, Blue 5%.

Going back to the red, green and blue image, add a channel mix layer, and tick the 'monochrome' box, the default ('custom') Photoshop settings are 40 per cent red, 40 per cent green and 20 per cent blue, giving a total of 100 per cent.

Whatever changes you make to the strength of each of these channels, you need to ensure they total 100 per cent, or you will end up lightening or darkening the image. On the properties palette, there is a drop-down options box set to 'custom'; there are a number of preset options, including red filter, blue filter, orange filter and yellow filter. Try a few of these, perhaps selecting the yellow filter, which will make the blue rectangle the darkest, then the red, and the green the lightest, by setting the various strengths of the channels at 66 per cent, 34 per cent and 0 per cent respectively for the red, green and blue channels. As adjustments can be made to the opacity of these channels, try changing the strengths to create the tones that you perceive as the red, green and blue in black and white.

Figure 7.5 shows the RGB channels as 25 per cent, 70 per cent and 5 per cent respectively (total 100 per cent), which made the red slightly darker than the yellow filter preset, the green slightly lighter, and added a touch of tone to the blue, rather than leaving it as total black.

There are times when the channel mixer layer is slightly more straightforward to use than the black and white conversion layers on certain pictures, especially summer landscape pictures where the amount of yellow in the picture is significant.

▲ Fig. 7.6
Black and white adjustment layer with RGB values altered from the default setting using finger adjustment tool.

Black and white conversion layer

This is the most recently added of the black and white conversion options offered by Photoshop. It is also pretty straightforward, although some landscape photos can cause it a little confusion.

Taking the reference RGB picture, add a black and white adjustment layer. You will notice that the red, green and blue sliders default settings are again 40 per cent, 40 per cent and 20 per cent, giving the same appearance as in the default channel mixer layer. The black and white adjustment layer doesn't need the percentages to add up to 100 per cent though, making it quicker and easier to make changes. At the top of the properties palette, there is a hand logo. Click on that and position the cursor on

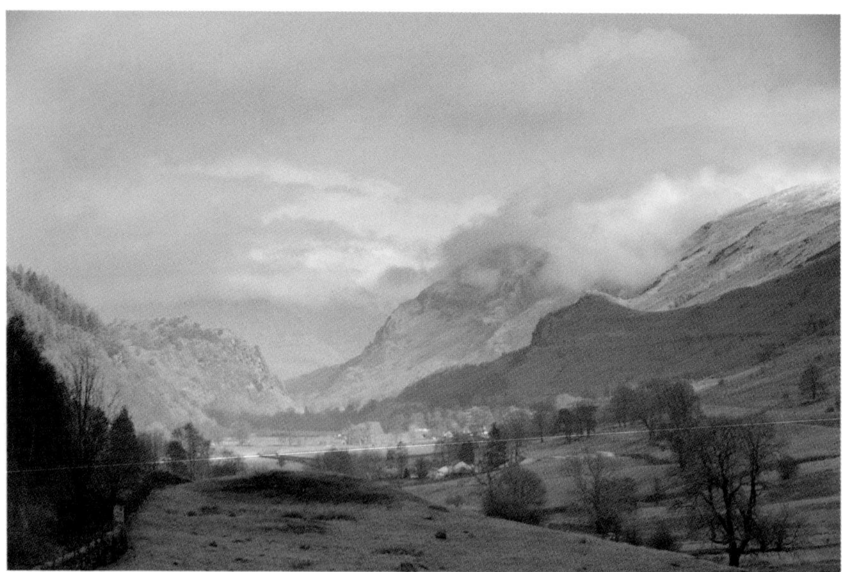

◀ Fig. 7.7
Original image of St John's in the Vale, showing low contrast throughout, but good data from shadow areas to highlights.

any of the three (R,G,B) colour blocks on the picture itself; click (and hold) the cursor on any of these blocks and slide the cursor right or left to lighten or darken the block. Note that as you click on the green block, the green slider on the properties palette becomes highlighted. By using the black and white adjustment layer in this way, different colours within any picture can quickly and easily be altered in tone.

In addition to the ability to change tones using the sliders, there is a large selection of drop-down filters to give the effect of regular black and white filters.

That sums up the basics of the various ways of converting a colour image to a black and white photograph. Now a few examples putting the theory into practice.

Example 1 – Creating an air of drama

Figure 7.7 was taken on a hazy February day, and exposed fairly well 'to the right' to maximize data, and create a file that could be worked on easily.

When you choose to convert it to black and white makes little difference, but you may find it is desirable and effective to add slightly more punch and contrast to a black and white image, than you might do to a similar colour image, especially when you are conveying a sense of mood and drama. This picture, despite being a very gentle-looking, soft original, would create a really powerful and dramatic image with the right processing.

Before processing a picture like this as a black and white, try looking at the various tones on each of the red, green and blue channels (which will help you decide which filtration to use). The red and green channels look to give the most contrasty result, so perhaps a yellow or orange filter might be good. However, before converting this (or any other) picture to black and white, there are some colour modifications that might work to the picture's advantage:

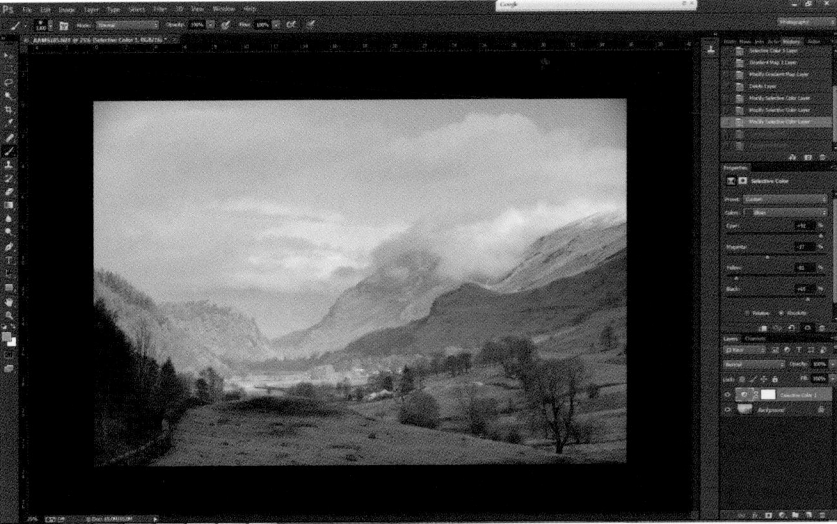

Fig. 7.8
Selective colour adjustment layer used to deepen the blue sky by adding black to blues and cyans.

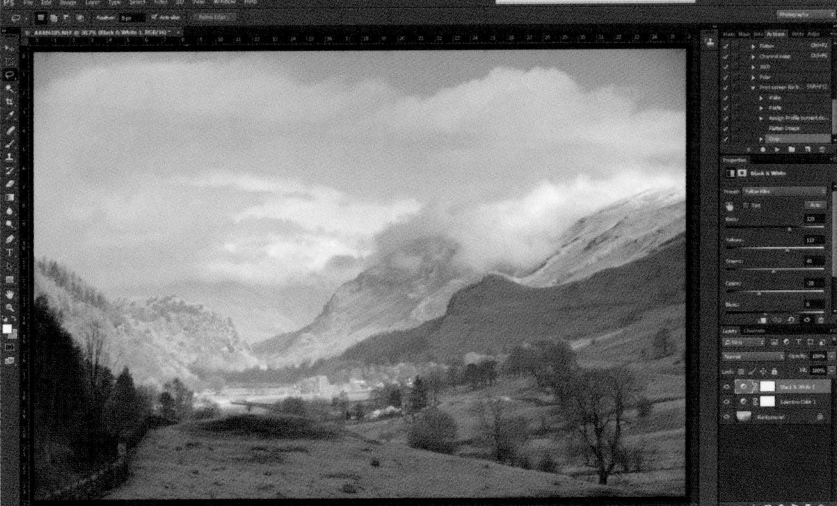

Fig. 7.9
Black & white adjustment layer added, using preset yellow filter.

- The blue sky looks a touch insipid, and a selective colour layer can be used to deepen the blues and cyans by adding black to them.
- Add a black and white adjustment layer – the red or yellow filter seems to give the best middle distance separation on this image.

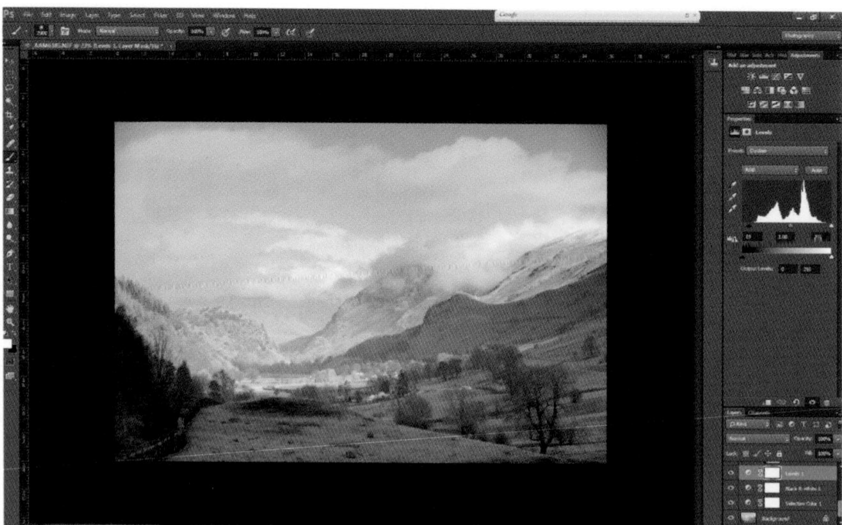

Fig. 7.10
Levels 1 layer added, shadows and highlight sliders moved in towards the edges of the histogram to increase overall contrast.

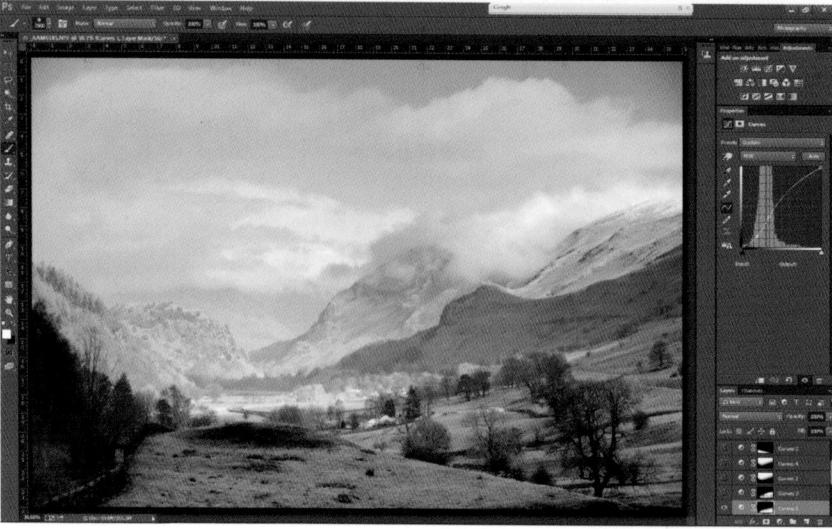

Fig. 7.11
Curves 1 layer added to increase contrast to grasses in the lower left of the picture (see Layer 1's layer mask).

- A levels layer allows the white and black points to be set – a slight increase in contrast.

The next stages are localized adjustments – as in previous chapters, use the quick mask (Q) tool in conjunction with the gradient tool (G) or the brush tool (B) to select the appropriate area, then remember to exit the quick mask (Q) before applying the adjustment layer. If you forget to exit quick mask, you will be attempting to add an adjustment to a mask, rather than the selected area of the picture.

This example has ten curves layers, each making small adjustments to various areas of the picture. As with all localized selections of this type, it is important to keep the edges of the selections really soft (*see* Figures 7.11 to 7.19).

Curves 1: Gradient selection of the grass in the lower right of the picture – increase in contrast by steepening the curve through the relevant part of the histogram.

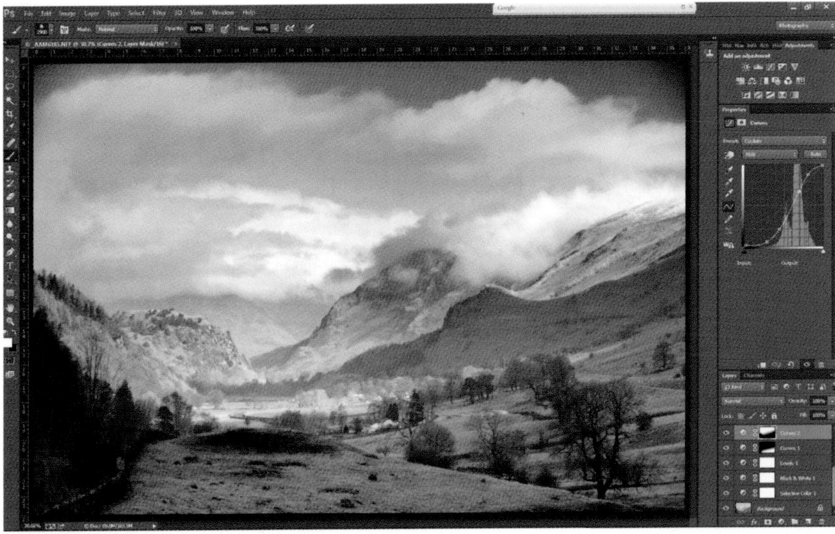

Fig. 7.12
Selected area of the sky (using quick mask) darkened and contrast increased by addition of Curves 2 layer.

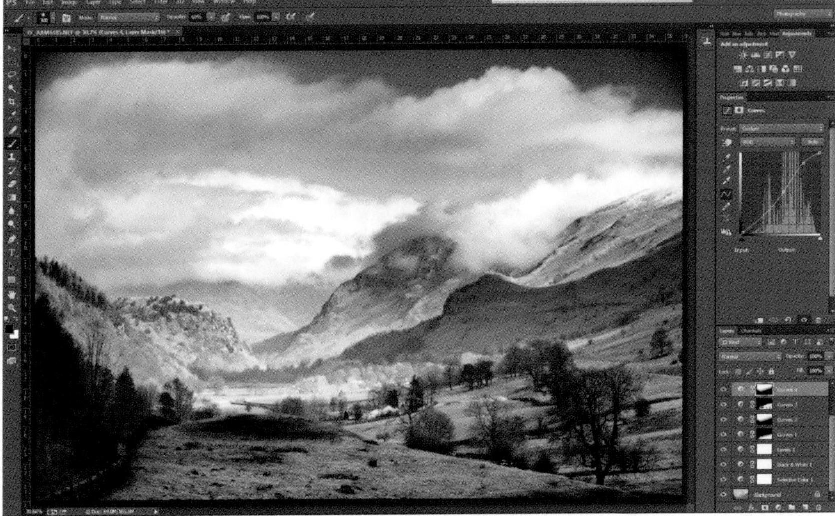

Fig. 7.13
Curves 4 layer – similar selection to Curves 3, adding more contrast to the sky by a slightly different shaping of the curve – by keeping the darker tones, but increasing the brightness of the lighter tones.

Curves 2: Gradient tool and brush tool used to select the sky, curves layer to increase the depth of tone of the mid-dark tones in the sky whilst preserving the brightness of the lighter clouds.

Curves 3: Another selection of the grassy areas at the bottom of the photo, but with the trees excluded from the selection. Allowing a slight darkening of the grass, without blocking up the tones in the tree areas.

Curves 4: Another sky selection adding contrast just to the mid-tones within the sky, It's often easier to add this as a second layer (the selection is identical to the curves 2 layer) but this is working on a defined part of the histogram for the sky, and it would be more difficult to shape the curves line on a single adjustment layer.

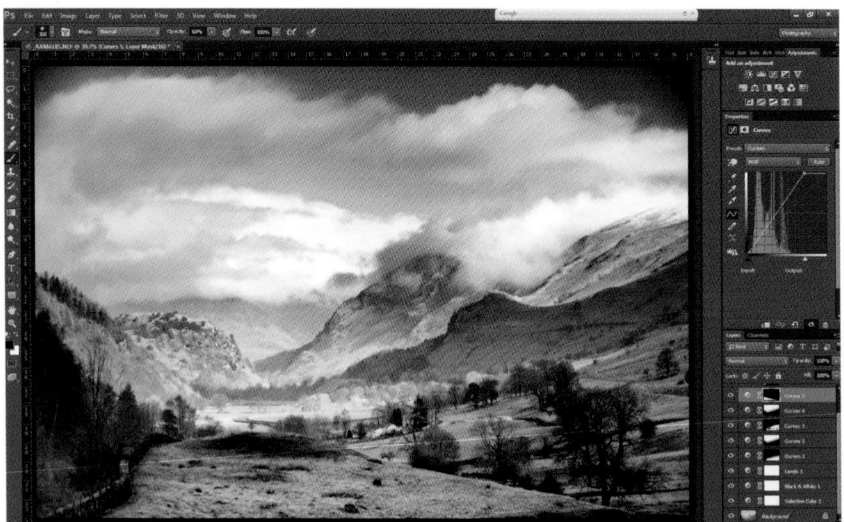

◀ Fig. 7.14
Curves 5 layer to slightly further lighten the grass mid-tones in the foreground.

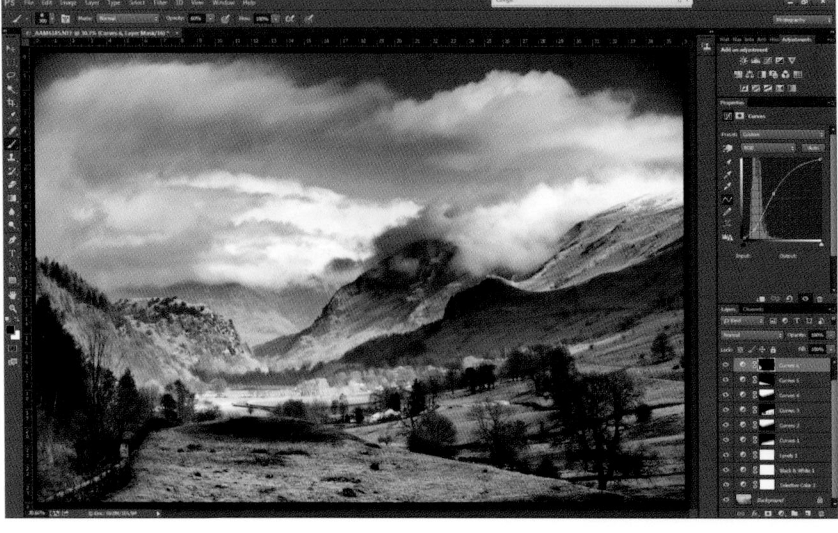

◀ Fig. 7.15
Curves 6 layer to add contrast to the bush in the lower left corner; note how dark the original tones were by looking at the histogram behind the curves properties palette.

Curves 5: Gradient selection of the lower left section of grasses, to lighten the mid-tones slightly.

Curves 6: Selection (by brush) of the tree and fence in the lower left of the picture, to get better separation through the darker tones by lightening the mid-tones on the branches.

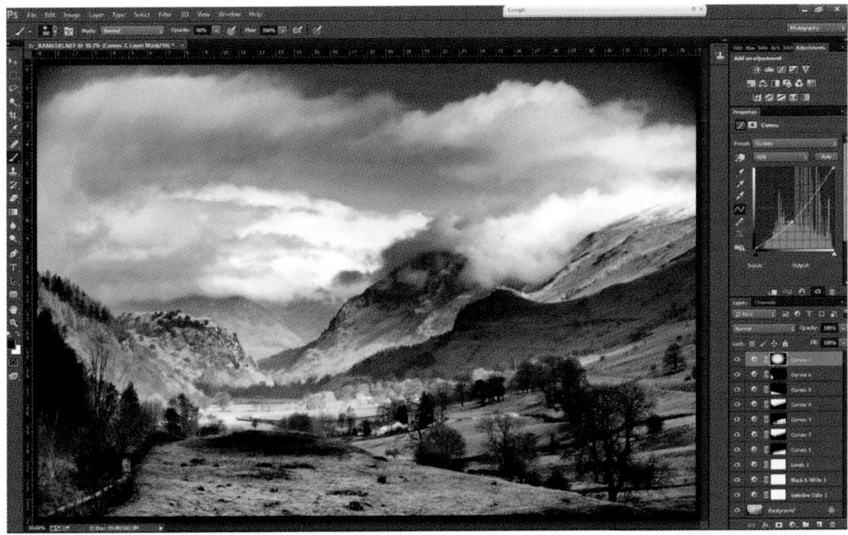

Fig. 7.16
Curves 7 layer to deepen the central tones.

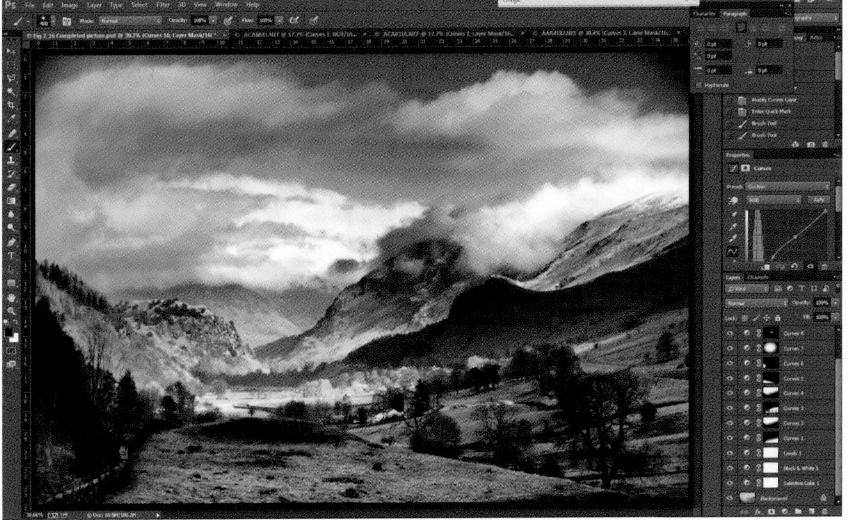

Fig. 7.17
Curves 8 layer used to lighten mid-distance mountain top and cloud (originally darkened by the graduated filter used to retain detail in the sky.

Curves 7: Large selection of the centre of the picture, which can be made by using a large brush in quick mask, or by using the radial gradient tool with the default colours exchanged – to go from white to black. The selection is to lower the darker tones in the area, as the original was a little too light in the centre of the image. The darkening adds drama and strength to the picture.

Curves 8: Small selection (by brush) of the top of the rock in the centre of the image, to lighten it slightly (the grad used in shooting the original image, whilst capturing sky detail well, did darken the rock) but equally to bring up the small white cloud drifting across the rock face.

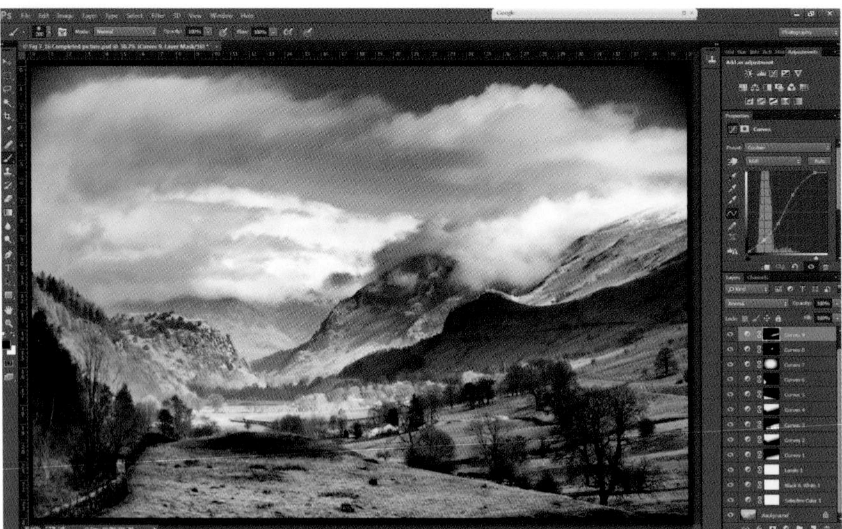

Fig. 7.18
Curves 9 layer to create a slight increase of contrast on right-hand mid-ground shadows, by separating them from the mid-tones within the same area.

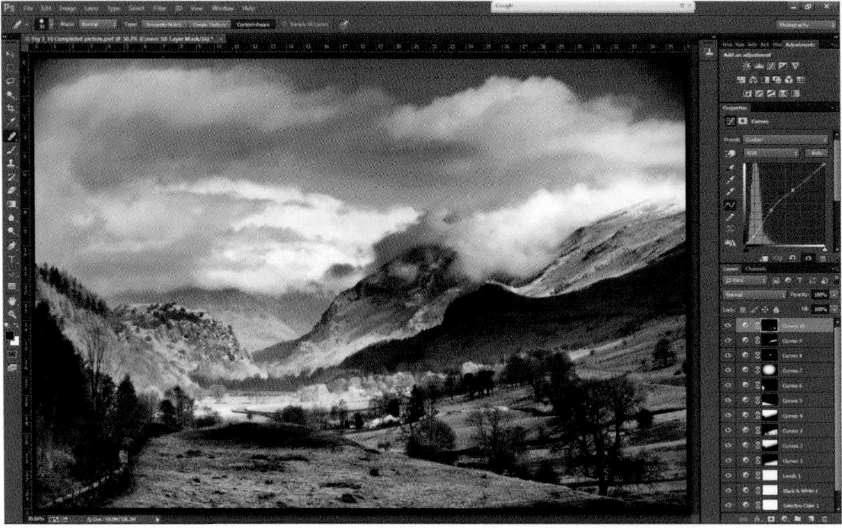

Fig. 7.19
Curves 10 layer used to lighten foreground trees.

Curves 9: Long thin selection (brush) of the shadow area on the right mid-distance, to increase the contrast locally and bring out the tones there.

Curves 10: Very small (round brush) selection of the central area of the individual foreground trees in the lower right of the picture, just to lift the mid-tones slightly.

Whilst more could easily be done to the picture, these relatively straightforward steps show the colossal change from the original data as shot, and the final result.

Fig. 7.20
Original file used to create high-key image.

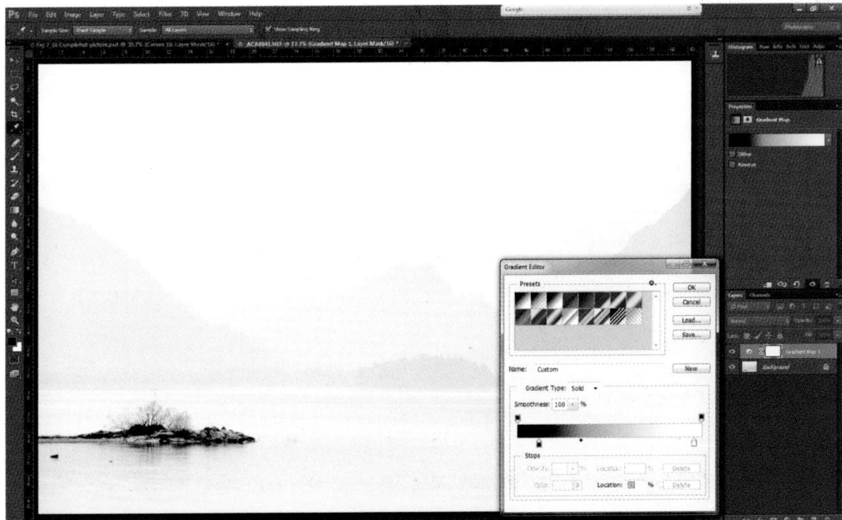

Fig. 7.21
Conversion to black and white using gradient map adjustment layer.

Example 2 – Creating a high-key image

Figure 7.20 was taken shortly after dawn on another hazy day, but this image lends itself to interpretation as a delicate, high-key image.

The black and white adjustment layer or the gradient map layer could both be utilized on this image. Both methods will be addressed to give alternatives.

Gradient map method

Make sure your histogram palette is visible for this conversion technique.

Add a gradient map adjustment layer, click on the drop-down arrow at the end of the default gradient and select black to white. A gradient editor dialogue box will open; click on the lower left black box at the end of the gradient line and drag it to the right. Pay close attention to the histogram and ensure that you do not clip the black detail. Do the same at the highlight (right) end. Finally, as soon as you make any change to the shadow or highlight sliders, a small diamond-shaped icon appears centrally just below the gradient. This is the colour midpoint

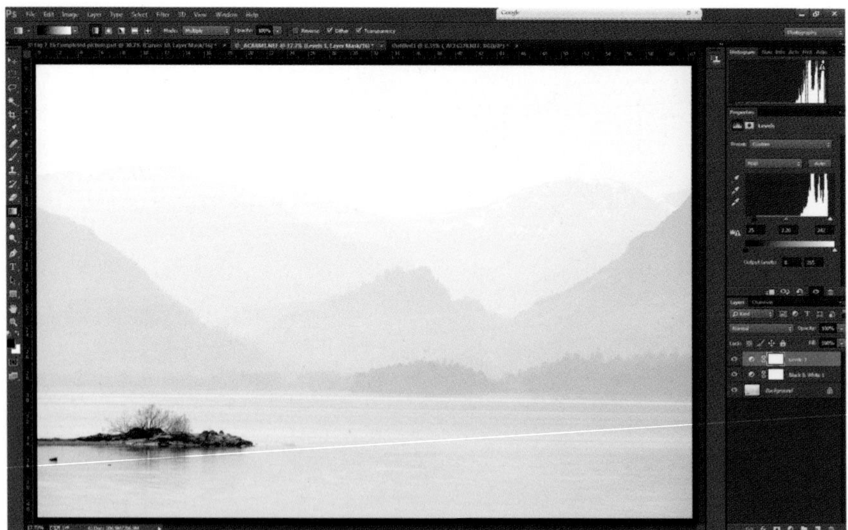

Fig. 7.22
Levels 1 layer added, shadow slider moved to the right to darken black tones, whilst mid-tone slider moved to the right to preserve and enhance mid-tones.

Fig. 7.23
Curves 1 layer used to deepen the dark foreground tones without having any pronounced effect on mid-tones or highlights.

slider. To get a feel of really high-key delicacy on this image, slide the colour midpoint slider to the left. (Figure 7.21) Quick, simple and very effective.

Black and white conversion method

From the basic image (Figure 7.20), add a black and white conversion layer. There is so little colour in the original that the default filtration setting will be the same as any other. Add a levels layer and slide the shadow and highlight sliders in to create a good black and a bright, but not blown, white. To lighten the mid-tones, as with the gradient map method, slide the grey (mid-tone) slider to the left until you achieve the high-key effect you want.

If the foreground headland is slightly light, add a curves layer and adjust the curve to deepen the dark tones in the image.

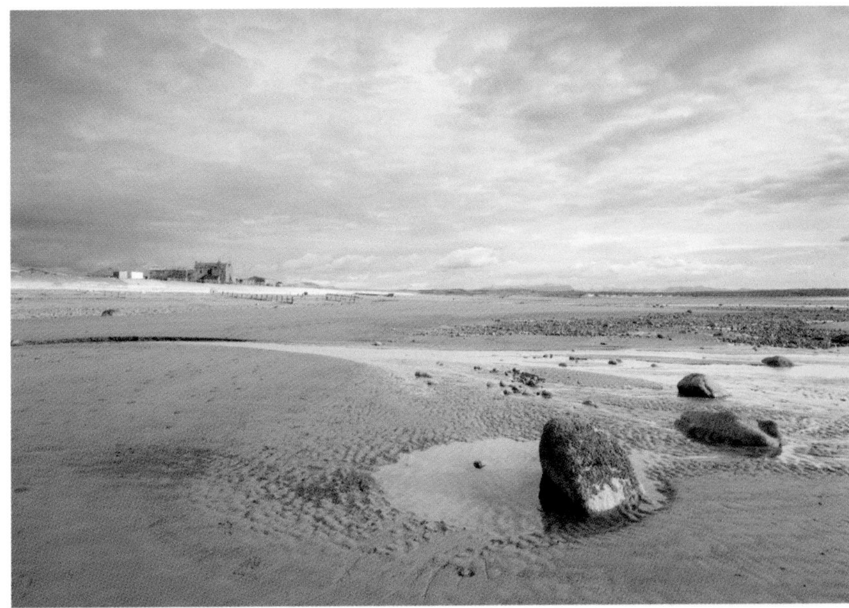

▶ Fig. 7.24
Original image of Cumbrian coastal view.

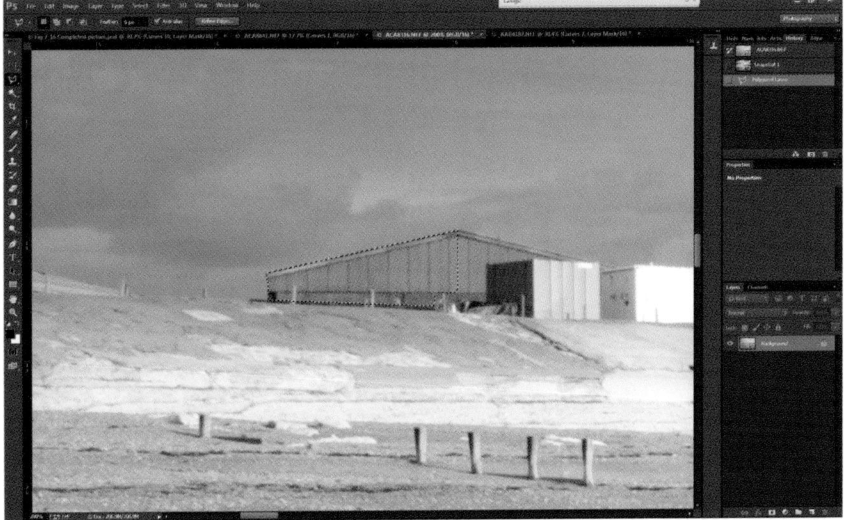

▶ Fig. 7.25
Select left-hand roof line of the barn using polygonal lasso tool.

Example 3 – Bringing out detail that you could see when you took the picture, but doesn't seem to be on the photograph

Figure 7.24 shows a picture taken on the Cumbrian coast. Towards the left side of the picture, by the farm, are a couple of builder's store buildings and some cones. Ideally these need removing.

Content-aware fill might not get this right straight off, so try selecting the left slope of the roof line (Figure 7.25), copy it to another layer (Ctrl-J) and *Edit>Transform>Flip horizontal*. Line the roof line up with *Edit>Transform>Rotate* and *Edit>Transform >Scale*, (Figure 7.26) and this successfully covers up a good deal of the store. A bit of simple cloning finishes off the job (Figure 7.27), though remember, if you are cloning, always clone

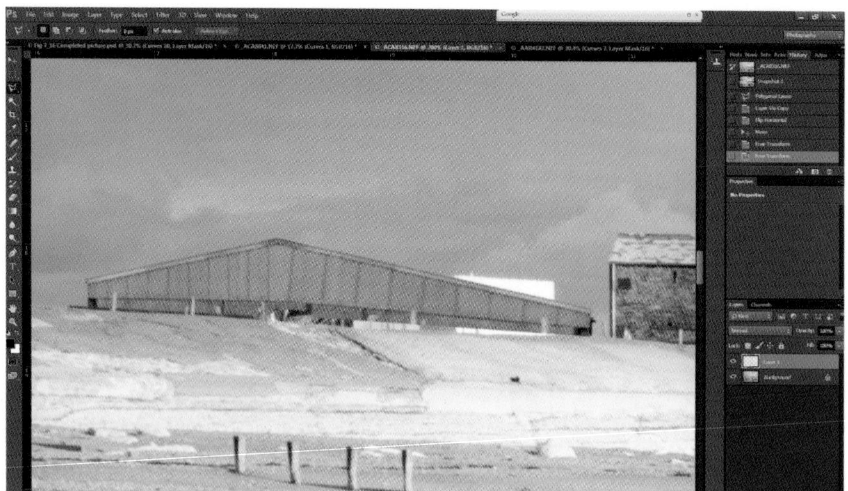

Fig. 7.26
Roof selection duplicated to new layer (layer 1), flipped and rescaled.

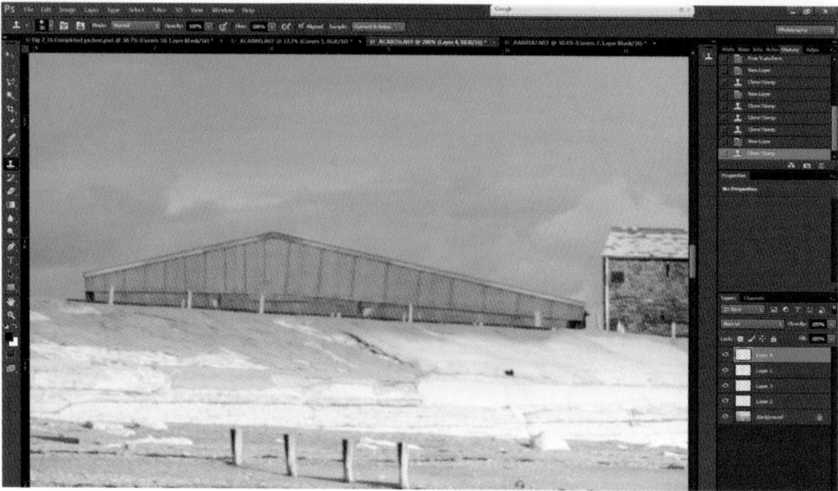

Fig. 7.27
Cloning on three layers to remove the remaining undesirable parts of the building works not covered by the 'new' roof.

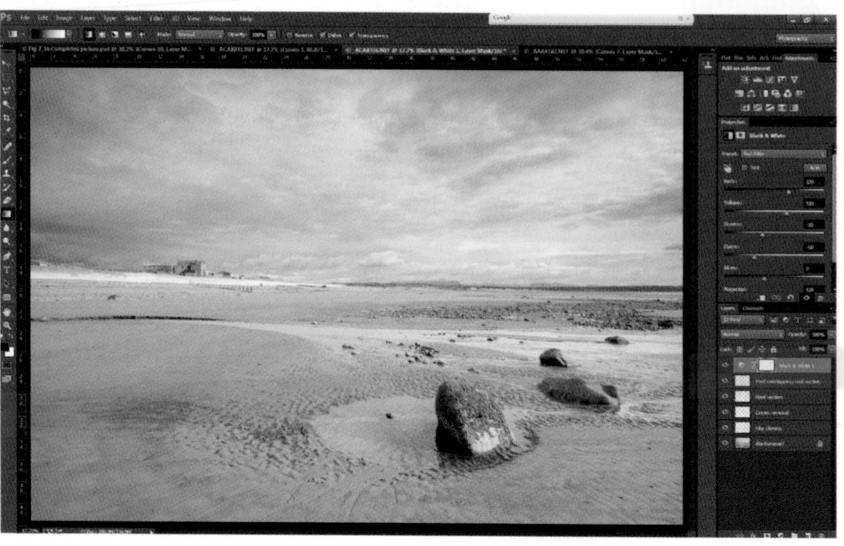

Fig. 7.28
Black and white adjustment layer added, (using preset red filter to maintain contrast, prevent the sky from lightening and keep good tone in the sand).

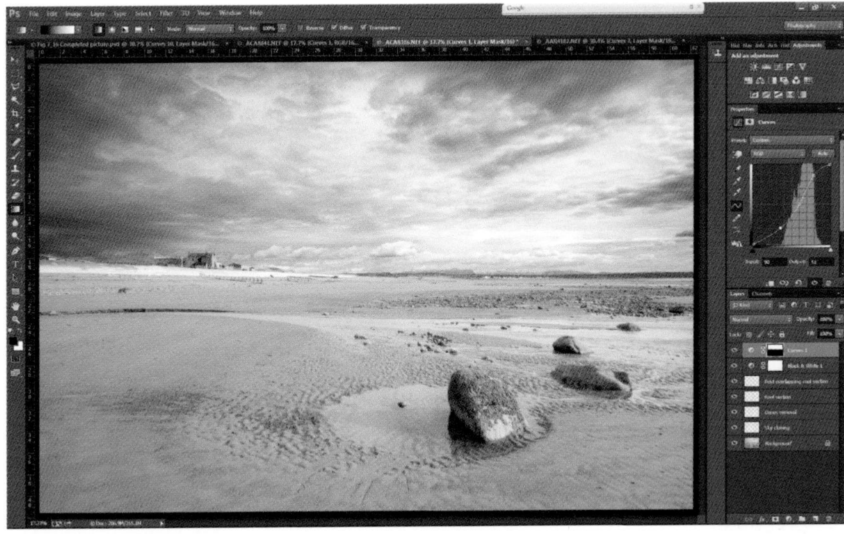

Fig. 7.29
Curves 1 layer added to increase contrast in the sky.

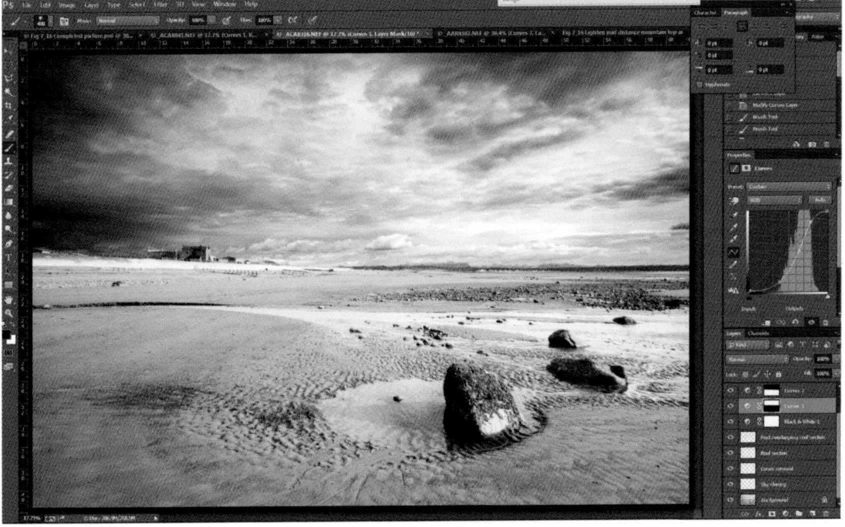

Fig. 7.30
Curves 2 layer added to increase contrast in the sand in order to bring out he texture – by steepening the curve line through the width of the histogram.

onto a separate layer, so any realigning can be carried out by moving *just* the cloned section you need to move, *not* all the cloned sections.

A final bit of cloning (content-aware fill would be perfect for this, as there is a large source area for content-aware fill to select from, and there are many footprints) could be carried out in the lower left of the photograph to remove unsightly footprints from the beach. Remember, if you miss any cloning out at this stage, by adding a new layer below all the adjustment layers and above the background layer, further cloning can be carried out at any time.

Again a few stages to convert to black and white and add the necessary contrast to bring out the textures of the sky and sand:

Add a black and white conversion layer – try a red filter to emphasize the cloud textures more.

Select the sky with quick mask (Q) and a gradient tool. A curves layer, with the curves line steepened through the central part of the histogram, will bring out the texture of the sky. Be careful not to lose detail in the bright highlight areas at the top end of the curve.

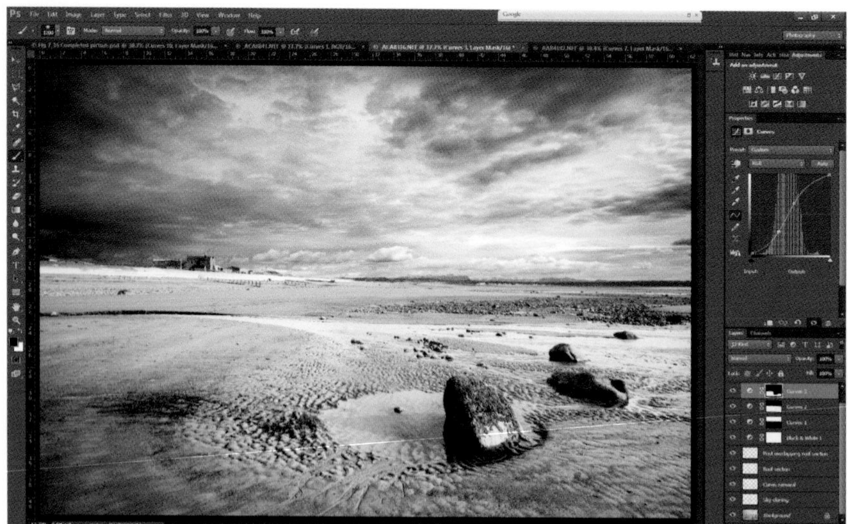

◀ Fig. 7.31
Curves 3 layer added to create stronger sand contrast to the smoother sand areas – note the different shape of the layer mask.

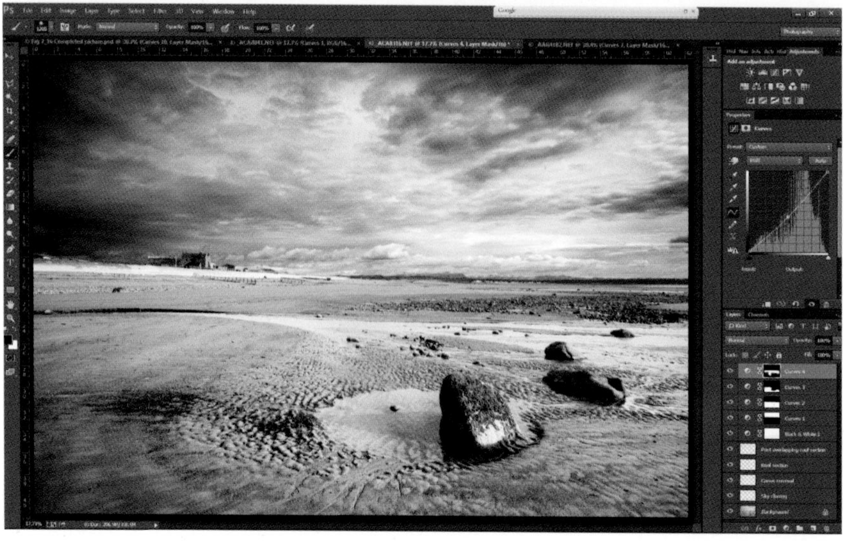

◀ Fig. 7.32
Curves 4 layer added to darken the central area of the sand thereby completing the picture.

Next, select the beach in the same manner as the sky, add curves (2) layer and increase the contrast similarly. The reason for working on these two areas separately rather than on a single overall curves layer is that the brightness of the sky (shown on the curves histogram), is lighter than that of the beach, and the section of the curve you are steepening is slightly different on each section. (Figure 7.30) If increasing the contrast of the whole beach makes the shadow areas of the rocks too dark, paint over them (on the layer mask) with a 30 per cent opacity black brush until you judge them to have enough detail.

Then select the fairly uniformly toned sandy area around the foreground of the picture, add a curves layer and increase the contrast significantly – this is the layer that really brings out the texture of the sand.

Finally, use a quick mask brush to select any areas in the centre of the picture that still appear slightly too light, a very slight central adjustment on the curve should suffice.

Hopefully, these worked examples demonstrate the huge interpretation possible when going from a colour original to a black and white final photograph.

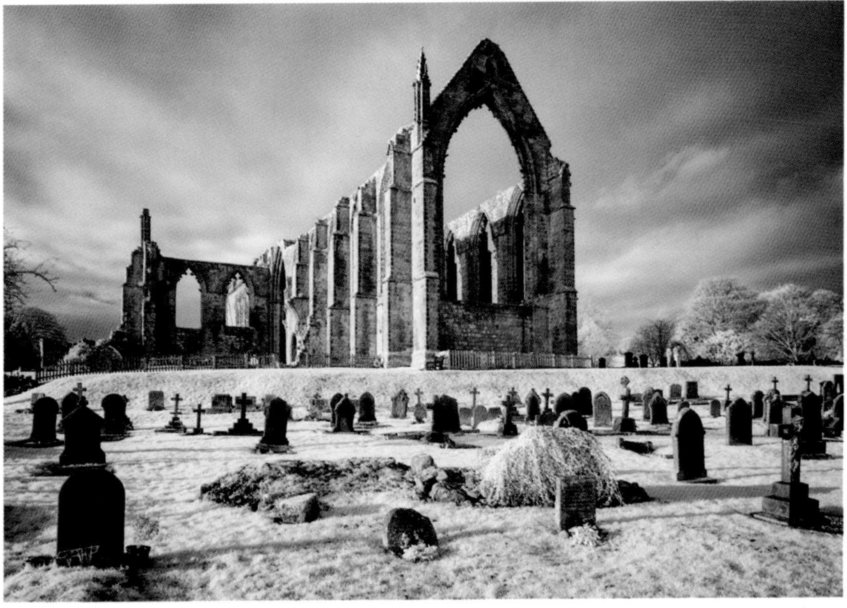

Fig. 7.33
Original 16-bit Infrared monochrome picture processed and flattened as a 16-bit RGB file.

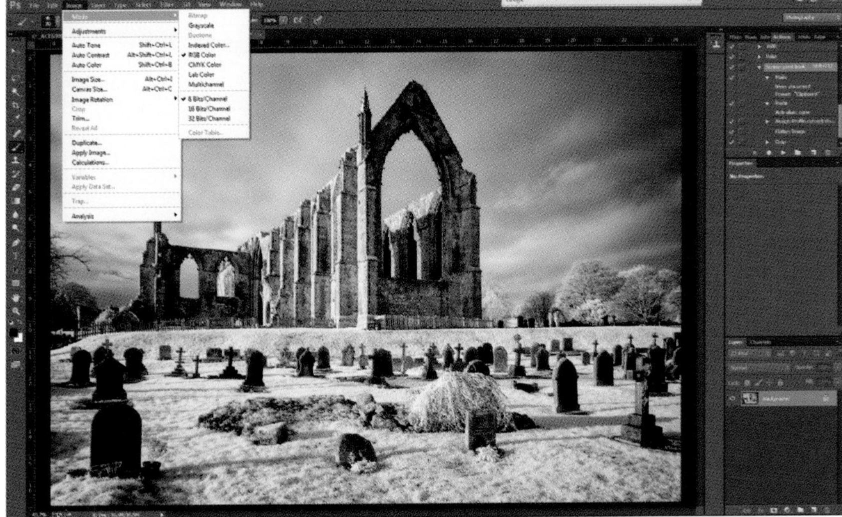

Fig. 7.34
Convert to 8-bit greyscale image (You will lose all colour data).

DUOTONE IMAGES

Duotone (and tri-tone) images can work well in adding a split-tone effect to your photographs. Figure 7.33 shows an infrared shot converted to black and white.

In order to turn a photograph into a duotone, it has to be in 8-bit depth and greyscale – you do lose a lot of data, but it is the only way. (Figure 7.34) Make sure you do as much work on editing the photograph in 16-bit RGB as possible prior to converting to greyscale; the less work done on the smaller file the better, as the quality might suffer.

Until your photograph is an 8-bit greyscale image, 'Duotone' is greyed out on the drop-down menus. Click on Duotone, and a dialogue box will appear with a black square. You'll notice that 'type'

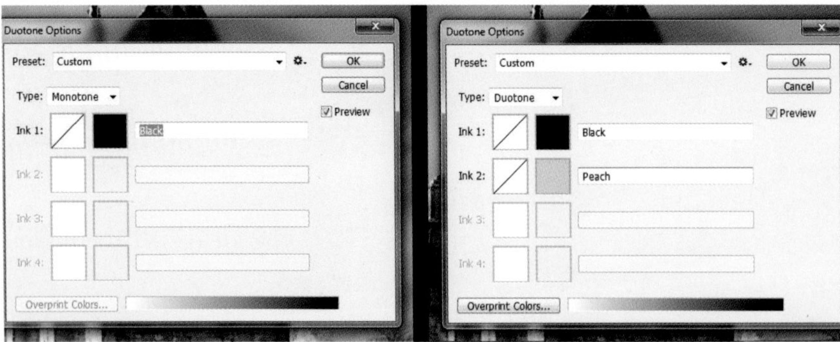

Fig. 7.35
Change monotone to duotone and select (and name) a secondary colour.

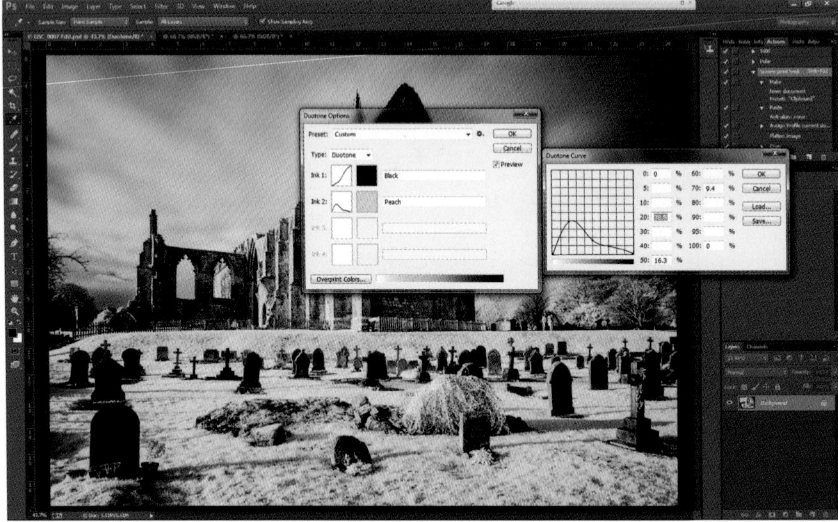

Fig. 7.36
Radical curve applied to the peach tones to create a split-toned image where the peach tones mostly affect tones around 25% grey values.

is set at monotone; click on the drop-down arrow and select duotone (tritone and quadtone are other options). Click on the clear (second) box and select a colour that you want as your split tone/tone in the picture. This photograph is being worked to look like a darkroom lith print, so a peach tone synonymous with lith printing has been selected. Whatever colour you choose, it has to be given a name, or it will not save.

The left-hand box adjacent to each of the colour boxes has a diagonal line running through it. This is in fact a curves layer that relates to the colour box. Whilst major alterations to the black tone will have a detrimental effect on the picture – in this case a little extra contrast in the blacks has been added – the curve relating to the peach box has been changed dramatically, (Figure 7.36) effectively applying the peach tones to the lighter tones within the picture, giving a split-toned effect. (Figure 7.37) You might find that to save the file you need to revert to RGB mode (*Image>Mode>RGB*).

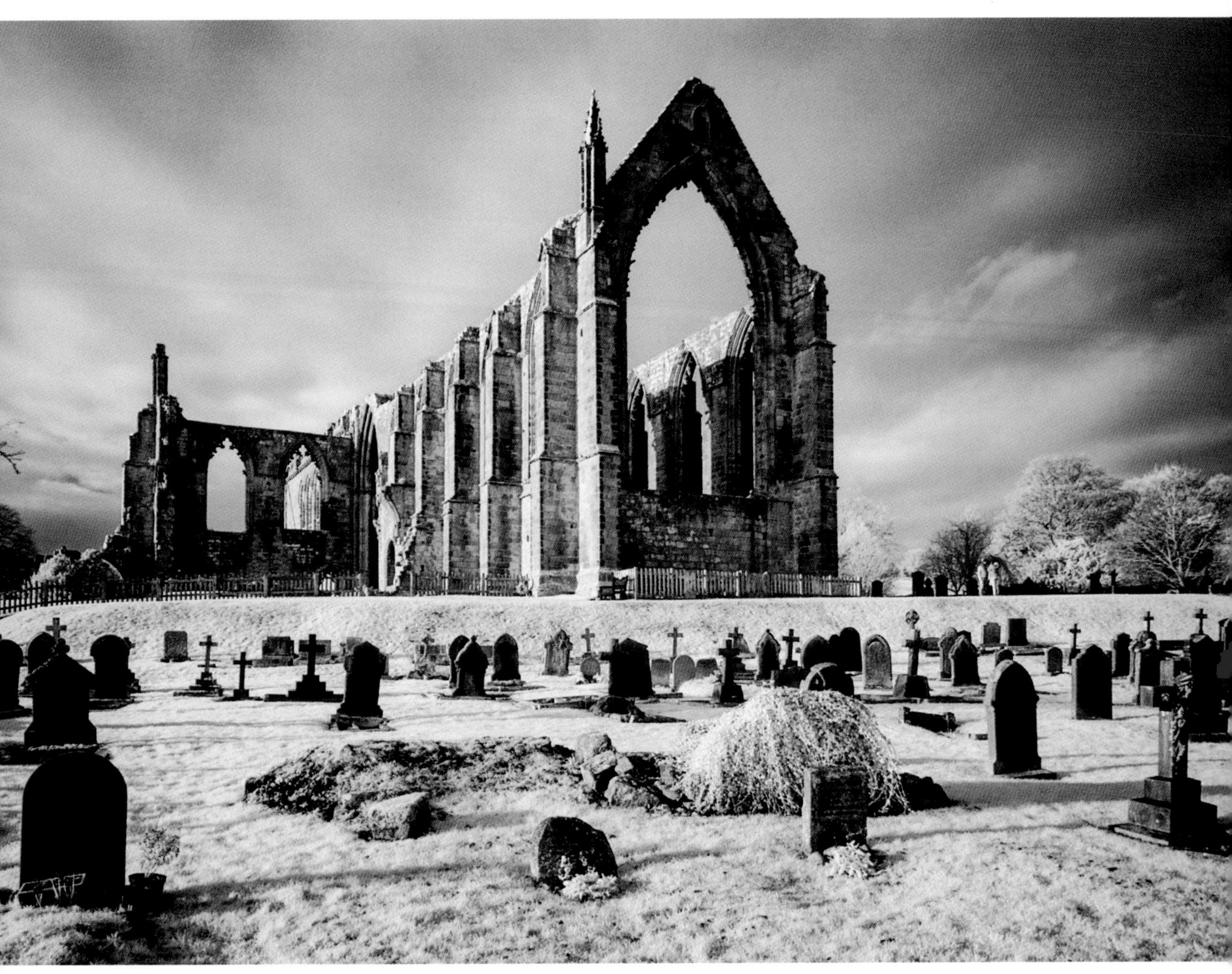

▲ Fig. 7.37
Completed lith-style image using duotone for split toning.

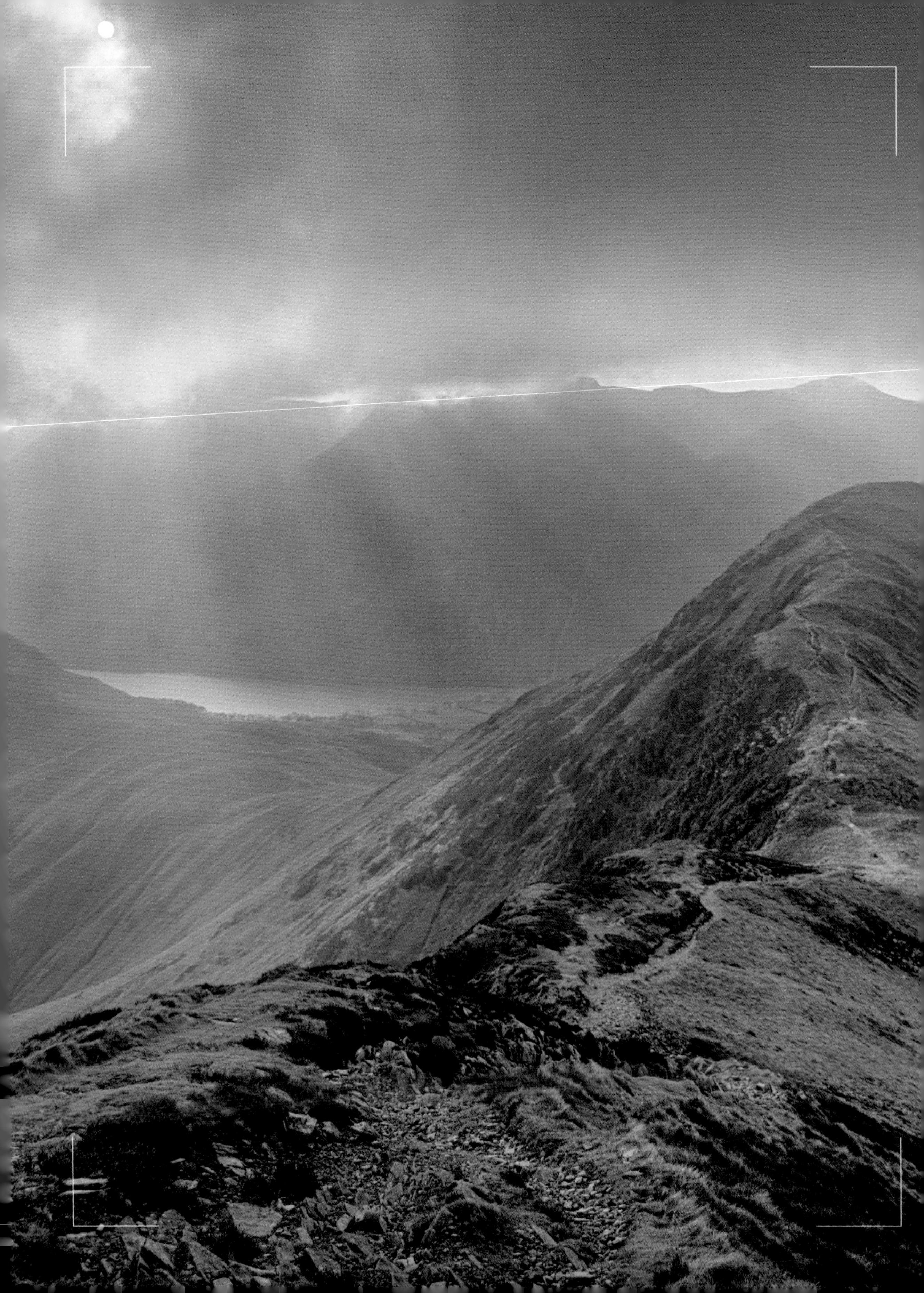

Chapter 8

Combining images

In some instances in photography, it is not always possible to achieve the desired effect with a single image. If the dynamic range of the brightness of a scene exceeds the 6 or so stops that the camera is capable of recording, a range of bracketed photos can be combined using the high dynamic range (HDR) facility within Photoshop. On occasion, the sky can be so bright that it might be preferable to drop another sky into the picture in its place. If the photographer is looking to create a long, thin image (either vertical or horizontal) a number of overlapping images can be joined together to create a panorama. Finally, in an image that requires greater depth of field than the camera can produce with the lens in use, it is possible to take pictures focused at different distances and join them together to increase depth of field by focus stacking.

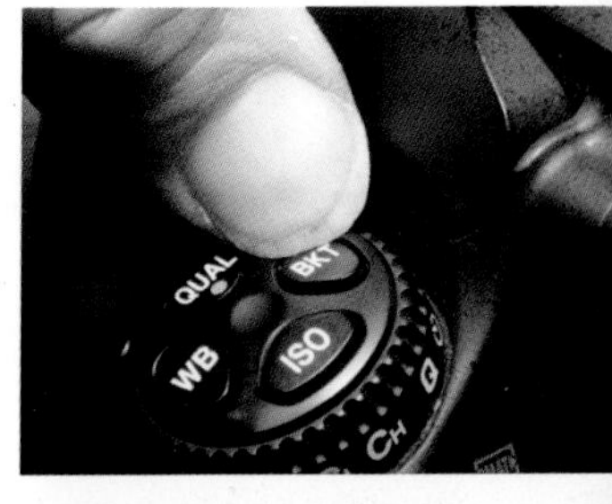

▶ Fig. 8.1
Bracket (Bkt) button on the Nikon D800.

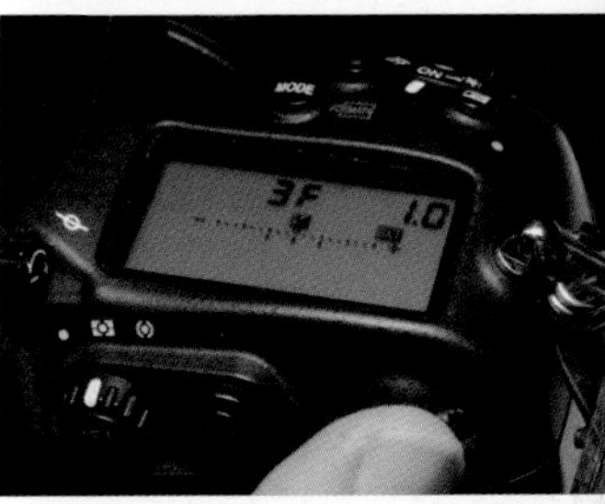

▶ Fig. 8.2
Bracketing set to 3 exposures at 1 stop increments.

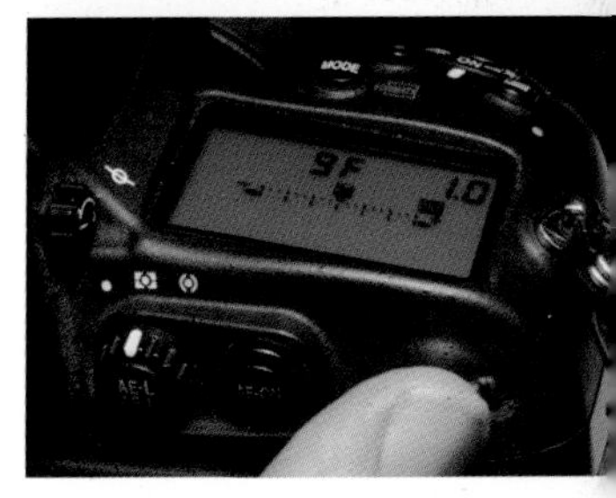

▶ Fig. 8.3
Bracketing set to 9 exposures at 1 stop increments.

HIGH DYNAMIC RANGE

So often in landscape photography, the brightness range between the sky and the land is too great to be encompassed on a single image file. We often manage to contain the dynamic range onto one file by using graduated filters in the field, but even then, the land areas are often rendered very dark and require a great deal of lightening in post processing. Where the contrast is particularly great, it is often better to bracket your exposures and combine the images in post processing. Most cameras offer a bracketing facility, referred to on Nikons as BKT (bracketing) and on Canons as AEB (auto exposure bracketing).

Most work in similar ways; the Nikon in Figure 8.1 shows the bracketing button, which must be held down, whilst simultaneously turning the thumb control wheel. It offers 3, 5, 7 and 9 exposures (3 and 9 are shown in Figures 8.2 and 8.3) at 0.3, 0.7 and 1.0 stop increments. Other makes offer three exposures only at up to 3-stop intervals. On most cameras, you have to fire the shutter for *each* of the required exposures. Some models allow you to set the self-timer and the camera will automatically fire the required number of shots.

In addition to the automatic exposure bracketing (which works with aperture priority, shutter priority and programmed modes) exposures can always be

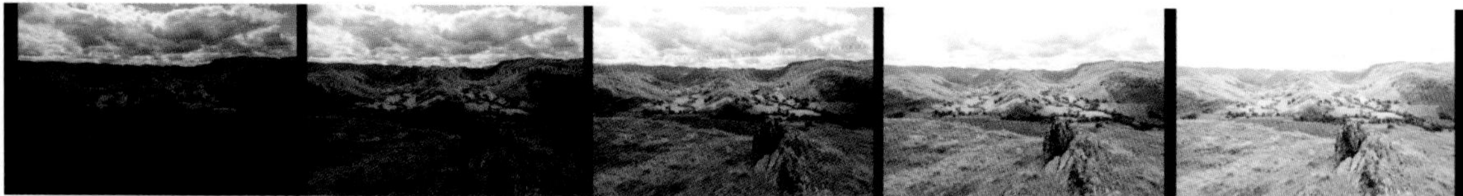

▲ Fig. 8.4
Bracketed sequence of 5 photos at 1 stop intervals.

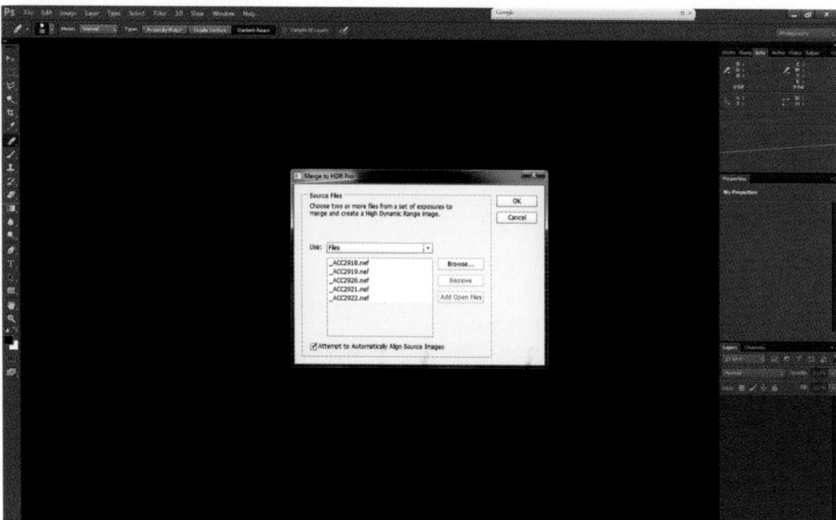

◄ Fig. 8.5
HDR Pro dialogue box opened in Photoshop.

altered manually as well. How you achieve a range of different exposures is not relevant; the important thing is that you end up with the lightest exposure offering really good shadow detail, and the darkest exposure retaining detail in the highlights. Figure 8.4 shows such a range of five bracketed pictures, each taken at one-stop intervals.

The centre picture is the 'metered' result, and the sequence from left to right is therefore –2EV, –1EV, 0, +1EV, +2EV. To get the best results on HDR images, it is advisable that all pictures are shot on a tripod, at the same aperture – this ensures that the pictures line up accurately and the depth of field is the same in each picture, which it wouldn't be if the aperture was altered. It is recommended that all bracketed sequences are shot on either manual exposure, or on aperture priority. The software will attempt to line up pictures that are slightly misaligned, so although not generally recommended, hand-held HDRs are (at a push) possible.

Under *File>Automate>Merge* to HDR Pro, a dialogue box appears on the workspace and allows you to browse for the bracketed pictures. Once you have selected your RAW files, ensure the box 'Attempt to align source images' is ticked, and click OK.

The HDR Pro box will open, combining your images. Usually the resulting image on screen will appear a little dark. In the top right corner of the screen is a drop-down menu for mode, the default setting is 16-bit, but for HDR work it is always best to work in 32-bit. The screen cannot display the huge dynamic range that a 32-bit image will contain, but it gives a massive amount of data to work with.

Ensure the box 'complete toning in Adobe Camera RAW' is ticked, and click on the button in the bottom right of the screen, 'Tone in ACR'.

The Adobe Camera RAW page opens and this image requires some processing. Both highlights and whites sliders need to be moved to the left to retain detail in the lighter areas of the cloud, and

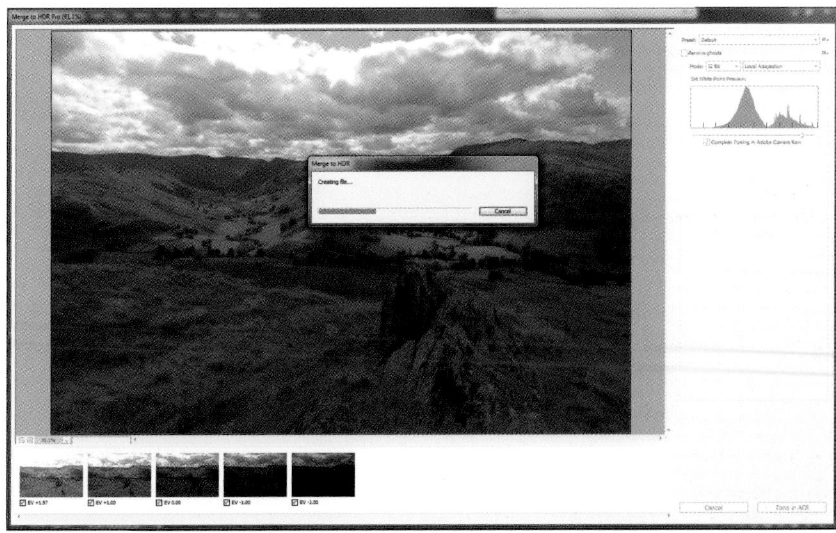

Fig. 8.6
Merging five images as an HDR 32-bit file (See 'mode' at top right of window).

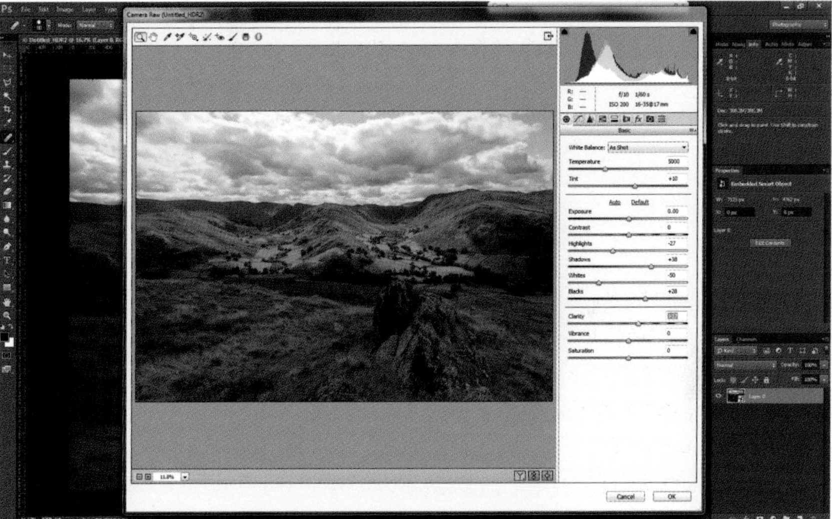

Fig. 8.7
Alterations made in camera RAW to the combined images.

blacks and shadows sliders need to be moved to the right to lift the darker tones. This tends to make the image as a whole look a little flat and dull, so perhaps an increase in the clarity to add a little definition to the tones. Remember, any adjustments made at this stage are to ensure dark tones are not blocked up and light tones are not blown – further alterations can be made in Photoshop, and often this can avoid the overdone 'HDR look' that we are all so familiar with.

When you are satisfied with the adjustments, click 'OK'.

The image will be processed and the file will open up as a 32-bit photo in Photoshop. At this point it is worth saving your file as a PSD (or TIFF if you prefer). Keep this 32-bit file as a reference file, because you may go back to it later.

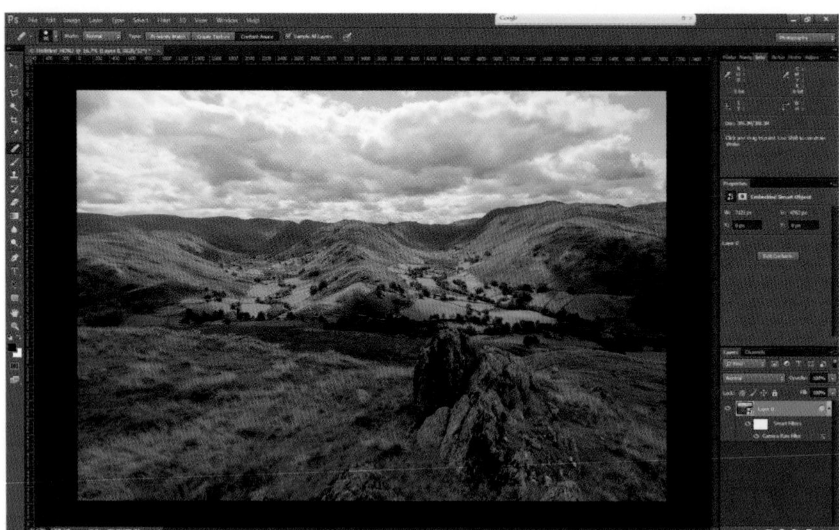

Fig. 8.8
32-bit HDR file.

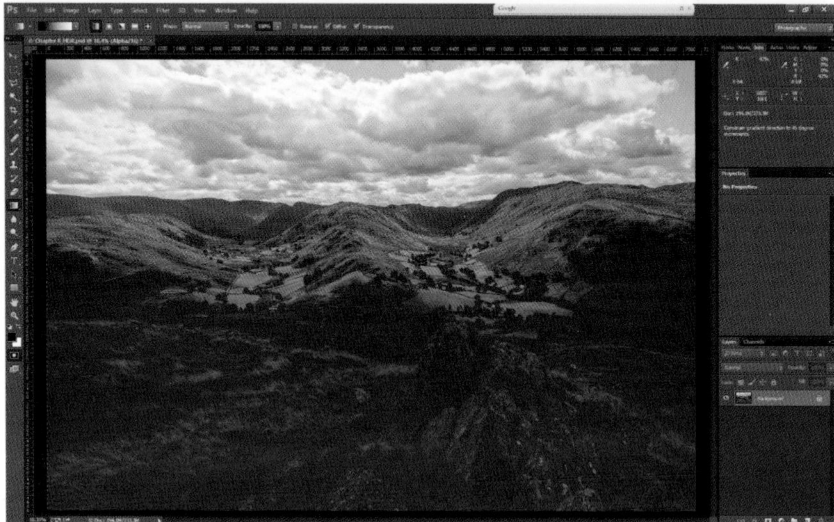

Fig. 8.9
Quick mask selection of ground on resulting 16-bit HDR to select it for further editing.

You cannot work on the file as a 32-bit; it is necessary to change it to a 16-bit file. If you just use *Edit>Mode>16Bit* you will get a warning dialogue box starting 'document appears to have active smart filters. Some filters may not work properly in the converted document depth'. Either click 'OK' and click 'Merge' on the subsequent dialogue box, or flatten the image, then convert to 16-bit. An HDR Toning box will open – if further changes are needed, they can be made here, but if you were happy with your adjustments in Camera RAW, there shouldn't be much need for change to the overall picture.

When the picture is converted to a 16-bit file, it can be worked on in exactly the same way as any other picture opened in Photoshop. In this case, the ground needs brightening slightly. A gradient selection with quick mask (Figure 8.9) will select the ground at the base of the picture, which, with the addition of a curves adjustment layer (after exiting quick mask) will allow the ground to be lightened.

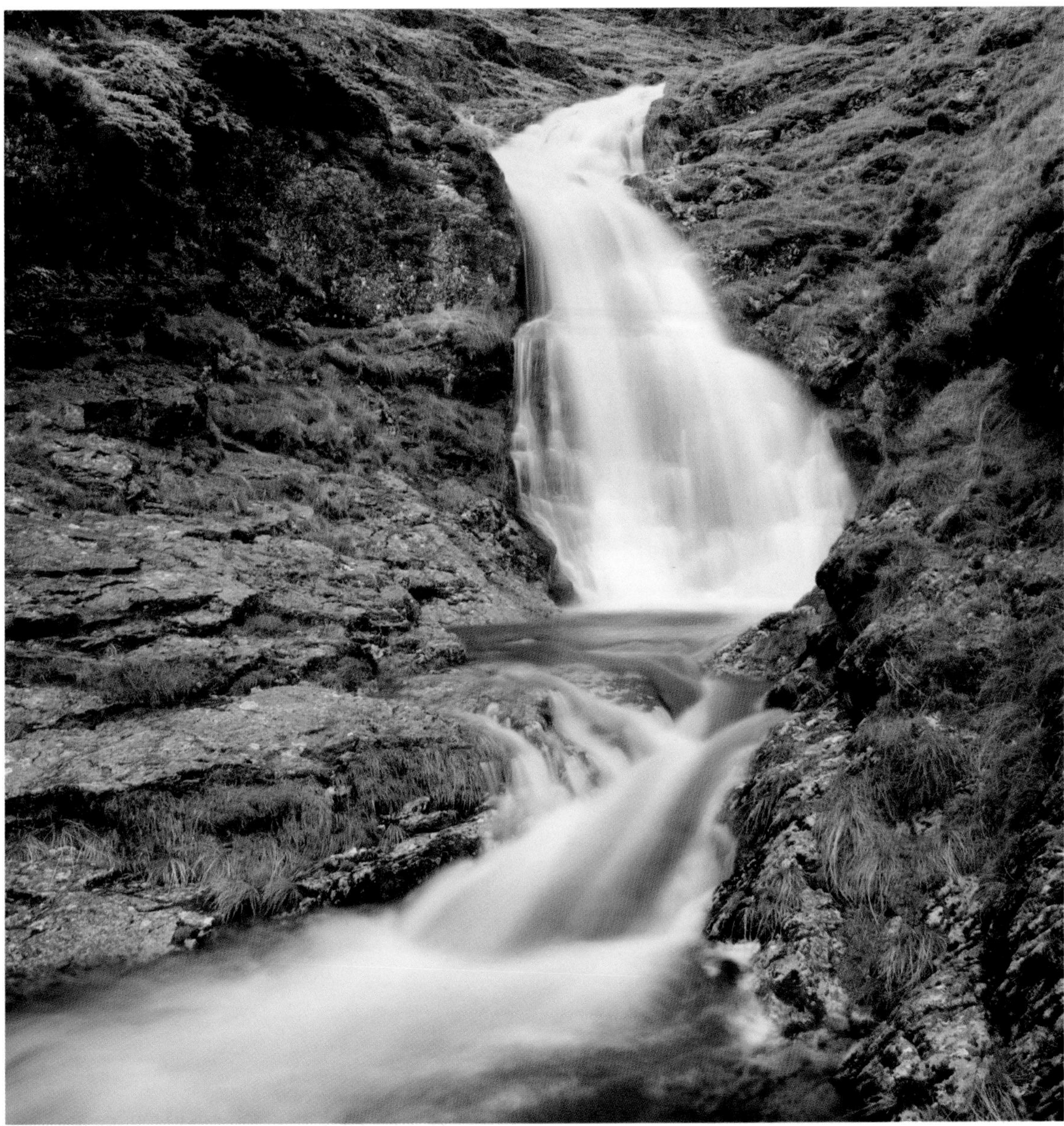

▲ Fig. 8.15
Vertically stitched panorama used to create a wider-angle image than was possible with a single image.

possibly needing only three or so images to combine. Vertical panoramas, although less commonly seen, can be really effective.

Panoramas don't always need to be excessively long and thin. Shooting a waterfall recently, I didn't have as wide a lens as I required. Ideally, I needed about an 18mm lens shot portrait to get the picture I was after, but the widest lens I had with me was a 28mm. Three overlapping shots taken in landscape format but panned vertically gave me the coverage I needed (and a larger image in terms of pixels) so I could print it really large.

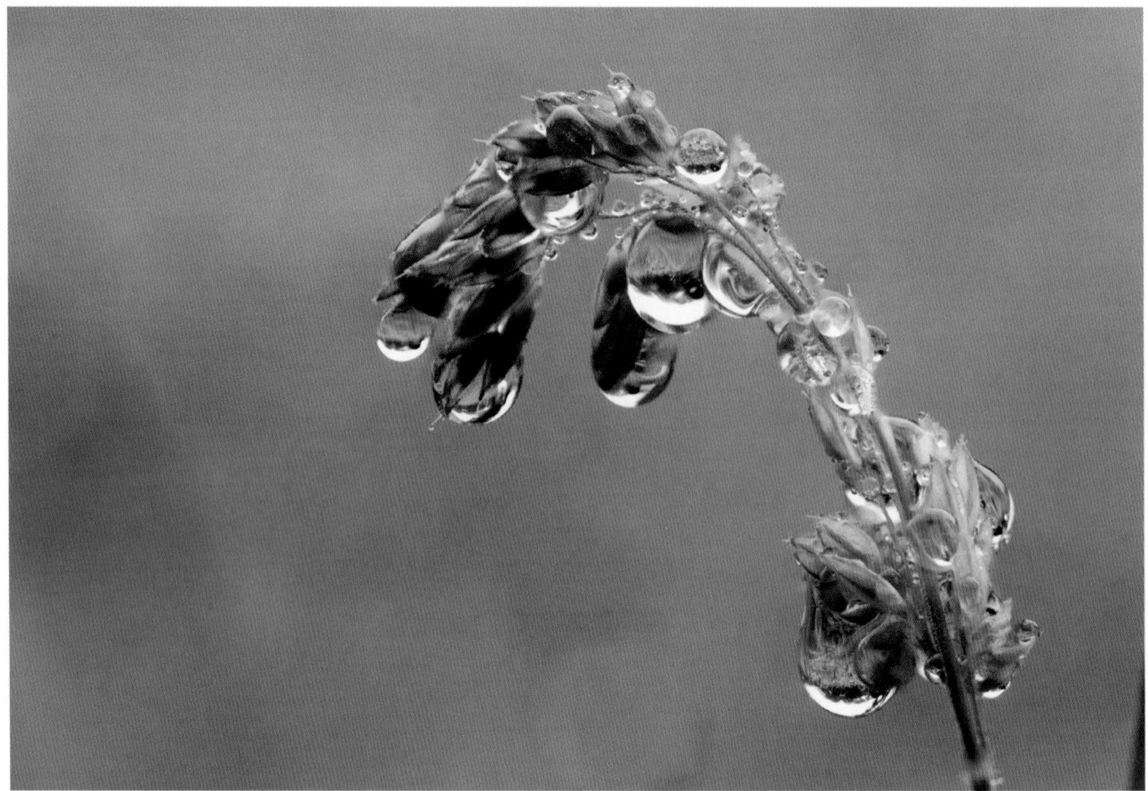

▲ Fig. 8.16
Focus-stacked image of a dew-laden grass head.

FOCUS STACKING

Achieving great depth of field in landscape photographs is something we all strive for on certain pictures. But shooting at *f*22 or smaller isn't always getting the best quality out of your lens, and many photographers, particularly with some of today's high mega-pixel cameras, prefer to shoot at apertures of no more than *f*11. Shooting an expansive landscape with foreground detail can, in these circumstances, prove difficult to achieve sufficient depth of field (sharpness from foreground to background). Focus stacking is a technique usually used in close-up photography, designed to extend the depth of field in a photograph, by taking a series of in-focus slices, and layering them together, to create a picture with a greater depth of field than would be possible with a single image. The sequence of pictures are best taken on a tripod, and as with panoramic photography, best at the same exposure, or the various 'slices' won't match up seamlessly. In general landscape photography, it can be used to give incredible depth of field, literally from a few inches to infinity. The easiest way to capture the set of pictures to be stacked is to use manual exposure, and manual focus. It's probably easier to start by focusing at the nearest point, then manually shift focus slightly further into the picture, and keep going until you have got a set of pictures that covers the depth of field you need. For practical purposes, two will be the minimum, and there is really no maximum, as the number of steps of focus will depend on the aperture you are shooting at; it isn't unheard of to have as many as thirty or forty pictures in a focus-stack, though that would be really unusual.

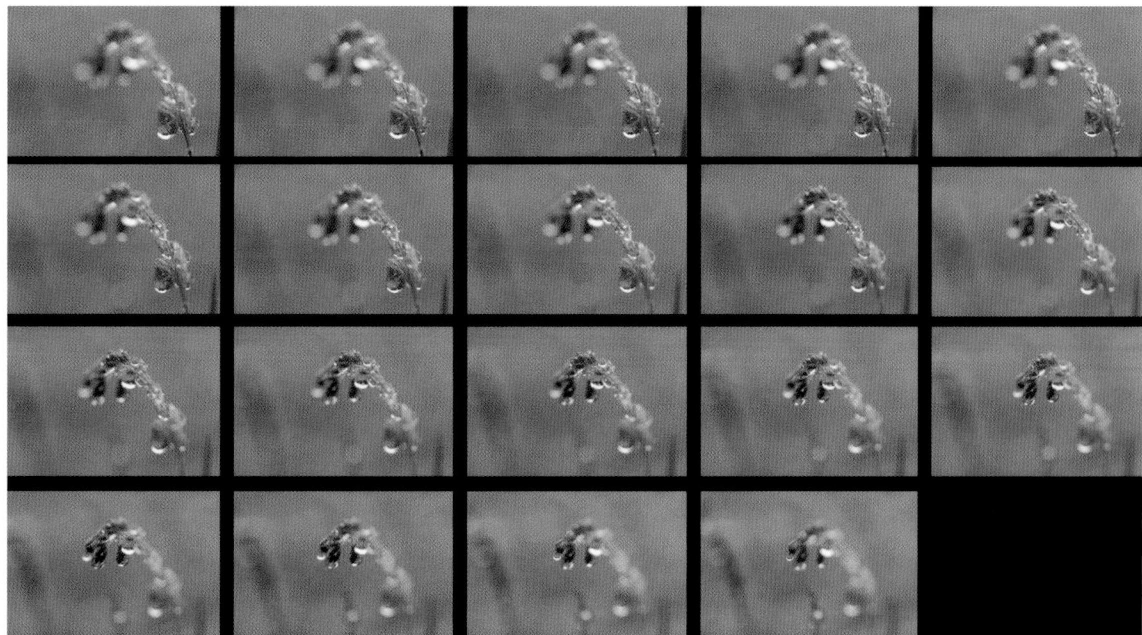

▲ Fig. 8.17
The 19 images used to create the focus-stack of the grass head.

The worked example here is more a close-up than a landscape, but serves to show another great use of focus stacking.

It was taken on a very still, but rainy day, and water droplets were hanging off the grass head. Shooting at an angle on the grass head gave the most pleasing, soft background at *f*9, but this close to the subject gave almost no depth of field. Even shooting at *f*32 didn't get the whole grass head in focus, but did make the background more easily recognized and distracting. Shooting at *f*9 to keep the background out of focus and manually focusing at the front of the grass (on the stem) and taking the first exposure, then nudging the focus further back through the grass head, photographs were taken continually until the far end of the head was in focus. A total of nineteen images were used.

To open them up and line them up in Photoshop, click on *File>Scripts>Load files into stack*; the dialogue box will give you the ability to browse for your selected pictures.

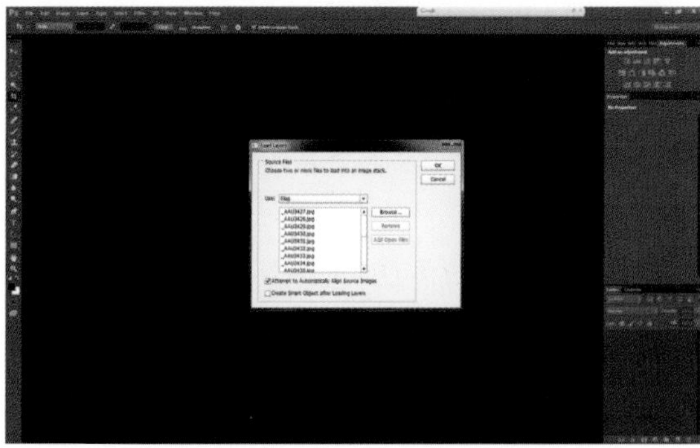

▲ Fig. 8.18
Focus-stack (Load files into stack) dialogue box used to browse for the pictures to include in the stack.

The tick box marked 'Attempt to automatically align source images' should be ticked. (Note: If you do forget to tick the box, aligning images can be performed as a separate action afterwards.) The reason this box has to be ticked is that as a lens is focused from infinity to close focus, it changes slightly in effective focal length. So elements within the picture grow or shrink according to the lens design. The align function will resize each layer to allow features

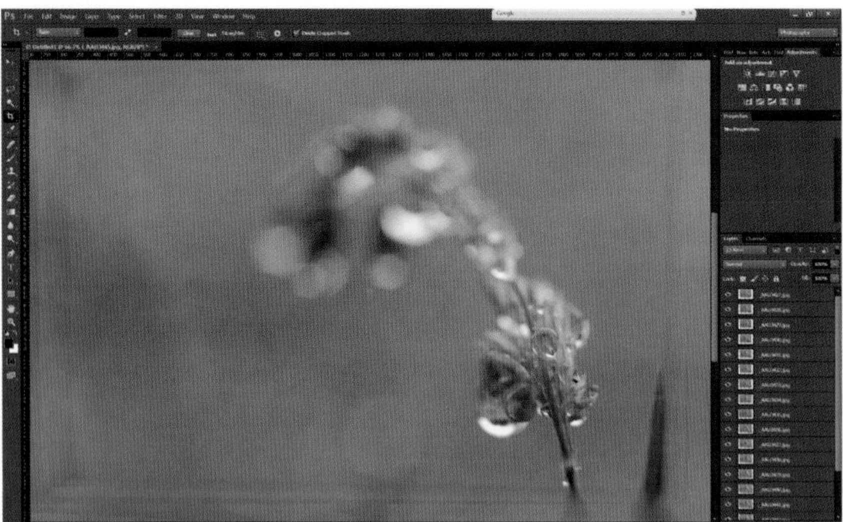

Fig. 8.19
Images loaded in stack and auto-aligned.

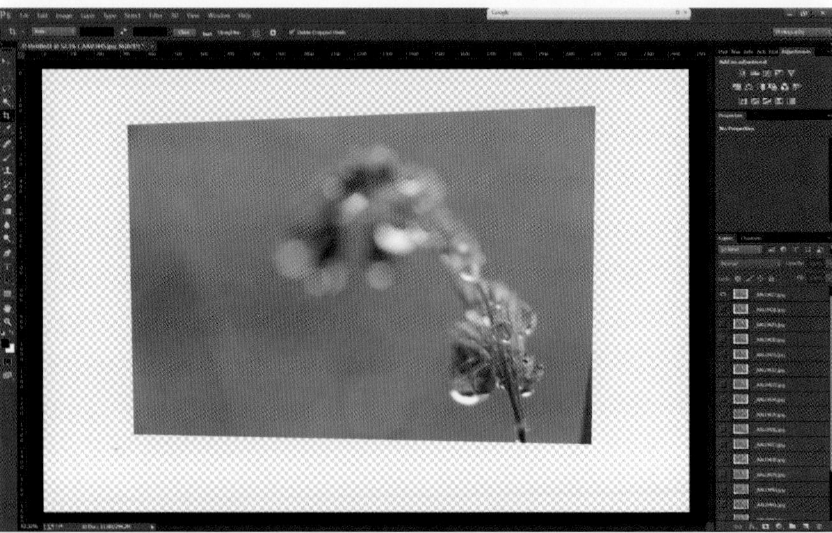

Fig. 8.20
Top layer visible only indicating how much the image changed in size during refocusing and giving a guide for cropping the image so that all layers are full of data.

within the picture to line up perfectly. Click 'OK' and Photoshop will load all the images into one picture, keeping each as a separate layer.

Try switching off all but the top (or bottom) layer, depending on how the images have been resized, just to see how much they have been scaled to fit.

The image needs cropping to the size of the smallest layer – remember this when you are shooting in the field – otherwise the background will look messy.

Once you have cropped the image, ensure all the layers are switched back to visible (eye showing) and select all the layers; do this by clicking on the top layer, scrolling down to the bottom layer (on the layer palette), holding the Shift key, and clicking on the bottom layer; they should all become selected/ active layers.

Finally, click on *Edit>Auto blend layers* and ensure the 'stack images' box is selected, along with the 'seamless tones and colours' tick box. Click OK and Photoshop will create the full focus-stack, by creating layer masks for each layer.

When working with large files and a lot of layers, this can take a few minutes, depending of course on

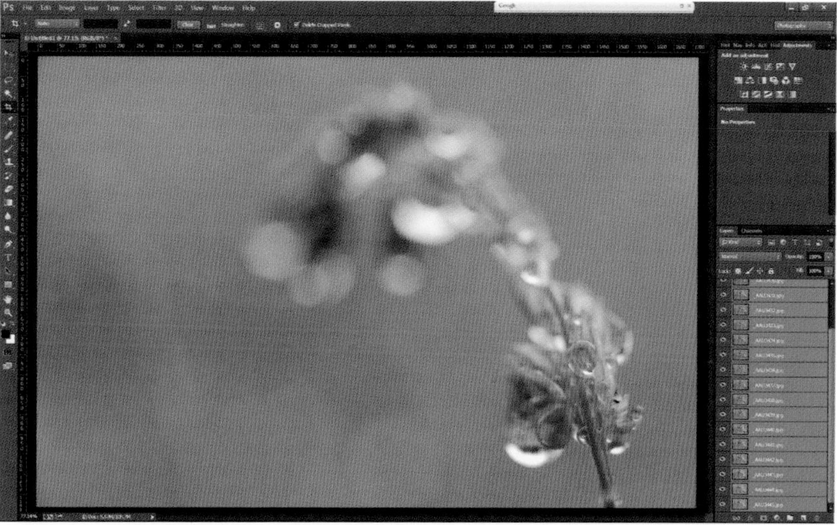

Fig. 8.21
All layers selected (shown by blue colour of each of the layer tabs).

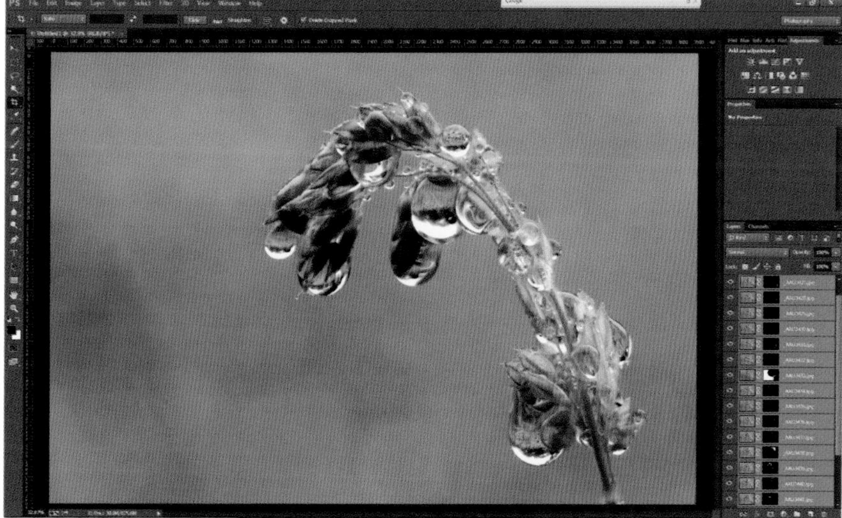

Fig. 8.22
Completed focus-stack showing layer masks on each layer.

your computer's processing power – just let it get on with it. If there are any areas that don't line up right in the final image, run it again from scratch – it isn't infallible, but it does a really good job 95 per cent of the time. If there are slices in and out of focus through the picture, it means you didn't overlap the in-focus zones between adjacent images, and nothing can be done in Photoshop. It is the most common error in focus stacking.

REPLACING SKIES

A technique that is all too often done badly, with the border between the new sky and the landscape having an obvious join, or an inappropriate sky, light coming from the wrong direction, incorrect white balance, perspective mismatches between the sky and the land; the list goes on.

As a recommendation, skies should only be replaced if there really is no other option; the sky being 'dropped in' needs to have similar perspective

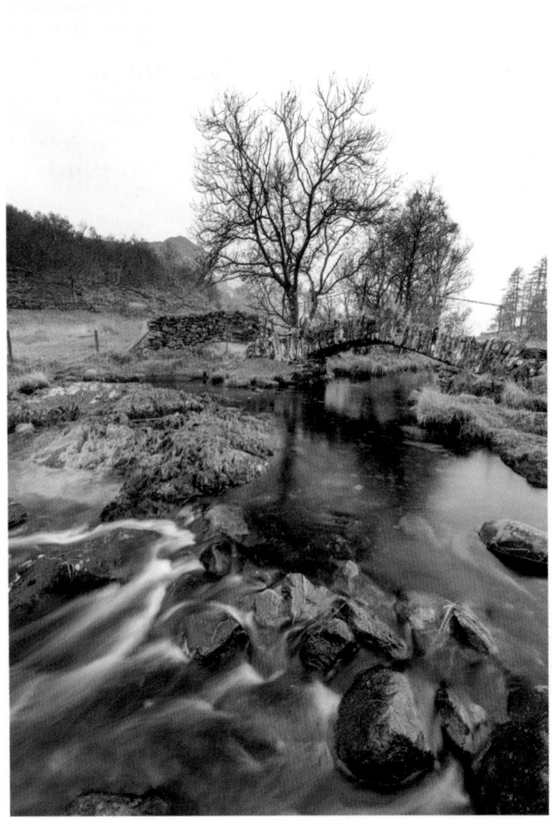

▲ Fig. 8.23
Slater's bridge with featureless sky, which would benefit from a sky with more detail.

▲ Fig. 8.24
is the sky above the previous photograph, taken a few seconds after the first, and exposed to keep the sky detail.

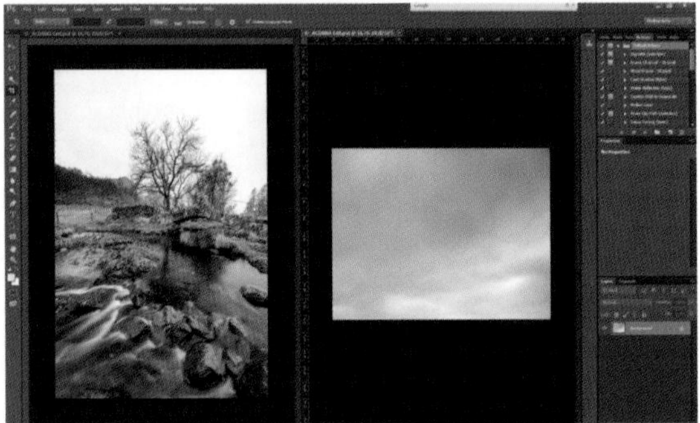

▲ Fig. 8.25
Split screen showing both the picture of the bridge and the one of the sky.

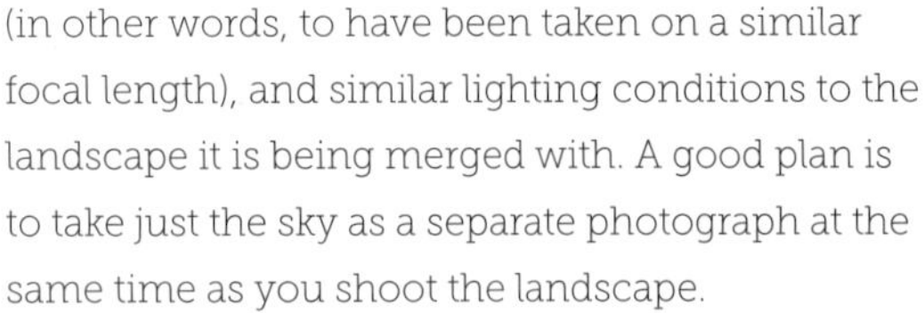

(in other words, to have been taken on a similar focal length), and similar lighting conditions to the landscape it is being merged with. A good plan is to take just the sky as a separate photograph at the same time as you shoot the landscape.

Figure 8.23 shows Slater's Bridge with a sky that was almost impossible to retain any detail in – back-lit, with the silhouetted tree blowing in the wind. Because of the tree movement, it wouldn't lend itself to an HDR, and because of the tree, a graduated filter strong enough to hold the sky, made the tree far too dark.

Figure 8.24 is the sky above the previous photograph, taken a few seconds after the first, and exposed to keep the sky detail.

Open both files in Photoshop and click on *Window>Arrange>2 up vertical* and you will have a screen like Figure 8.25.

Select the move tool (V) and select the window with the sky by clicking anywhere on the window. Drag the sky layer across to the picture of Slater's Bridge; if you hold the Shift key before releasing the mouse button, you will place the sky centrally within the picture. Keeping the move tool selected, drag the sky layer to the top of the picture.

The sky layer, being above the landscape of the bridge is, of course, obscuring the top half of the picture completely.

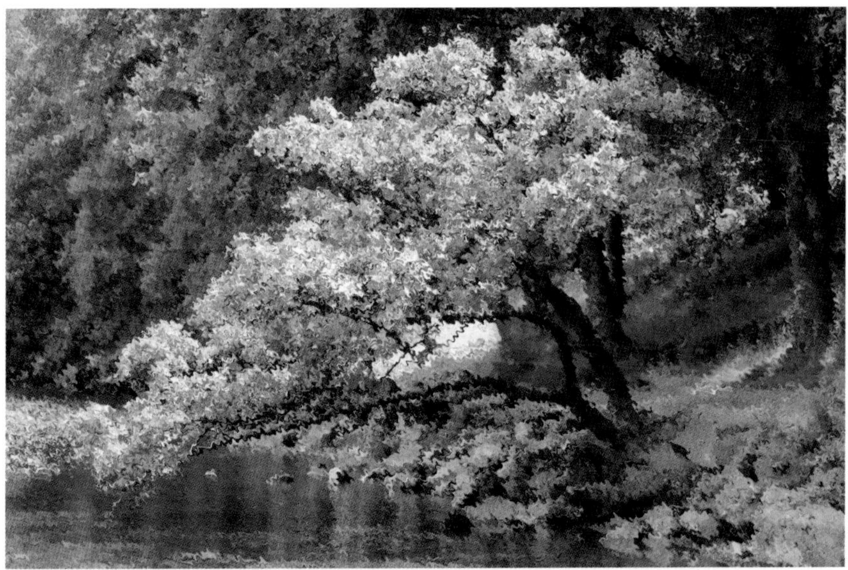

Fig. 9.5
Ripple filter.

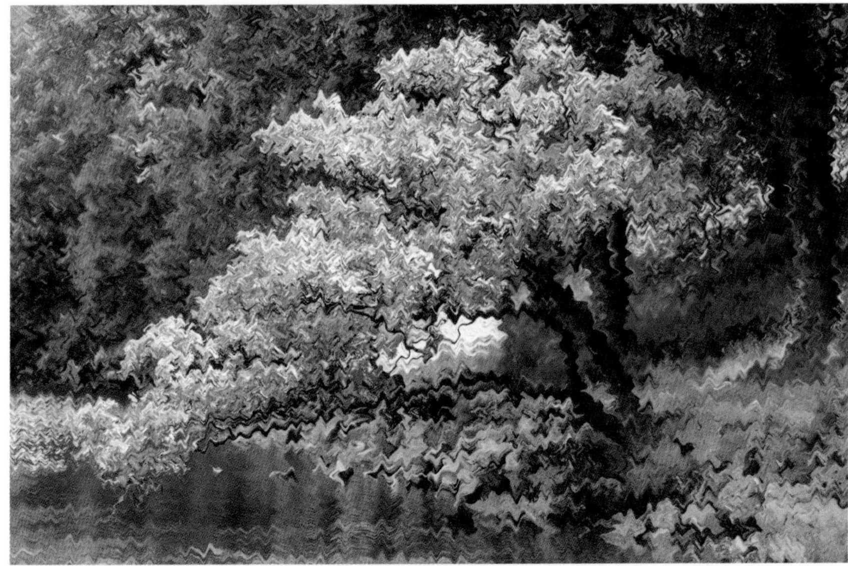

Fig. 9.6
Wave filter.

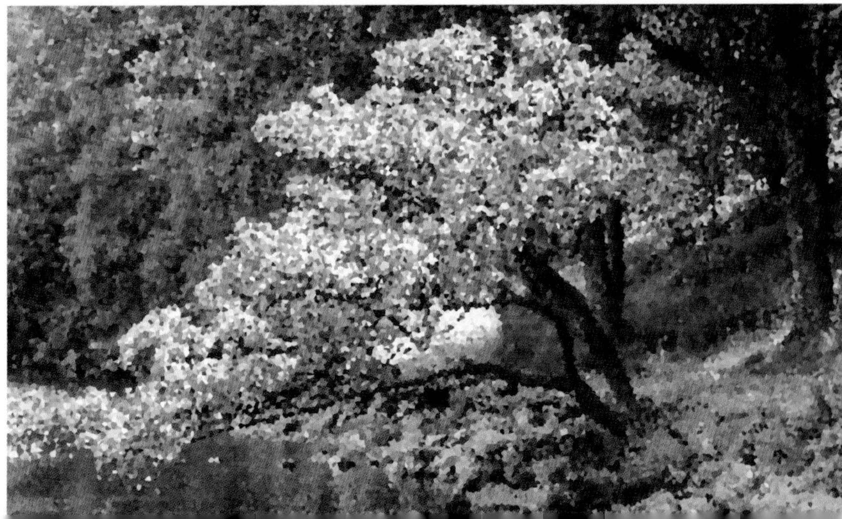

Fig. 9.7
Crystallize filter.

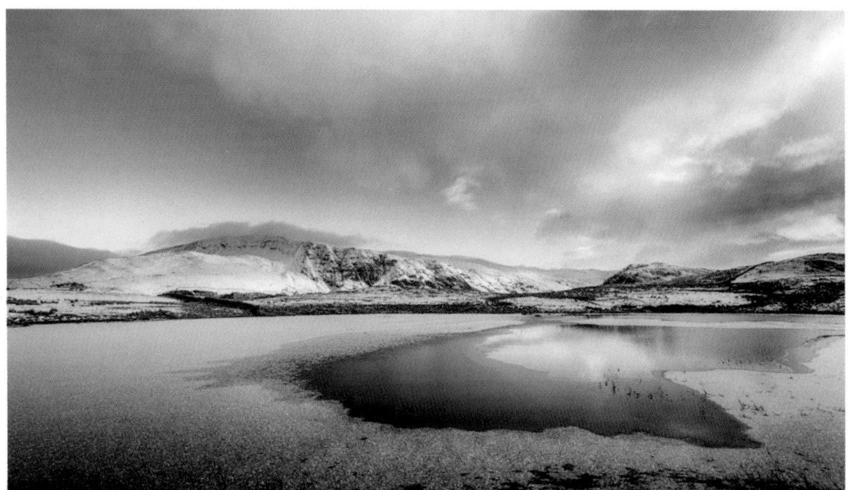

Fig. 9.8
Tewet tarn with blue cast.

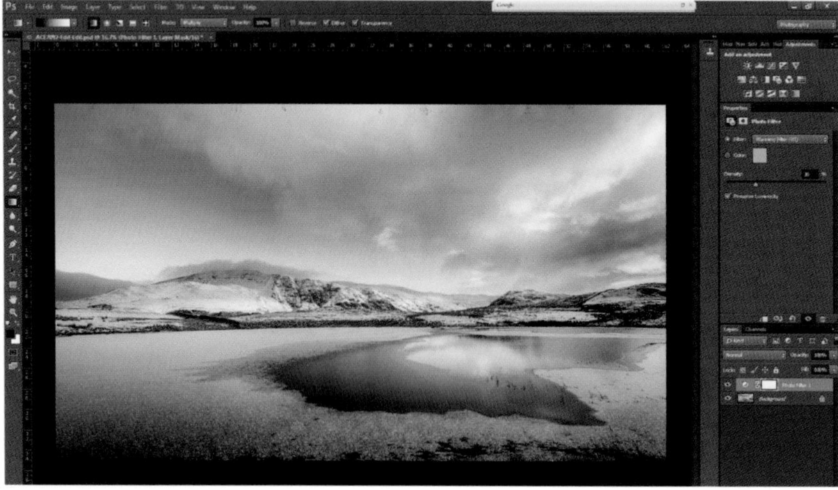

Fig. 9.9
Photo Filter 81 set at 30% used to correct cast.

are restricted to tiny prints. As the filter is being used to break up the image and simplify it in any case, there is less need to print at really high resolutions, meaning that the file can simply be enlarged more for printing (more about this in the next chapter).

OTHER FILTERS

The following filters are applied to the mid-sized file (15Mb/2,000 pixels wide):

Some (but not all) of these filters contain adjustments within them, enabling them to work with larger file sizes, but others do not. You will have to experiment to see what suits your personal taste.

The filters illustrated are not an exhaustive list – more an example of some of Photoshop's effect filters. Their use is no more than personal choice and they are not recommended as a means to enhance a landscape.

Photo filters

Exactly like adding colour-correction filters to your camera in the days of film, photo filters allow you to warm up, cool down or change the colours in your pictures to anything you like.

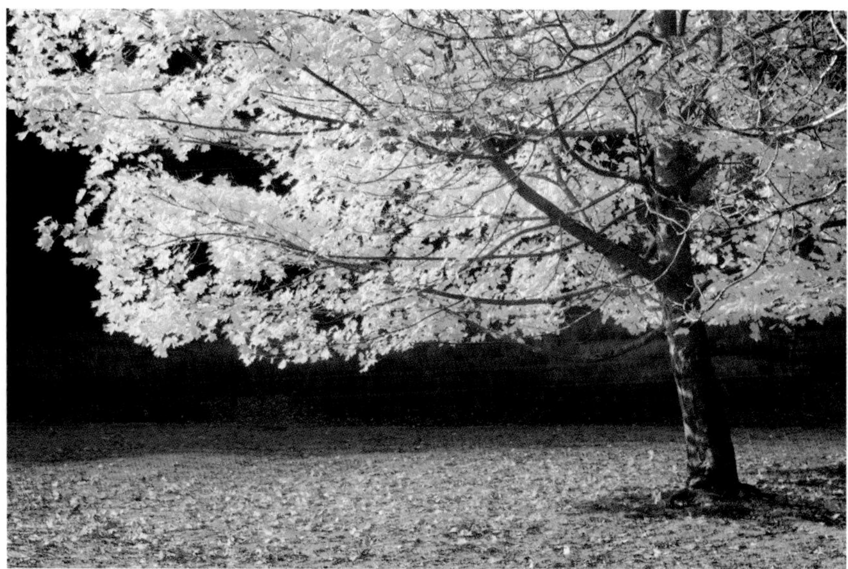

Fig. 9.10
Autumn tree original file.

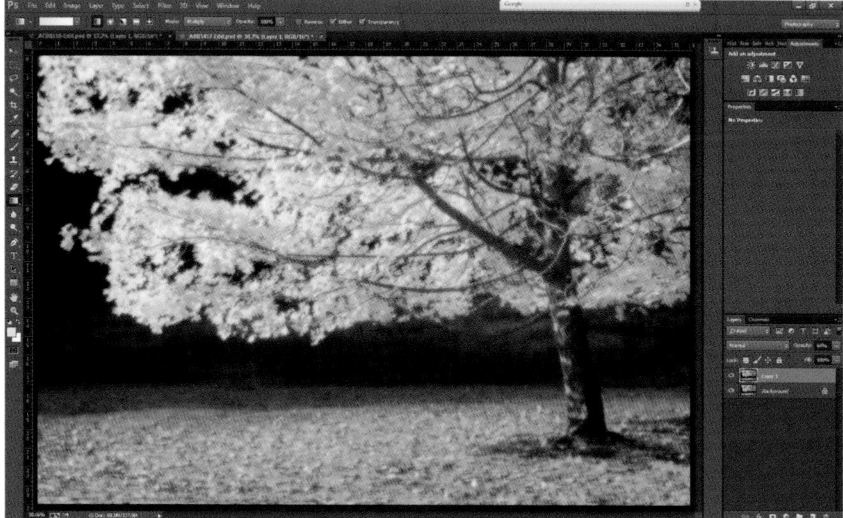

Fig. 9.11
Soft focus by blurring duplicate layer and reducing opacity (to 64%).

Figure 9.8 displays a winter shot, showing the all too familiar blue cast, especially in the shadow areas. Simply by adding a photo filter adjustment layer, selecting one of the warming filters (81 series), and adjusting the density to around 30 per cent, the cast is removed and normal colours are restored.

Whilst casts like this can be easily removed using Adobe Camera RAW when you open your file, it is a very useful alternative way of correcting or adapting colours.

Soft focus

Although more often thought of as a portrait-style filter, soft focus was often used in the more romantic black and white era of landscape photography. Many of Ansel Adams' earlier landscapes taken in Yosemite were shot on soft-focus lenses. It is now a simple technique that can be applied to photos, and a change of blending modes can give totally different picture styles.

Starting with the autumn tree shot, (Figure 9.10) make a duplicate layer (Ctrl-J) and click

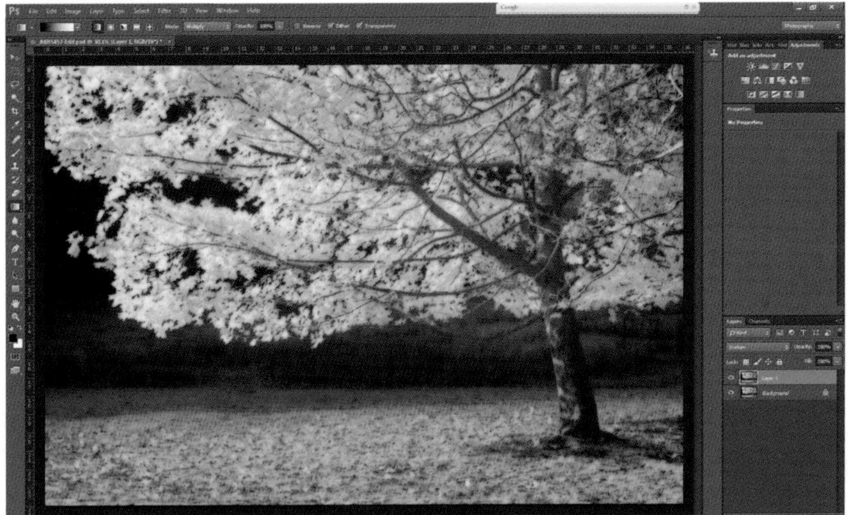

Fig. 9.12
Different soft-focus effect created by using darken blending mode (at 100% opacity) on the blurred layer.

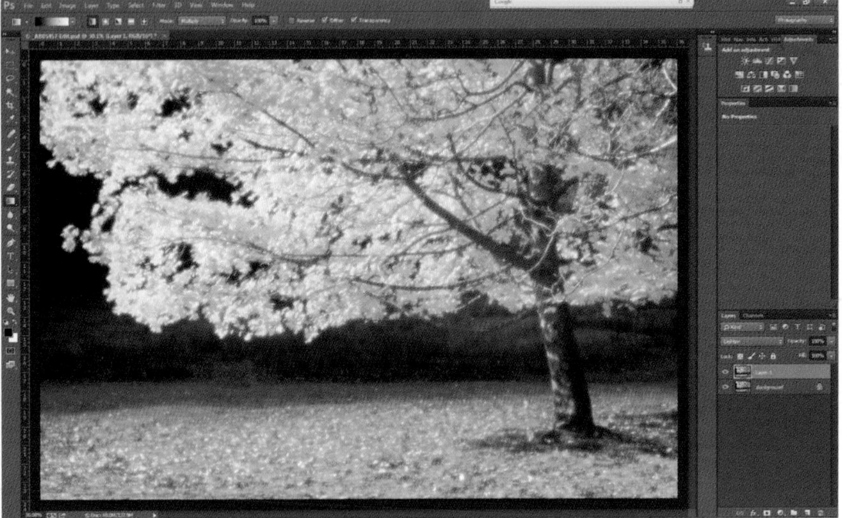

Fig. 9.13
Alternative soft focus by using lighten blending mode (at 100% opacity) on the blurred layer.

Filter>Blur>Gaussian blur. Add a moderate radius to the blur using the slider on the dialogue box. Between 10 and 20 should work depending on file sizes, but experiment with lower and higher values, as they will give different effects. The top layer is now simply out of focus.

Firstly, try reducing the opacity of the blurred layer to allow a proportion of the sharp layer to show through. On this picture around 65 per cent gives a pleasing image.

Different effects can be obtained by changing blending modes.

HOW TO CREATE HIGH-KEY LANDSCAPES

There are many definitions of 'high-key' from 'a range of tones from mid-grey through white' to 'a reduced contrast ratio used to create an upbeat mood'. For the purposes of this book, it could be described as 'a light-toned photograph still exhibiting a full range of tones, processed to give a feeling of delicate, pastel tones'.

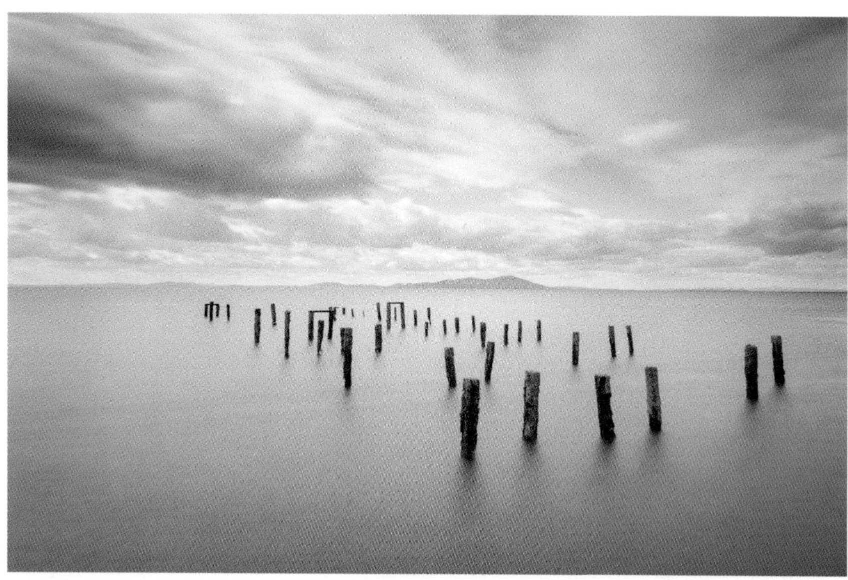

Fig. 9.14
Original image of oyster beds at the Solway Firth.

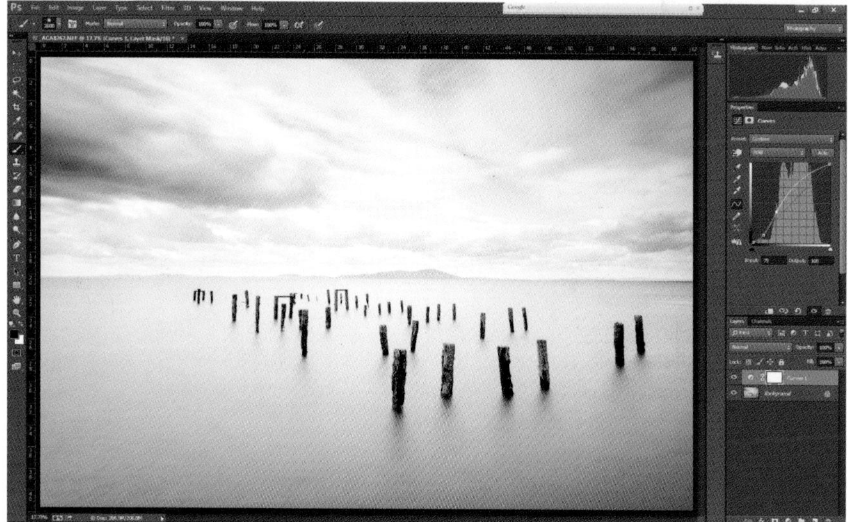

Fig. 9.15
Curves 1 layer added and mid-tones lightened by lifting the centre part of the curves line.

Figure 9.14 shows a coastal scene of oyster beds as shot. This is the kind of image that would make a great high-key landscape. As it is, it appears a rather grey, slightly dull-looking image, but if the posts of the oyster beds were kept fairly dark whilst the whole of the rest of the image was lightened to a delicate pastel tone, it would be very effective.

As you need to preserve the dark tone detail, adding a curves layer to push up the top end of the curve would be more effective than starting with a levels layer.

Partly due to fall-off with the wide-angle lens, and partly due to the use of a 10-stop neutral density filter, the photograph is slightly darker at the edges than in the centre. In any case, this type of high-key shot looks better fading to lighter tones around the perimeter of the photograph. A selection of the darker edges can be made with a large, very soft-edged brush in quick mask mode (Q).

This does not have to be very accurate; the key is to use a really large brush with a very soft edge. It doesn't even have to be an even border around the

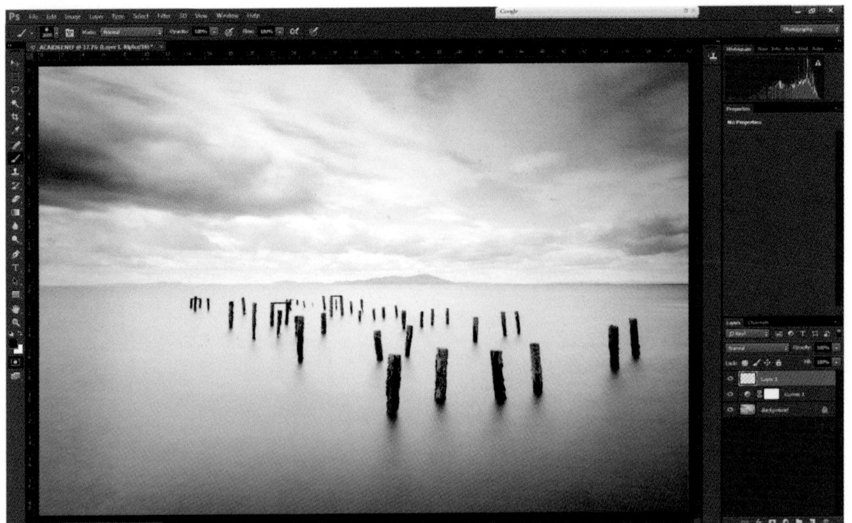

Fig. 9.16
Quick mask selection of darker edges by using brush tool set to 2500 pixels wide with soft edge.

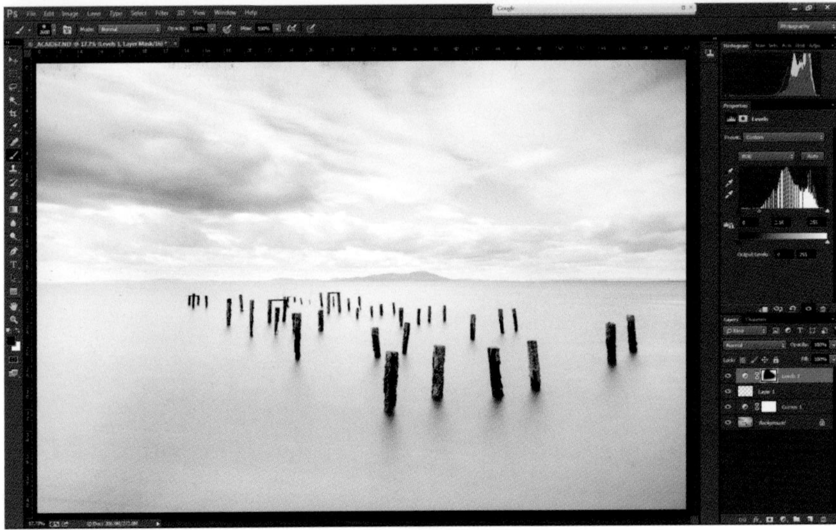

Fig. 9.17
Lightening mid-tones on levels 1 layer to fade the edges and lift the cloud tones.

edge of the picture – use it to select those areas that are a little dark – such as the cloud base at the top left, or the water and sky lower right and top right as well as a small selection round the entire picture.

Add a levels layer (as we only want to change mid-tone brightness, not alter contrast in any way), and selecting the mid-tone slider, move it to the left as far as you think necessary – it might be a lot further that you expect – in this case moving it from 1.00 to 2.16 gives a good result.

Another method of achieving a high-key result is by using a soft light layer. Figure 9.18 shows a view across Derwentwater which is again a little grey and flat-looking.

This would perfectly suit a more pastel, high-key treatment. The foreground rocks, although very dark, do have detail in them, as can be seen from the histogram. A quick and easy way of achieving a high-key result is by adding a new layer (*not* an adjustment layer), by clicking on the new layer icon – second from the right at the bottom of the layers palette – which will appear as a chequerboard layer of transparency. Fill this with white, either by choosing:

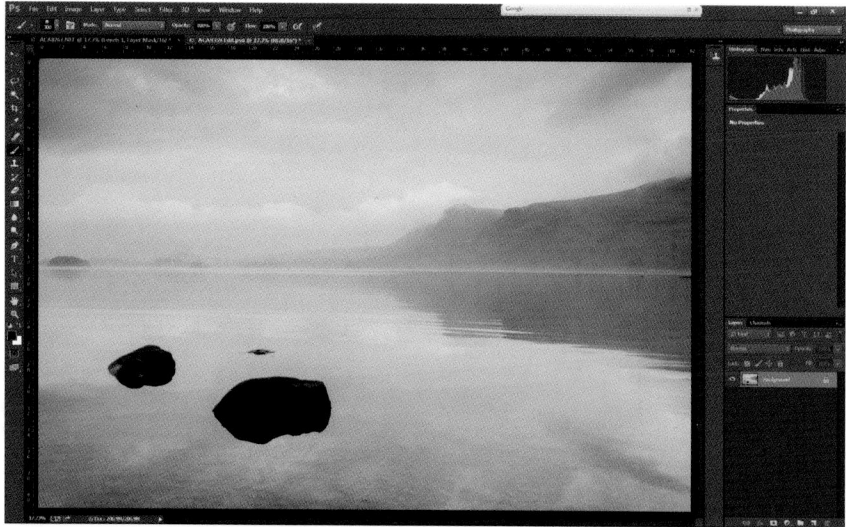

Fig. 9.18
Original image of lake view with dark foreground rocks.

Fig. 9.19
Layer 1 added and filled with white (at 100% opacity).

- *Edit>Fill* and either choosing *foreground*, *background* or *white* as your fill (ensure that fill opacity on the dialogue box is set at 100 per cent and the blending mode is set to normal – both Photoshop default settings), or
- by using the shortcut Shift-F5, which will bring up your fill dialogue box and continue as above, or if your foreground or background colours are already white, the quickest shortcut is Alt-backspace to fill with the foreground colour, or Ctrl-backspace to fill with the background colour. These may seem awkward to remember, but once you are used to them, they are a great way to fill layers or even layer masks with solid black or white, and will prove to be among your most useful shortcut keys. The layer will fill with white and the image will – for the moment – disappear.

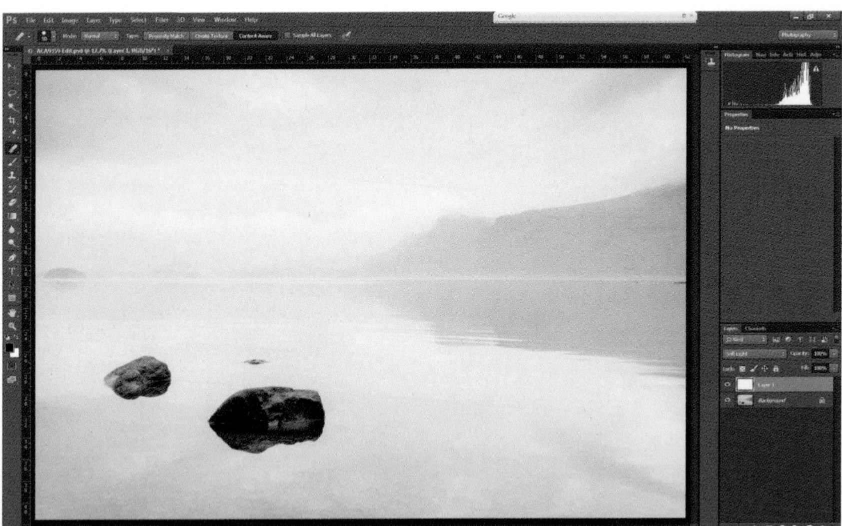

Fig. 9.20
Blending mode of white layer (Layer 1) changed to soft light – strength of effect can be adjusted by changing the opacity of the white (soft light) layer.

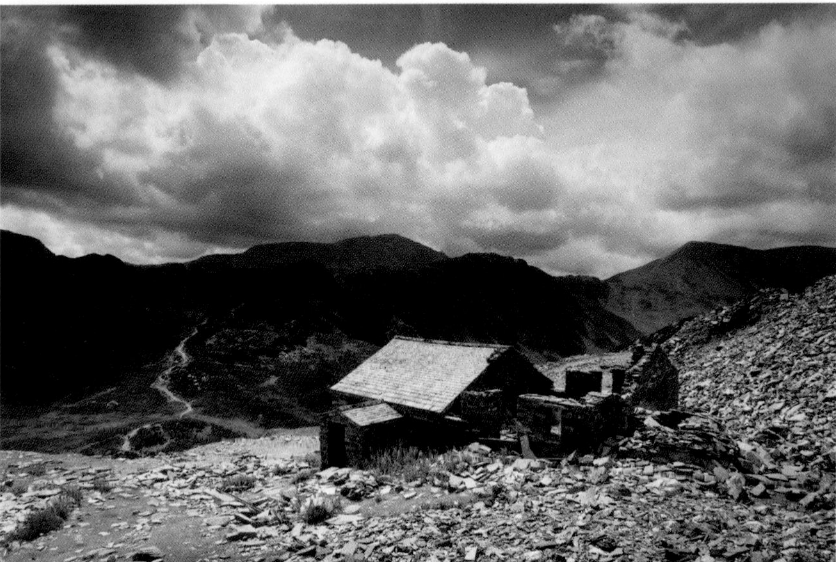

Fig. 9.21
Original image of Dubs Quarry.

Change the blending mode to soft light and the effect of the layer is simply to lighten the tones of the background layer below.

This is the same way of using the soft light blending mode as was covered with dodging and burning, and can be very effectively used to create a high-key image very simply.

HOW TO CREATE LOW-KEY LANDSCAPES

Dark, moody, dramatic landscapes are not simply the result of underexposure. That goes against everything that has been covered on exposure. Whilst low-key pictures do rely on a lot of dark areas in the photograph, they need small areas of bright tones to make them come to life.

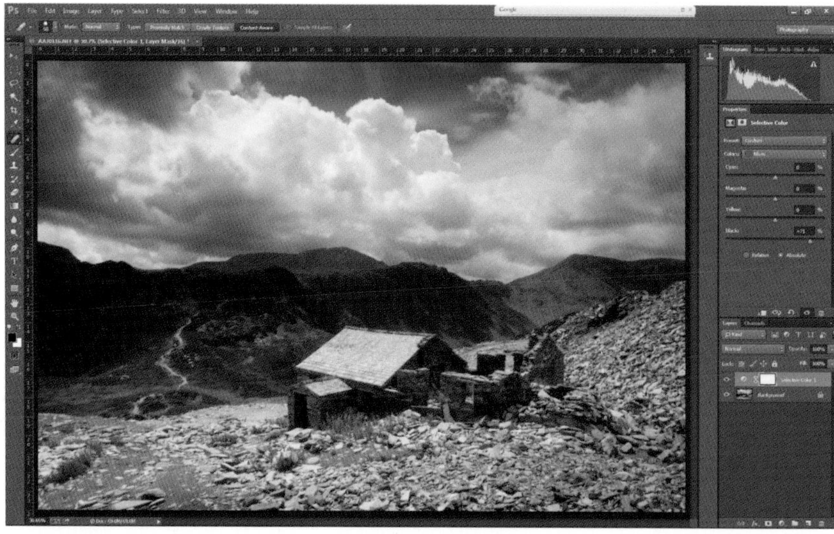

Fig. 9.22
Selective colour used to darken the sky and the grass by adding black to greens and blues.

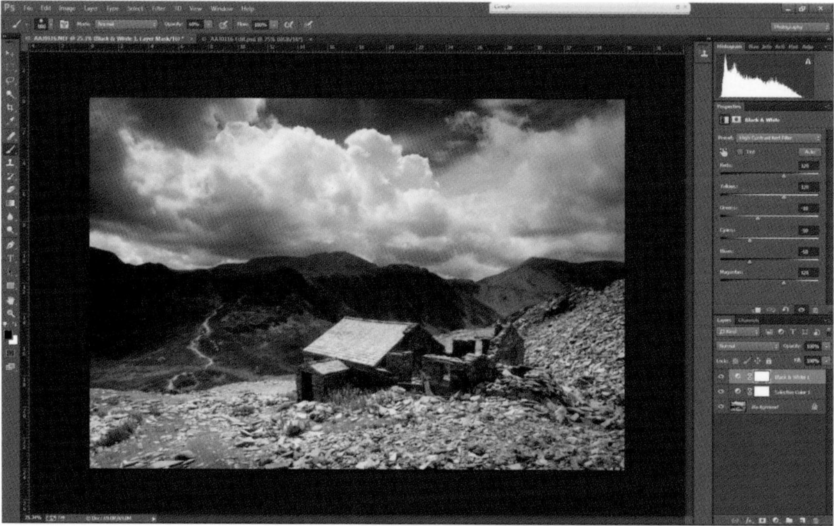

Fig. 9.23
Black and white layer added using high-contrast red filter.

Figure 9.21 is a photograph of Dubs Quarry on Haystacks, which exhibits good dark tones, and excellent highlight details on the brighter clouds and the slate roof of the building. Though this will look more dramatic as a low-key black and white image, there are a couple of things to do before converting the image to black and white. As there is blue sky at the top of the picture that could be rendered really dark and dramatic, add a selective colour layer and add black to the blues, also darken the grass tones by adding black to the yellows (yes, it's an odd thing in Photoshop that grass almost always reacts better to changes in yellow tones than changes in green tones), as the grass colour contains a lot of red values as well as green.

Next, add a black and white layer and set the drop-down preset to high-contrast red filter.

The slate at the bottom of the picture still needs to be more dramatic. Using a very wide, soft brush in quick mask (Q) select the base of the picture, add a

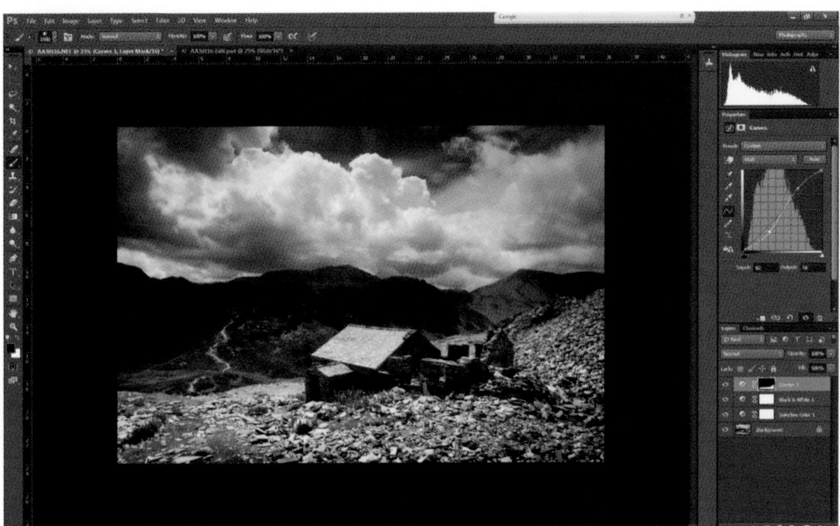

Fig. 9.24
Curves layer 1 added with layer mask to select bottom of picture to darken slate base.

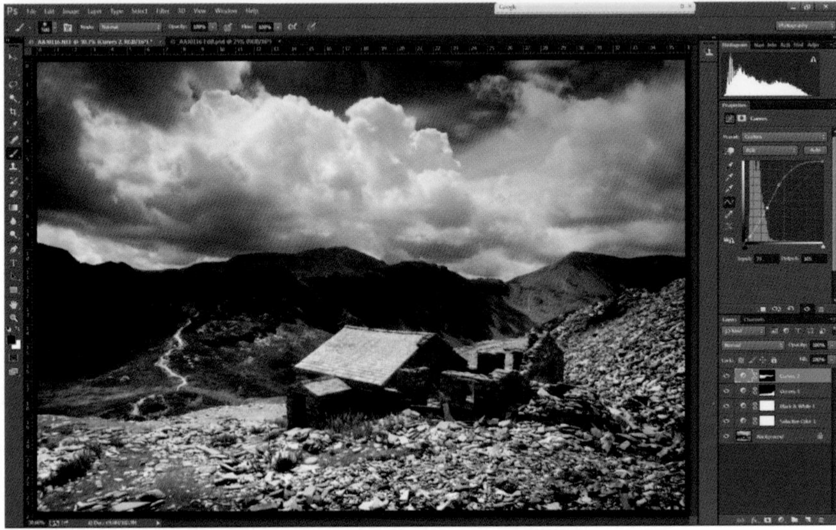

Fig. 9.25
Curves layer 2 added with layer mask to increase the contrast and lighten the fell behind quarry building.

curves adjustment layer and darken the lower tones of the slate, a slight S-curve through the curves line will preserve some sparkle in the lighter tones there.

Next, a selection of the dark fell behind the quarry building, again made with the quick mask tool. You might find it easier to select a broad swathe with the brush, then by exchanging the brush colour to white, paint out the areas you don't want selected, such as the roof of the quarry. A curves layer will allow you (again with an S-curve) to create more contrast within the dark tones, whilst still keeping the dramatic feel to the fell.

As a final curves layer, take a soft-edged selection of the lighter clouds, add the curves layer and by adding two points on the line as in the properties palette, pull the lower point down as shown in Figure 9.26. This will serve to preserve the highlights within the cloud, but darken the mid-tones to create more of a feeling of drama.

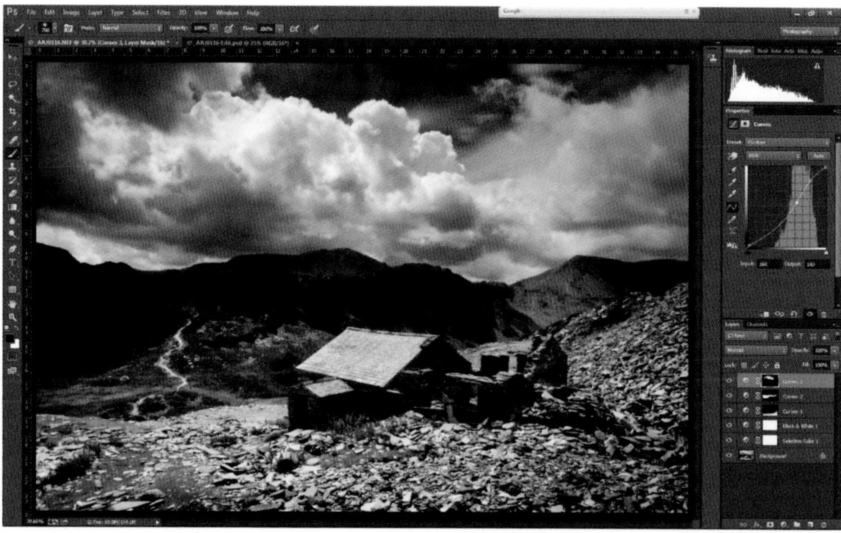

Fig. 9.26
Curves layer 3 added with layer mask to increase contrast of and slightly darken lighter cloud areas.

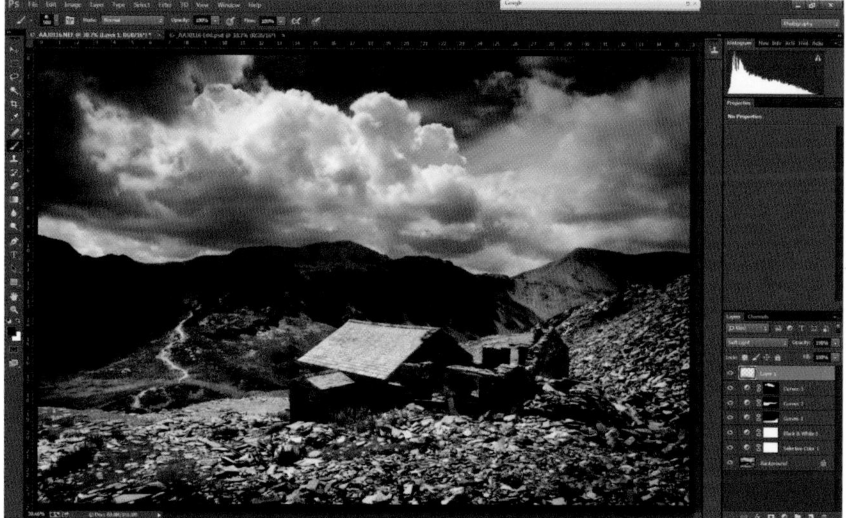

Fig. 9.27
Soft light layer added and 500 pixel brush used to paint round the edge of the picture to darken edges.

Finally, by adding a new layer with the blending mode set to soft light, and using a black brush set to around 20–30 per cent opacity, paint over the picture and darken the edges slightly. The final result (Figure 9.27) is a far darker, more dramatic picture than the original photograph, and brings across the mood of the scene.

Fig. 9.28
A high-key print with a white border and no keyline – the edge of the photo is undefined.

Fig. 9.29
The same picture with a narrow black keyline added helps separate the picture from the border.

PRESENTATION OPTIONS

Adding a keyline round your picture

Some pictures benefit from a thin keyline, particularly if they are to be presented on a border, and if there are tones within the picture that may appear to 'bleed' into the border. Figures 9.28 and 9.29 show the same picture set against a white background, without and with a thin black keyline. The difference between the two is immediately obvious.

Creating the keyline is very simple. Starting with your completed picture, add a new layer (to keep your editing separate from the background layer), select the entire image area (Ctrl-A). Marching ants will enclose the entire picture space. Click *Edit>Stroke* and a dialogue box will appear.

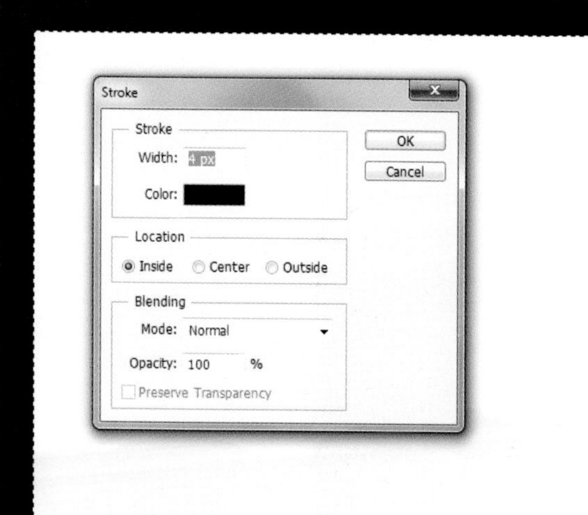

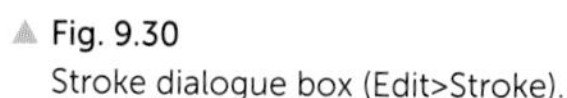
Fig. 9.30
Stroke dialogue box (Edit>Stroke).

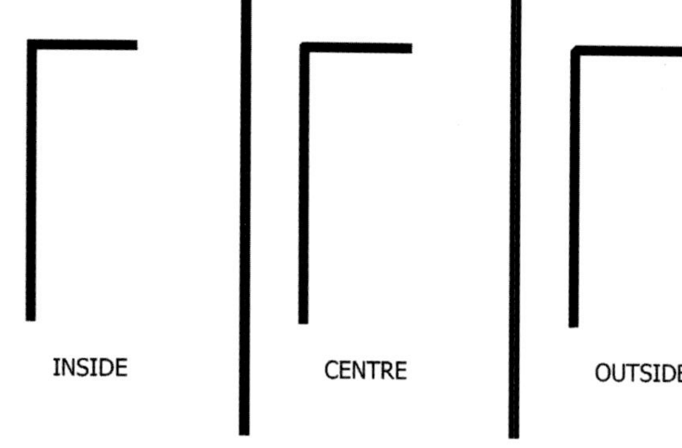

Fig. 9.31
Location of the stroke line in relation to the line of selection.

Taking the dialogue box options:

- Stroke:
    - Width: Of course down to personal choice, but with large RAW file sizes, try between 3 and 5 pixels.
    - Colour: Your choice, but black is the most neutral.
- Location: Strange though it may seem, always choose *inside*. Firstly, if your selection is on the edge of your image, it is therefore usually also at the edge of your canvas. If you place the line *centrally*, then half of it will fall off the edge of your canvas and not show. If you select *outside* all the line will be outside the canvas, and it will not show at all.

    There is, however, another reason to select *inside*, which is shown on Figure 9.31. The corner of the selection line is enlarged and it is clear that only when *inside* is selected, is the corner of the stroke even. This is hardly relevant when dealing with lines of 4 pixels wide, but the principle is the same if you are adding a wide feature line within the picture area.
- Blending:
    - Mode: normal.
    - Opacity: 100 per cent.

Printing a border on your picture

Should you want a wide border (rather than a keyline) on your photograph, adding a stroke line to the inside of the selection will only obscure part of the picture area. In this case, you want to extend the border around the outside of the picture area. The easiest way to do this is to enlarge the canvas that the image is on. When you do that, you see the extended canvas around the picture itself.

The canvas is always the colour of the *back-ground colour*, so make sure you have the appropriate colour selected *before* you change the canvas size.

Figure 9.32 shows a picture that might benefit from a wide border. As with all images, it is recommended that you leave the picture layer untouched and create a duplicate layer, which will remain as the picture (Ctrl-J). This will leave the original background layer to be used as a border. It's also worth adding another layer at this stage for a keyline, because once the canvas is enlarged, it will be more difficult to select the right area accurately. Select all (Ctrl-A) on the blank top layer and add a keyline (*Edit>Stroke>Inside*). If you don't want or need it later on, you can easily switch off or even delete the

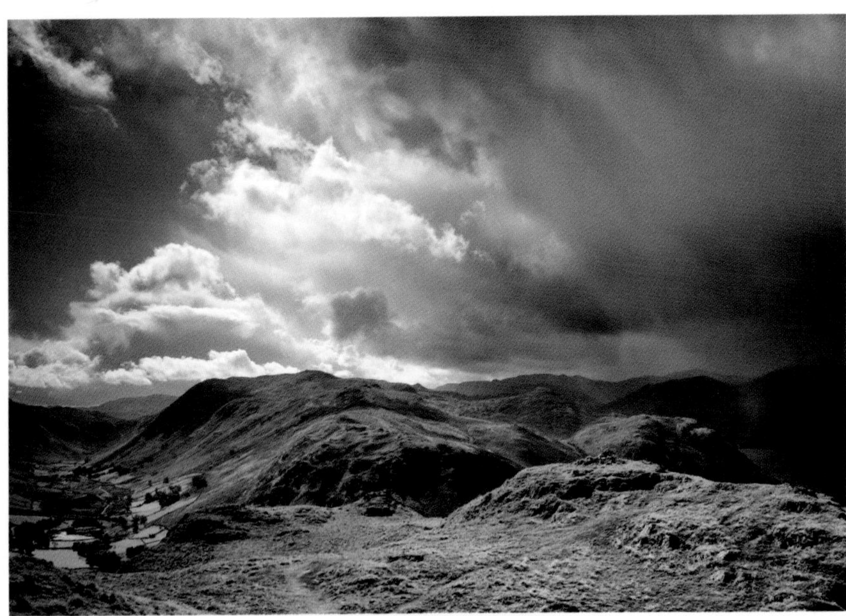

Fig. 9.32
A picture that might be suitable for a wide border.

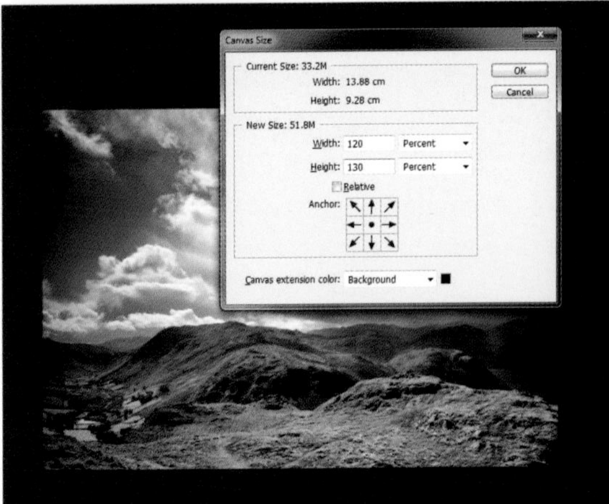

Fig. 9.33
Canvas size dialogue box (Image>Canvas size)/(Ctrl-Alt-C).

layer, and if you want it a different colour, it's easy to change.

Next, ensure the background colour (at the bottom of the tools palette) is set at the desired colour, and enlarge your canvas. Either *Image>Canvas size* or Ctrl-Alt-C (for canvas) will pull up a dialogue box.

The default 'new size' settings are in whatever units you have selected in preferences (Chapter 2), but are likely to be in centimetres, inches, or pixels. It is generally easier to work with borders using percentages, as it only takes a little mathematical knowledge to realize that if you are shooting 3:2 format, your new canvas needs to be enlarged 66 per cent more on the short dimension than the long, for example 115 per cent:120 per cent or (even easier) 120 per cent:130 per cent. For a 4:3 format, try 120 per cent:115 per cent or 140 per cent:130 per cent. This enlarges the canvas by the equivalent amounts on all sides. Of course, if you have cropped your photograph, you might find

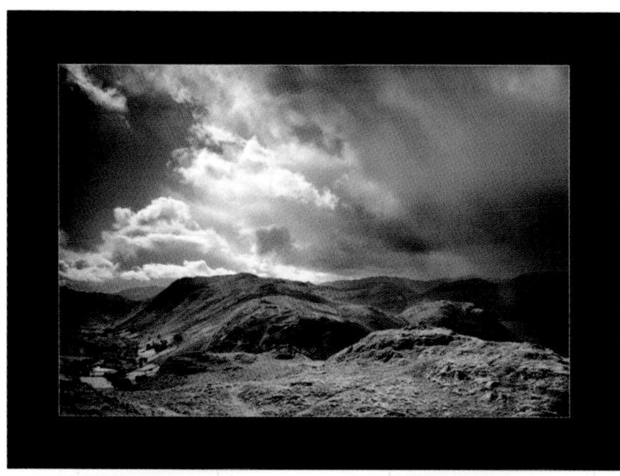

▲ Fig. 9.34
Picture with white keyline and black border.

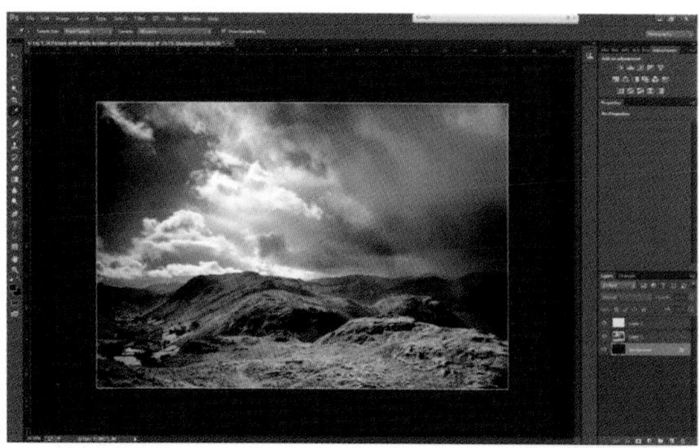

▲ Fig. 9.35
Blue border (colour selected from within the picture area) and the whole of the background layer filled with the colour.

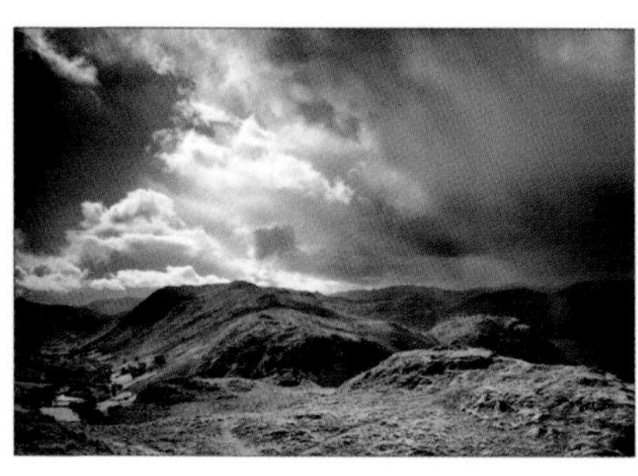

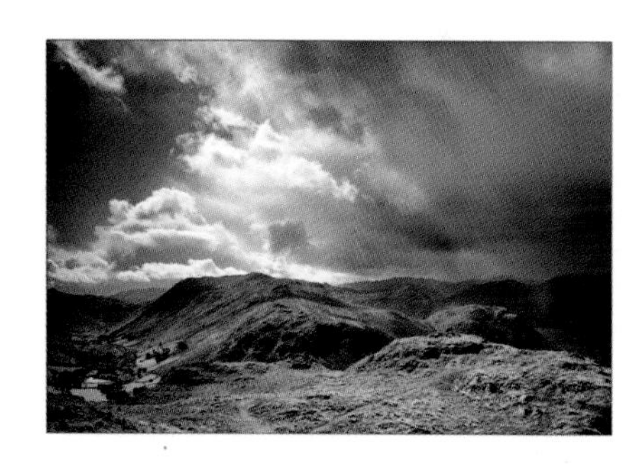

▲ Fig. 9.36
White border shown without and with external keyline.

it easier to work in centimetres and add on the same border width each side.

Figure 9.34 shows the picture with a black border and a white keyline. Because the border is on a separate layer to the visible picture (you duplicated the picture onto a separate layer), the background layer can be filled with any colour, in order to look at different border colours. You could choose a colour from within the picture, fill the background layer with it (Alt-backspace, to fill with foreground colour) use black, white, or anything.

Do remember, however, that if you choose a white border, unless you print a keyline round that it will still only print as blank paper, so there is no need to add a white border. Figure 9.36 shows a white border with and without a keyline.

Remember though, it is easy to get carried away with borders, and make them too fussy and ornate. The aim of any border is to put a simple frame on a picture, rather than to take over from the picture itself.

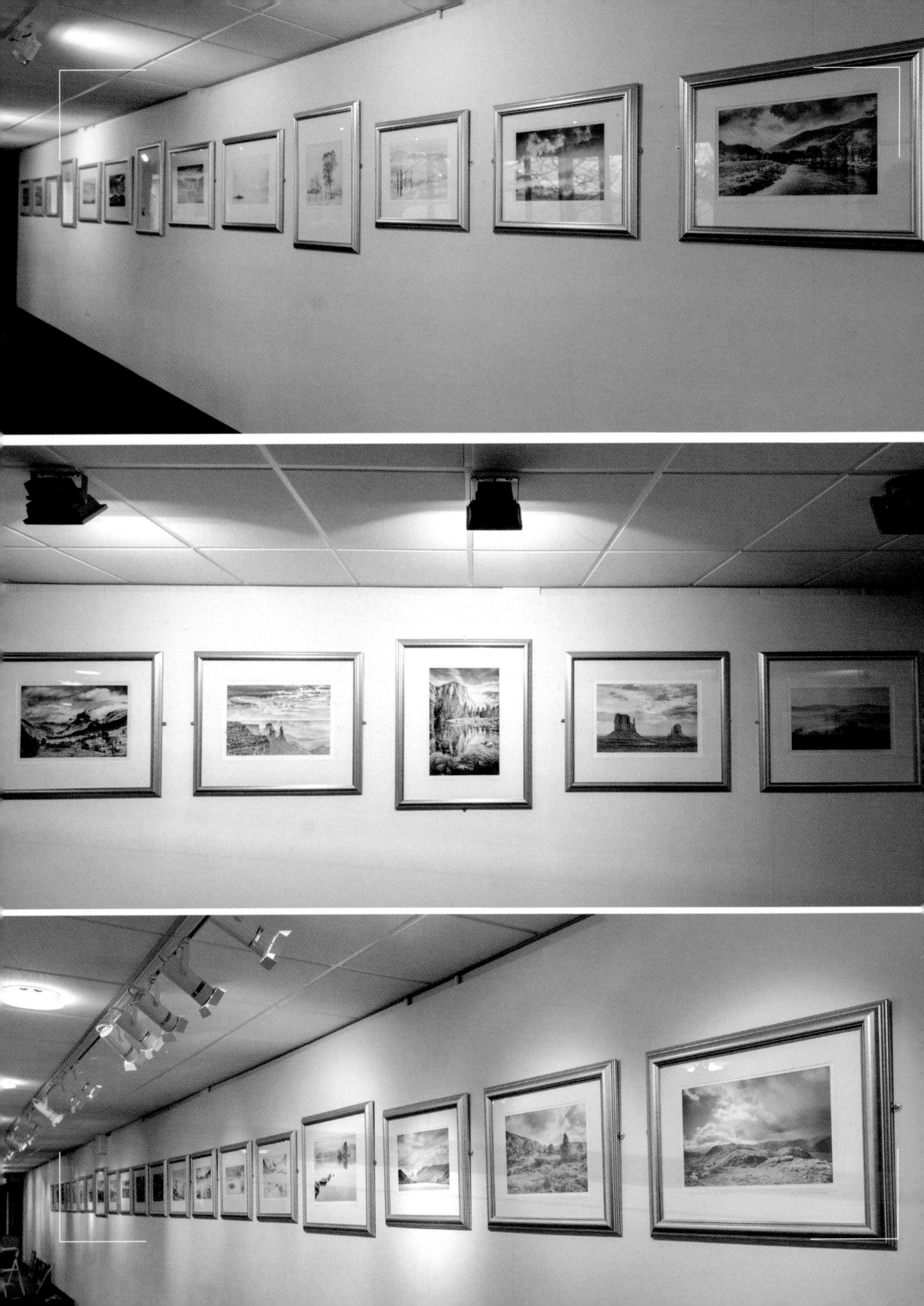

Chapter 10

Displaying, exporting and printing

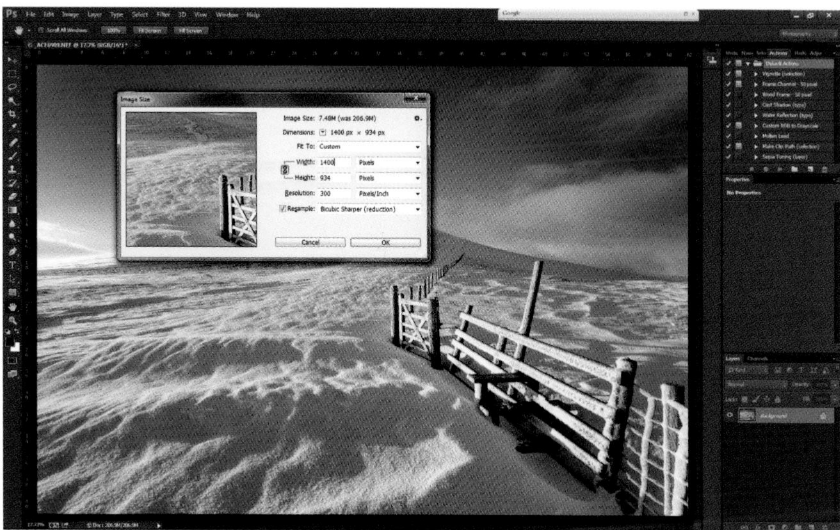

▶ Fig. 10.1
Image size dialogue box.

Too many people leave 99 per cent of their photographs on their hard drives, and do nothing to display or share them. There are many options for viewing or printing your pictures; some of them will be covered here.

EXPORTING PHOTOS FOR SCREEN DISPLAY OR PROJECTION

Digital picture frames are a popular way to display a series of pictures, and allow a lot of pictures to be displayed in a small space. Similarly, camera club projected image competitions and national and international projected exhibitions all call for the same treatment to your photographs. Posting photographs to Facebook, Flickr or any website is no different.

The primary elements that you need to attend to are image size, bit depth, colour space and file type.

Image size

Altered under *Image>Image size* (Alt-Ctrl-I), most good-quality digital projectors show an image of 1,400 pixels wide by 1,050 pixels high, which is the same size often required by national and international exhibitions. So the image needs to be resized.

Figure 10.1 shows the image size dialogue box; by ticking the resample tick box, the pixel sizes become editable. Change the width *or* height of the image to 1,400 (width) or 1,050 (height), but ensure the other dimension is smaller than the projector's maximum size. (In other words, if you alter the width on a landscape-format picture to 1,400, ensure the height does not exceed 1,050.) It is vital that the lock between the width and height of the image that constrains the aspect ratio remains active, or you will change the overall shape and perspective of your picture. You will notice from the dialogue box that this file has been reduced in size from its original 206.9Mg down to 7.48Mg. This file will perfectly fit the projector, with one pixel on the screen equating

OTHER IMAGE SIZES TO CONSIDER

For display on a normal HD television	1,920 x 1,050 pixels
For display on a 4K television	3,840 x 2,160 pixels
Most digital projectors	1,400 x 1,050 pixels
Digital picture frames	Between 480 x 234 – 1,024 x 768 pixels

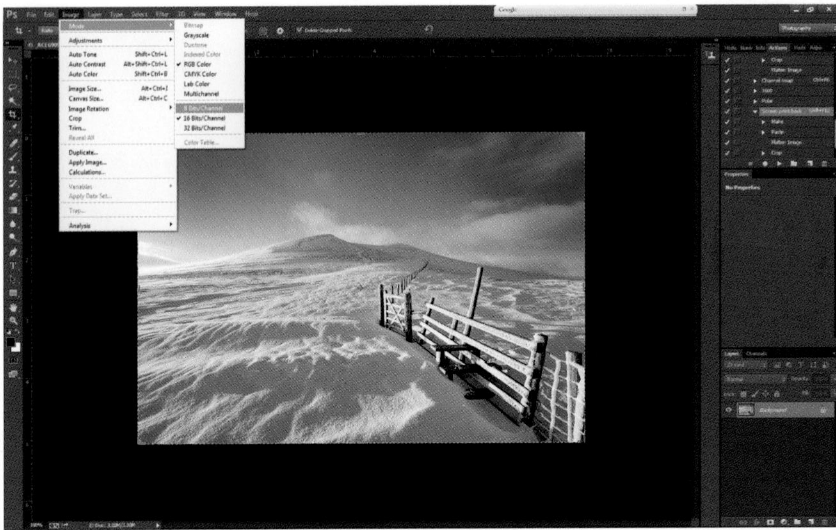

Fig. 10.2
Changing bit-depth from 16-bit to 8-bit for web display.

to one pixel on the image, therefore giving as sharp a projected image as it is capable of showing. It also means that the file is a much more manageable size to deal with. Whatever you do, do *not* overwrite your master working file with this new, much smaller file. Always keep files for exhibition, projection, display and the web separate from your originals.

Resizing pictures for the internet will depend on what size you want them to appear on the screen; for a full-screen picture 1,920 pixels wide will give plenty of quality, but remember, the larger the file size, the longer it will take to load. Photos displayed on the web are usually at 72PPI (pixels per inch).

Understandably, there are concerns when loading your pictures onto the web, especially social media sites, regarding image security. Many websites have settings that prevent other people from downloading your images, and whilst the more determined may be able to bypass these security measures, it is enough to put off many. Thinking before uploading them can also alleviate image theft. Uploading a full-sized image to a social site will firstly take some time to load, and the sites may or may not resize the image for display, meaning that if a full-sized image is displayed, there would be the potential for its theft. Typically, resizing your image to 800–1,000 pixels wide will display more than adequately on any social media site, yet only be a file of around 400K by the time the other settings are taken into account.

Bit depth

Assuming you have started with a RAW file, opened it up in Photoshop through Adobe RAW, edited it and saved it as a PSD file, it should be in 16-bit depth.

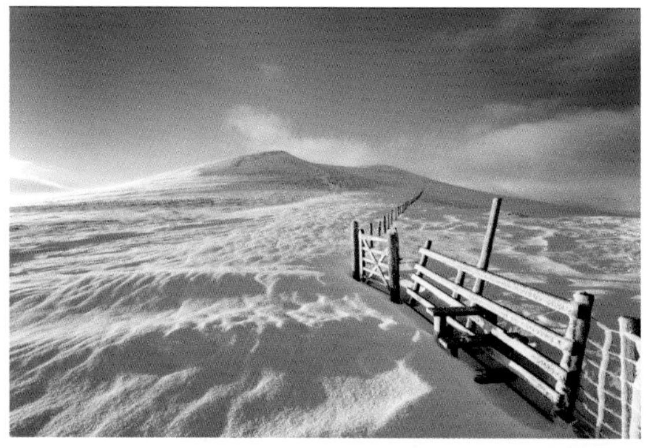

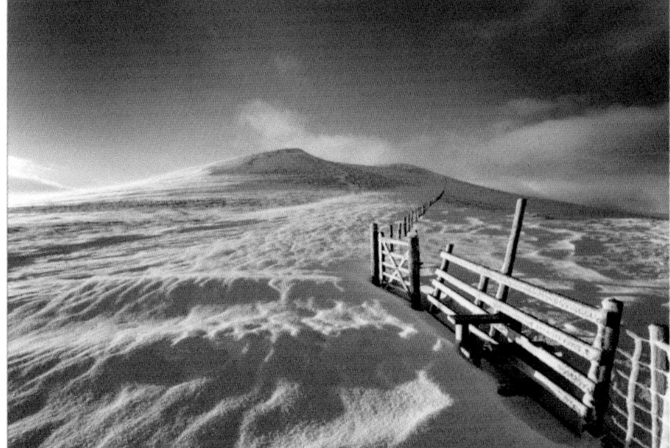

▲ **Fig. 10.3**
sRGB and ProPhotoRGB images web ready.

▶ **Fig. 10.4**
Convert to profile dialogue box (under Edit>convert to profile).

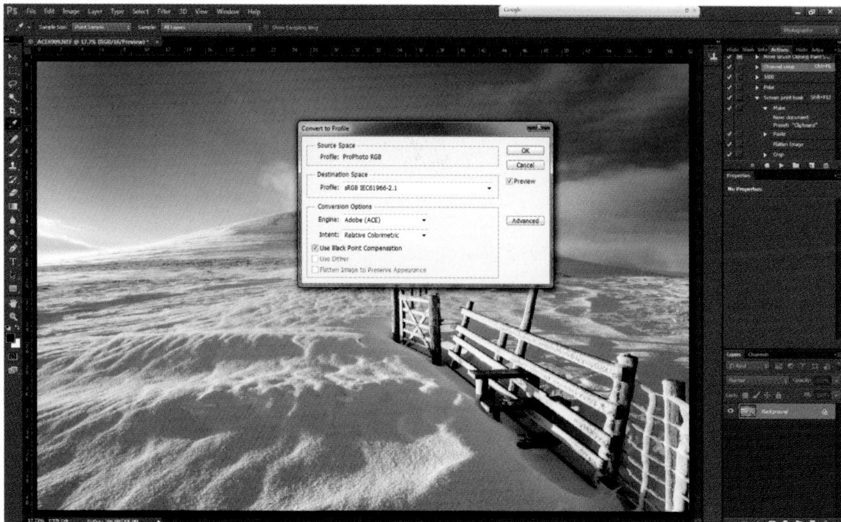

There is no need to keep it at this level of quality for projection or web images. *Image>Mode>8-Bits per channel.*

The difference between 16-bit and 8-bit files are the numbers of tones per channel contained within the file; the 8-bit has 256 tones per channel, the 16-bit has 32,769. Whilst a 16-bit is preferable for editing and printing, 266 tones per channel are more than enough for screen display.

Colour space

Colour space was covered in Chapter 2, with ProPhoto RGB being recommended as the colour space that offers the greatest colour gamut. However, posting a ProPhoto RGB picture on the web or most projection equipment will display an unpleasant colour shift. Converting the file to sRGB will allow the colours to display successfully.

Figure 10.3 shows the difference between the sRGB-converted file (on the left) compared to the ProPhoto uploaded file (on the right). The colours appear truer to the original on the sRGB file. This relates purely to the full spectrum of colours in the ProPhoto RGB file being incorrectly displayed as an sRGB. So, whenever the colour display is sRGB, make sure to convert your files to match.

Edit>Convert to profile pulls up the convert to profile dialogue box. Select sRGB and click OK. Be

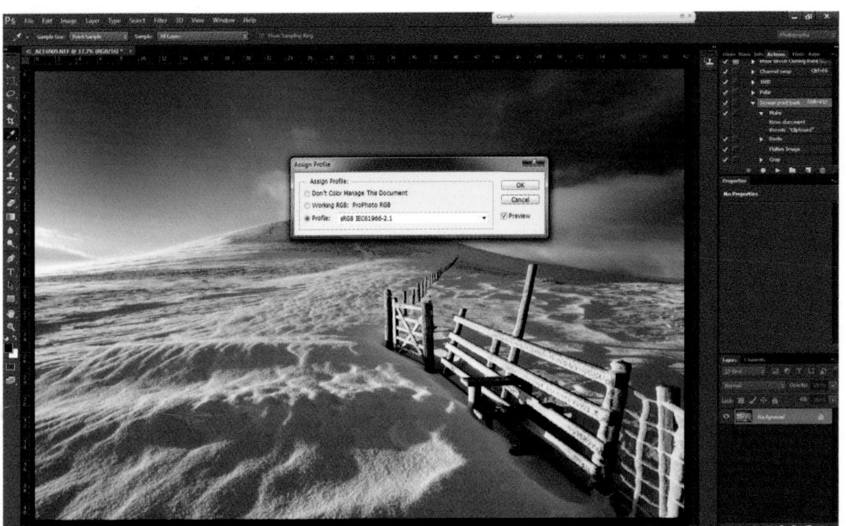

Fig. 10.5
Assign profile dialogue box.

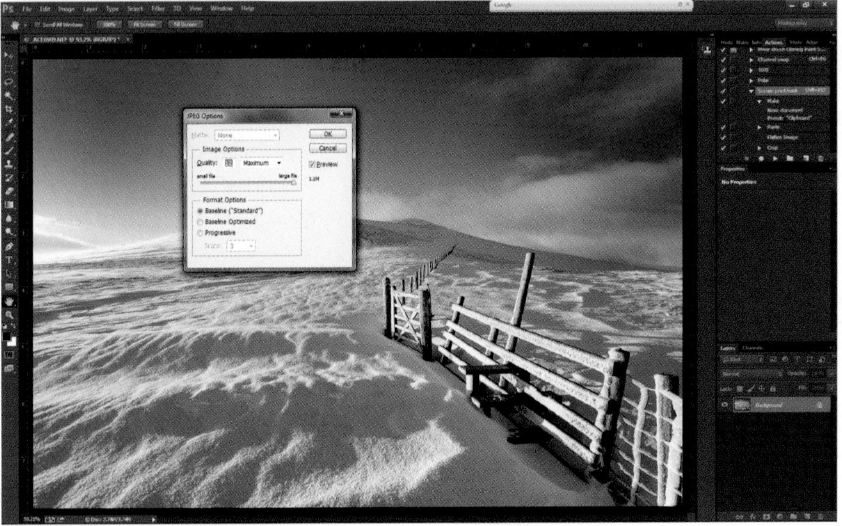

Fig. 10.6
JPEG options dialogue box, showing the file being saved as Maximum (12)~ quality.

careful to use *Convert to profile* (Figure 10.4) rather than *Assign profile* (Figure 10.5),

File types

For digital frames, exhibitions and projected images, the preferred file type is the humble JPEG. Keep your file as a 16-bit PSD until you have finished editing; once you have changed the size and the colour profile, reduce the bit depth to 8-bit, then save your file as a JPEG. Make sure you are not overwriting any other larger files.

In saving a JPEG, a JPEG options dialogue box will appear.

Unless there is a requirement to restrict the file size, leave the quality at 12 (maximum); this will give the lowest amount of file compression and maintain the quality. Some exhibitions where entries are emailed in put a restriction on file size, and it might be necessary to save at a higher compression (lower quality).

Format options are a mystery to most people; Baseline ('Standard') gives, generally, a pretty good result, and is compatible with all web browsers.

EXPORTING PHOTOGRAPHS TO EXTERNAL PRINTING COMPANIES

Not everyone will choose to print their own photographs, particularly large-size prints, as the financial outlay on a large printer is considerable, so many choose to send their files to an external company for printing. This can be fraught with problems, with screen profiling and colour space being the most concerning. Many quality printing companies will have a downloadable interface that you can instal on your computer (both PC and Mac compatible) to check cropping, sizes and colour balance. Some even have a proofing service where they can send you an 8 × 6 proof print by post the next day.

Just choose a good-quality company, use their apps to check colour, follow their instructions to the letter and you will get wonderful results.

Some maintain Baseline Optimized may save the colours slightly more accurately, and it does save about 2–8 per cent on file size, but is not supported by all web browsers. Progressive downloads the image first as a low-res image, with incremental quality improvements as downloading continues; this was relevant in the days of dial-up internet access, but now can be ignored. Either of the first two should give satisfactory results.

PRINT SIZES V DPI/PPI

The question of how large you can print from various file sizes is one of the most common that is asked. The confusion around the difference between PPI and DPI is also huge.

PPI: Pixels per inch. A direct relationship between the size of the image in pixels and the size of the printed picture.

Opinions vary as to optimum PPI figures for prints, commonly considered to be 300 PPI, although the default setting within Photoshop is 240 PPI, but Epson printers supposedly work at their highest quality at multiples of 360 PPI, in other words 360/720. The issue here is that these high figures might limit the size of print you can produce.

Of course, you can print at lower resolutions than 300 PPI, and within reason, it is unlikely you could see the difference at sensible viewing distances. At 180 PPI, there will hardly be a perceptible difference between that and 360 PPI, yet it would allow the 3,680 × 2,456 pixel image to be printed to 52 × 34.6 cm, almost an A2 print, from a 9 mega-pixel file.

DPI refers to the number of ink dots the printer applies to the paper, and printer settings of 360, 720, 1,440 and 2,880 DPI are often found. Many believe that 2,880 will give the best result, but in truth, little difference will be visible between all the settings. For high-quality prints on heavy printing paper, 1,440 DPI should be more than enough.

Size	Mb	Print size @ 300 PPI (in)	Print size @ 300 PPI (cm)	Max paper size
7360 × 4912	36.2	25.4 × 16.37	64.51 × 41.50	A2
5520 × 3630	20.3	18.4 × 12.1	46.73 × 30.73	Super A3 (A3+)
3680 × 2456	9	12.26 × 8.18	31.14 × 20.77	A4
2144 × 1424	3.1	7.14 × 4.74	18.13 × 12.03	Smaller than A5

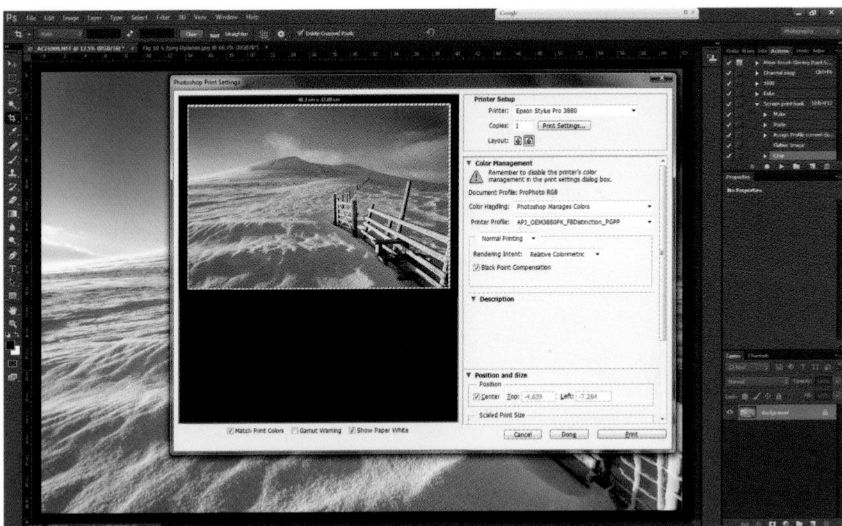

Fig. 10.7
Print dialogue box showing 'Photoshop manages colours' selected.

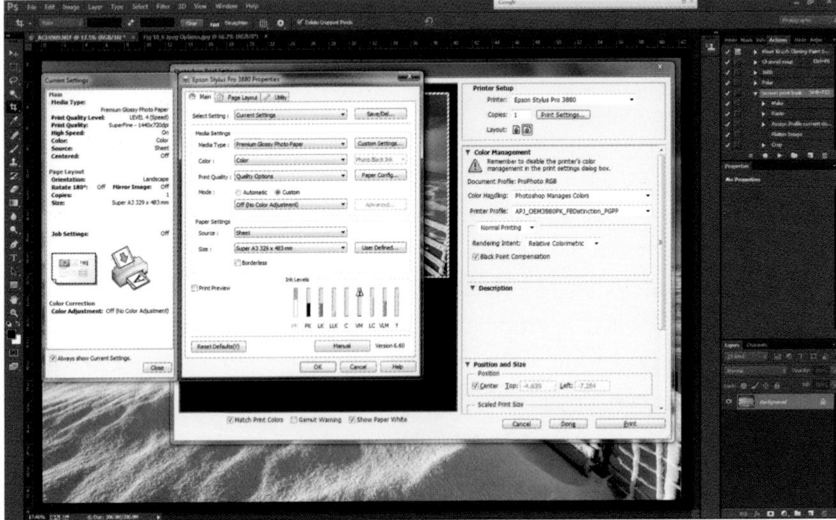

Fig. 10.8
Printer-specific settings.

PRINTER PROFILES AND PRINTING

Another area where there seems to be lots of confusion between photographers is colour space and printer profiles, with many claiming 'it's best to work just in sRGB, as that's what your printer sees anyway'.

It is vital that you work in the best colour space possible (ProPhoto RGB for 16-bit, Adobe RGB for 8-bit), to give the best-quality results.

Printer profiles are totally different from the colour space, relating to the way the PC 'talks' to the printer. Ctrl-P will bring up the printing dialogue box.

The top box (printer set-up) relates to your printer (or printers) – if you use more than one printer, ensure you have the right one selected. Clicking on Settings opens the printer-specific settings (in this case, the Epson Stylus Pro 3880).

Media settings

- Media type: Where possible (not always with matt black inks selected), choose premium glossy photo paper. The paper type you select

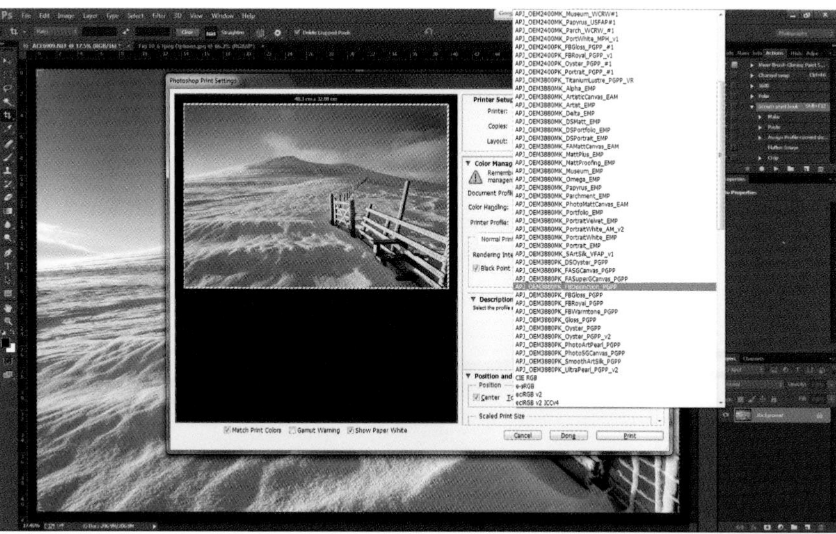

▶ Fig. 10.9
Printer profiles showing specific profile selected for printer, ink and paper to achieve maximum quality results.

makes no perceptible difference to print quality, but some settings simply throw more ink at the paper. Photo-quality glossy is the least ink-hungry setting.

- Colour: Normally colour (or advanced black and white photo).
- Print quality: Quality options will allow you to set 1,440dpi; this offers very high quality, and prints about twice the speed of 2,880dpi.
- Mode: Select Custom, and choose 'off' – you want to use a specific profile which will be set separately.

Paper settings

- Source: Sheet if not too heavyweight a paper, front or rear feed if the paper is likely to jam the printer.
- Size: Typically A4, A3, A3+ or A2.

Colour management box

- Colour handling: Photoshop manages colours (this is *vital*!).
- Printer profile: Many paper manufacturers offer ICC profiles for specific paper/printer/ink combinations, some will even create custom ICC profiles for your printer.
- Select 'Normal Printing' (rather than hard proofing).
- Rendering intent: Set to Relative Colorimetric (this compares the white of the source colour space to that of the destination colour space and shifts *all* colours accordingly. Out-of-gamut colours are shifted to the closest reproducible colour in the destination colour space. Relative colorimetric preserves more of the original colours than perceptual. Saturation option produces vivid colours at the expense of colour accuracy. Absolute colorimetric does not change in-gamut colours, but will change out-of-gamut to the closest reproducible colour. This can result in banding in areas of smooth colour and is not ideal for photographs.
- Black point compensation box should be ticked (ensures the full range of the source space is mapped to the print to give you deep, rich blacks).

Position and size

The easiest way to fill the print is to tick the box marked 'Scale to fit media', although if you are printing a set of pictures, it is often desirable to set them to a specific size. Remember also, if you are including a white border around your print, to leave size around the printed area. This depends on how you are intending to mount and present the print.

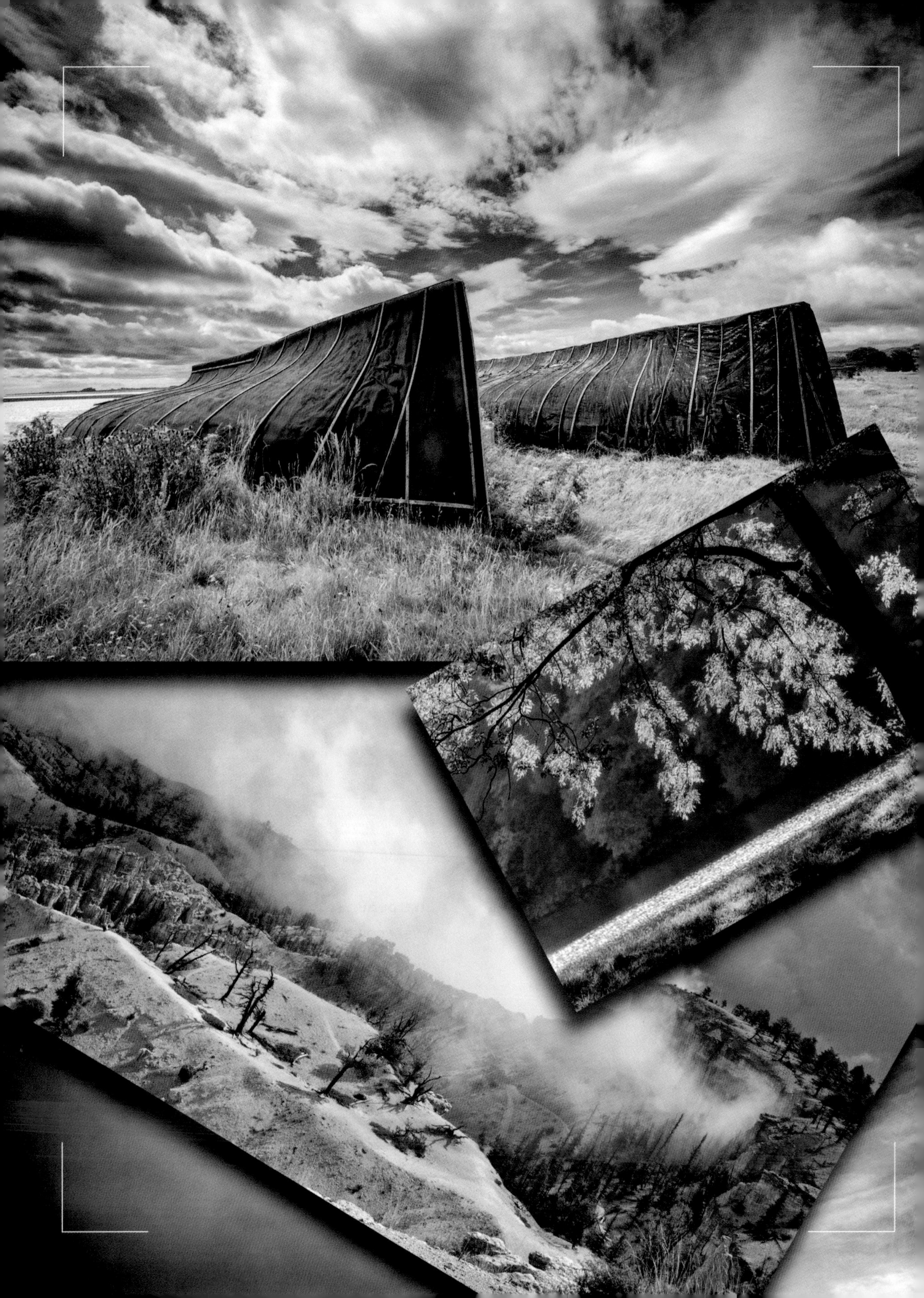

Chapter 11

The Google Nik Collection – the number one plug-in

Some years ago Nik software developed a series of plug-ins which formed the Nik suite. Initially they were very expensive; with each section of the overall package retailing at up to £199, the cost of the whole suite became a significant investment. A couple of years ago, Google acquired ownership of the Nik package, lumped it all together in what they called the Google Nik Collection, and sold it as a single, all-encompassing package, all for £95.

Since that price reduction, it has become the plug-in of choice for many photographers, and this chapter sets out to introduce the reader to the various applications within the package. On some, particularly those more applicable to landscape photography, it will go into greater detail. It should help those who have the collection, and inspire those who don't.

The full package comprises a range of applications, as summarized below:

Analogue Efex Pro/Pro 2

Allows you to mimic the look and feel of classic cameras and films, including faded colourways, vignetting and fall-off. Seems an odd choice for a landscape photographer trying to achieve sharpness, accuracy of colour and the like, but can have great applications in fine-art-style landscapes.

Colour Efex Pro 4

A comprehensive set of filters allowing colour correction and alteration, special effects and global retouching. A useful application, with some features ideally suited to the landscape photographer.

Silver Efex Pro 2

When the Nik package was sold as individual applications, Silver Efex Pro was the one that most photographers went for. It is a black and white conversion package that is very straightforward to use in its basic sense, and with a little more understanding, can create truly dynamic and impressive black and white images.

Viveza

Allows adjustments to colour, contrast and brightness to your image (all can be done just as well in Photoshop) but also structure (clarity) – very effectively.

HDR Efex Pro

Allows natural (or otherwise) HDR images to be created from a range of bracketed pictures, an effective alternative to Photoshop in some instances.

Also allows tone mapping of a single image, which particularly in conjunction with duplicate layers, can be very useful in bringing out greater detail in plain skies.

Sharpener Pro

A very powerful sharpening tool, which can be used to locally control structure, contrast and sharpness for the appropriate output results (screen or print).

Dfine

An extremely effective and useful noise reduction tool, which you can target at the noisy areas of an image to maximize detail either by using control points or masks.

The Nik selective tool can either be accessed from *Filter>Nik collection*, in which case it can

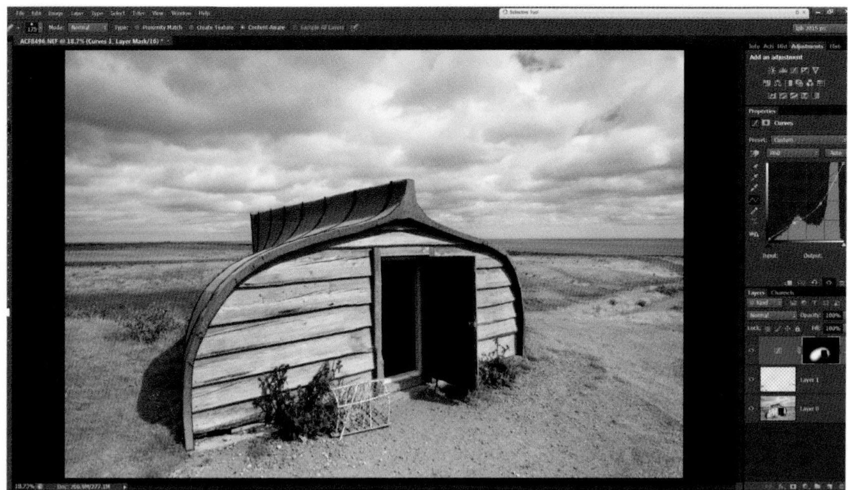

◀ **Fig. 11.1**
Basic cloning work and localized contrast adjustment (using curves).

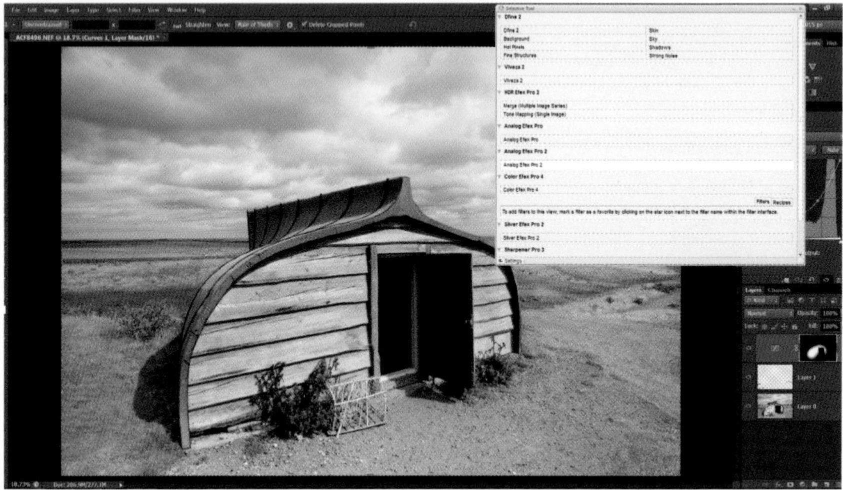

◀ **Fig. 11.2**
Nik Selective tool drop-down layer.

only be applied to a flattened image (or a pixel layer directly) or, more effectively, the selective tool drop-down can be added when installing the software, and by using the drop-down menu, (almost) all of the collections will add an upward flattened layer to the top of the layer stack. This allows the opacity of the Nik layer to be adjusted, blending modes to be used to change the effect of the layer and layer masks to be applied.

Analogue Efex/Efex 2

As with almost all of the Nik Efex collection, selecting Analogue Efex creates an upward flattened layer over the top of the layer stack.

Start with a photograph of one of the upturned boat huts on Holy Island.

As with any photo, process it as you choose (in this case, all that has been done is a touch of cloning and a levels layer – when adding Analogue Efex, it is often best to start with a simple image.

Note – it is not necessary to flatten the image at this point. Simply by clicking on the drop-down menu, Nik Efex will perform an upward flatten of all the layers in the image and add the appropriate Nik layer at the top of the stack.

By selecting Analogue Efex Pro 2, a large dialogue box appears.

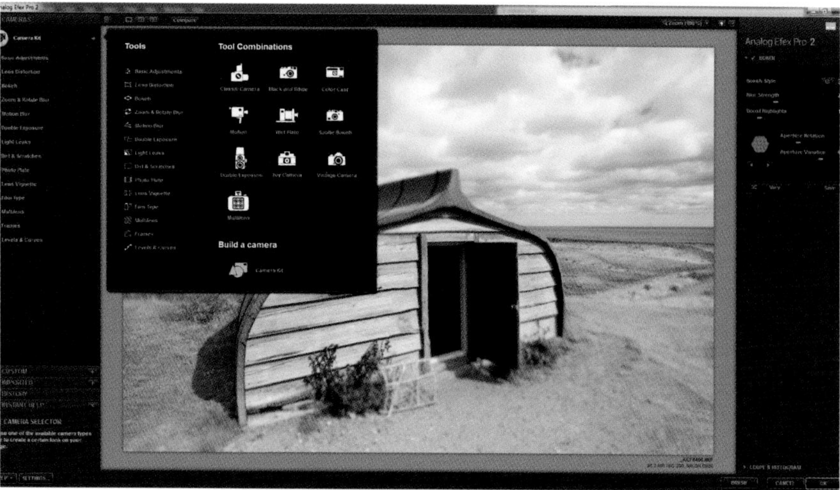

Fig. 11.3
Analogue Efex Pro dialogue box.

The default dialogue box for Analogue Efex Pro is for the 'classic camera', which offers a selection of analogue-style effects from faded low-contrast images, through contrasty images with a little edge fall-off. For many, the thought of spending hard-earned cash on a sharp camera and lens, taking huge care about taking the picture, and then applying a filter to degrade the image will be photographic sacrilege (on most images, I would agree). But sometimes, a certain image will just cry out for that treatment.

If you click on the right-hand arrow on the classic camera tab at the top of the thumbnails on the left side of the screen, other Analogue Efex options will appear on a further pop-up box:

Black and white offers a range of black and white options, some containing processing 'faults', dust marks, scratches etc.

Colour cast: As it 'says on the tin' – a range of processing colour casts, some of which mimic some old films that most will relish the passing of.

Motion: A creative effect, offering post-processing ICM effects, including lineal and circular 'camera' movements, also allowing sharp areas through the motion. Well worth experimenting with, if you are a fan of camera movement pictures.

Wet plate: A series of nine basic thumbnails, all of which can be customized, offering processing faults on 'wet plate' film effects. Might be useful if you are trying to create an aged Victorian-style image.

Subtle bokeh: A series of effects designed to smooth out background bokeh and add selective edge fall-off. Can be very effective with wide aperture work.

Double exposure: Quite a complex effect, allowing two separate files to be combined either in or out of register, differing opacities applied to the second exposure (thereby allowing the first to show through), and bokeh effects, vignetting, light leaks and similar effects all to be added in the one application. In effect, it does little that cannot be achieved within Photoshop and the other effects marked above, but can be really effective and quick to use on the right image.

Toy camera: There has been a huge interest in recent years in toy camera lenses, Lumo cameras, Holga cameras and lenses. I own a few myself, but never seem to have them with me when I want to create that kind of vignetted image with a sharp spot in the middle, softening at the edges with radial blur affecting the corners. The toy camera section allows these effects to be added – quite convincingly – at post production.

Vintage camera: Another series of effects creating an old film appearance, including light leaks, fading, vignetting and processing faults.

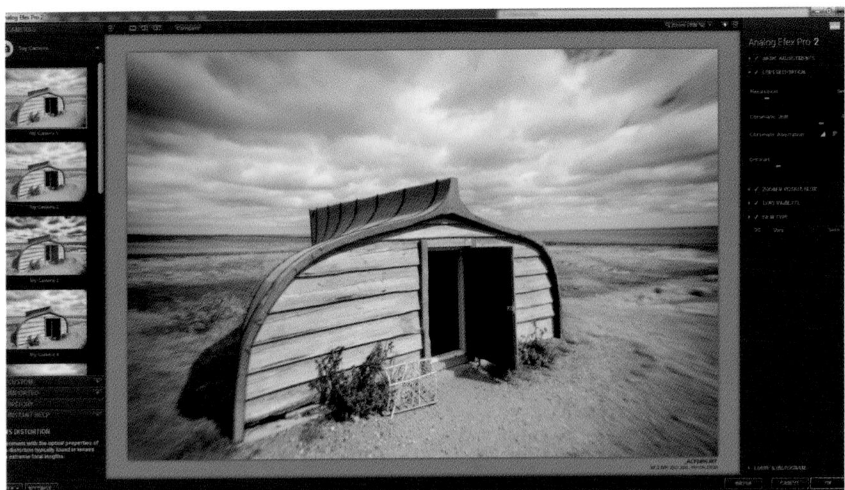

Fig. 11.4
Analogue Efex Pro 2 using toy camera settings.

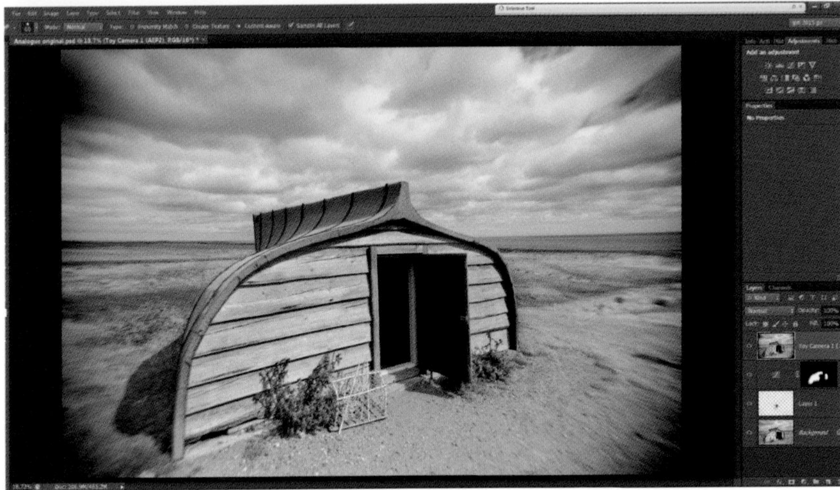

Fig. 11.5
Completed, unflattened image, showing the toy camera layer added automatically above the existing layers.

Multilens: An unusual effect – almost like a triptych, but using sections from within the same image and adding dirt and scratches to give the aged analogue effect.

Worked example, using toy camera

This example is a simple illustration of how easy it is to use one of the Analogue Efex Pro 2 components, by clicking on the Nik selective tool drop-down, then the Analogue Efex Pro 2 tab, and clicking on the right arrow adjacent to the classic camera and selecting toy camera.

There are nine different thumbnails offering different faded and contrast effects. This image seems to suit Toy Camera 1. To increase the toy camera look, and at the same time reduce the dark vignetting in the corner, try moving the pincushion/barrel distortion slider slightly further to the left – which has the effect of pulling the corners out further. In this example, the chromatic shift has been tweaked from 30 per cent to 44 per cent to emphasize the chromatic aberration and the defocus moved from 0 to 30, to introduce some blur in the corners. With this type of effect, there are no rights or wrongs. In fact, whatever you do, some will love it whilst others will not like it at all.

Every image on which you try Analogue Efex Pro/Pro 2 will need different applications and

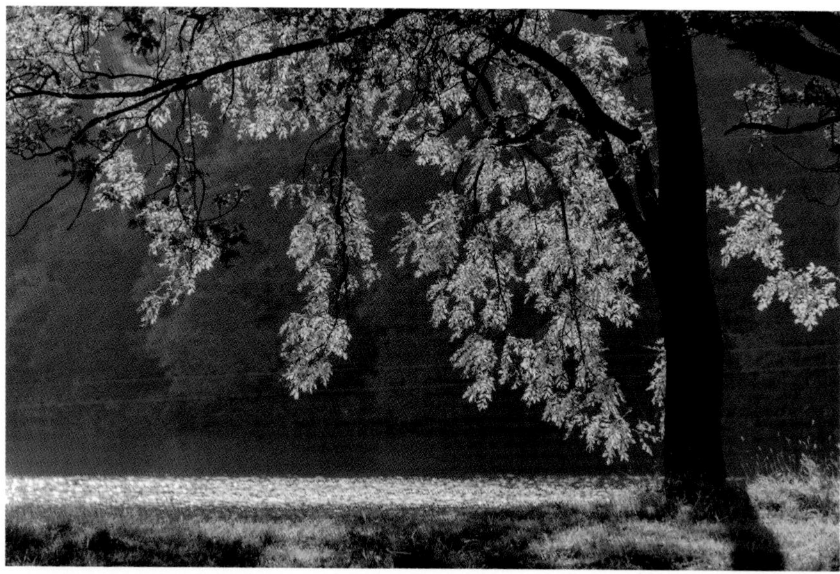

Fig. 11.6
Original image of overhanging trees at Buttermere.

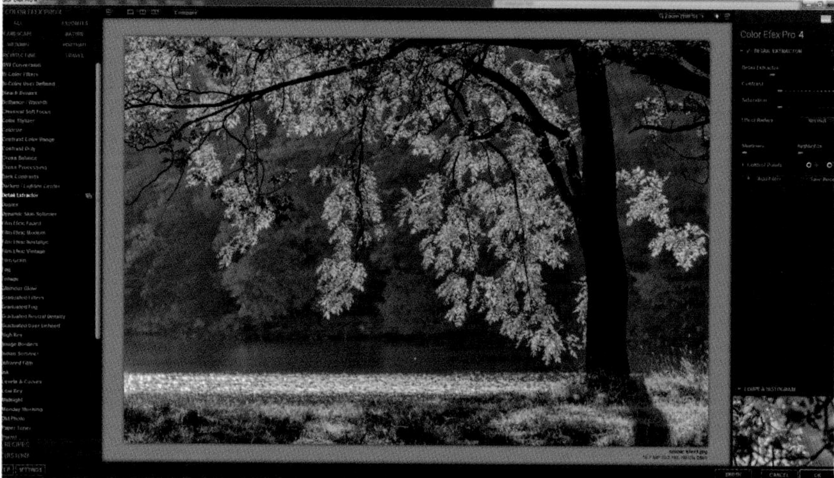

Fig. 11.7
Detail enhancer selected (as shown in the list on the left side of the screen).

settings; the best way to get familiar with this part of the Google Nik package is to practise.

Fig. 11.5 is the completed picture, showing the additional layer added by Analogue Efex Pro 2 at the top of the layer stack.

Colour Efex Pro 4

Similar in application to Analogue Efex in that, whenever Colour Efex Pro is selected, a new top layer is created. Colour Efex is a truly versatile application with the ability to affect colour, contrast, sharpness, soft focus, and countless different effects to enhance the image. If more than one effect is required on the same image, they can all be added in the same layer.

The worked example is a simple landscape shot of some overhanging trees at Buttermere. (Figure 11.6) The original image is a little more pastel in tone than might be desired, so by adding a Colour Efex layer simply by clicking on the drop-down menu and selecting Colour Efex Pro you pull up the Colour Efex pop-up screen. Colour Efex 4 defaults to the last filter used, so it's unlikely it'll be the one you want at first.

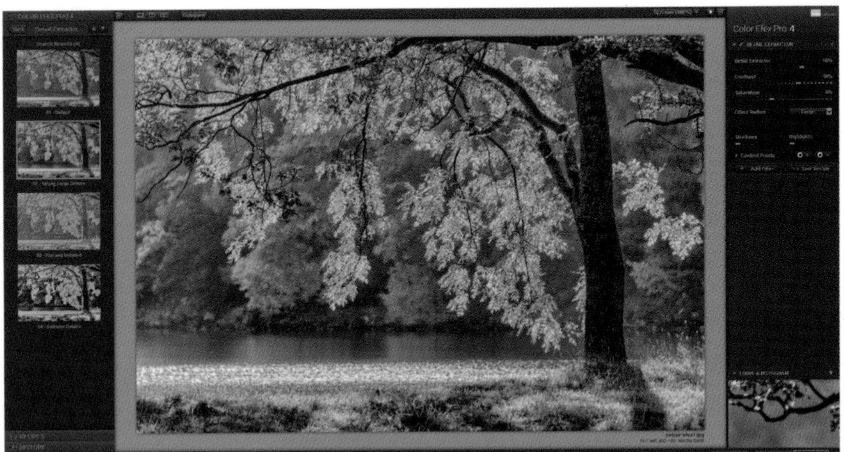

Fig. 11.8
Detail enhancer (strong large details) selected.

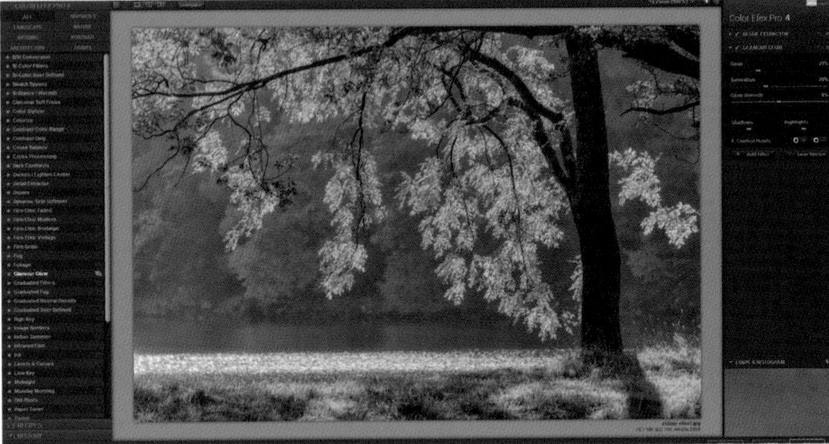

Fig. 11.9
Glamour glow added to detail enhancer.

The first thing evident in this picture is that, despite the limited vibrance range, the details in the shadows look a touch dark.

You will see, on the list on the left side of the screen, that 'detail enhancer' is highlighted, and the right side of the screen has a range of sliders to adjust the effects and settings to create your preferred effect. Adjacent to each of the effects on the left side of the screen is a blue icon, which when clicked on opens a series of thumbnail default settings. This is the same for every one of the available effects on Colour Efex Pro 4, giving a countless number of possible default adjustments. Figure 11.8 shows the default presets for detail enhancer, with the second option (Strong Large Details) selected. Note the more enhanced effect on the background details over Figure 11.7.

In this image, the default settings seemed to give the most satisfactory result, lifting the dark shadows in the foreground tree trunk, without overemphasizing the background details.

Having lifted these details, the sparkle of the sun on the leaves might be enhanced by a glow effect. By clicking on the 'add filter' tab at the right side of the screen, it preserves the adjustments made using the detail enhancer, and allows another effect from the left column to be selected. Click on the 'back' tab (top left of the screen) and select 'glamour glow'.

Again, selecting the blue icon next to 'glamour glow' brings up a series of default options.

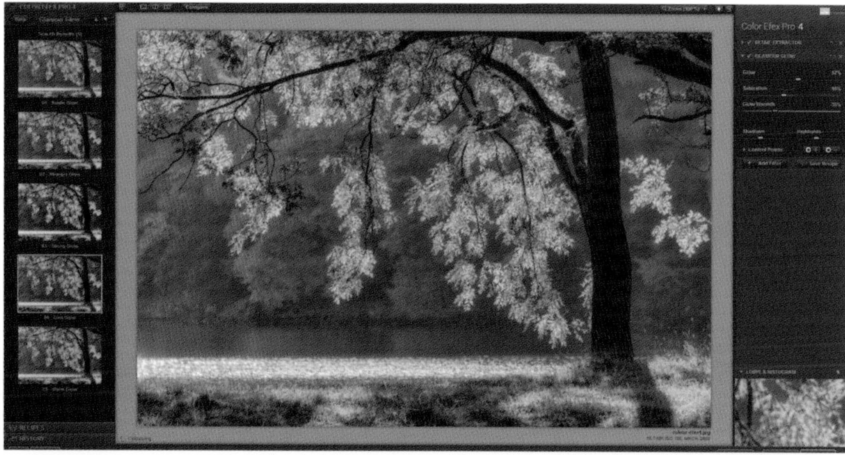

Fig. 11.10
Glamour glow (cool glow) selected.

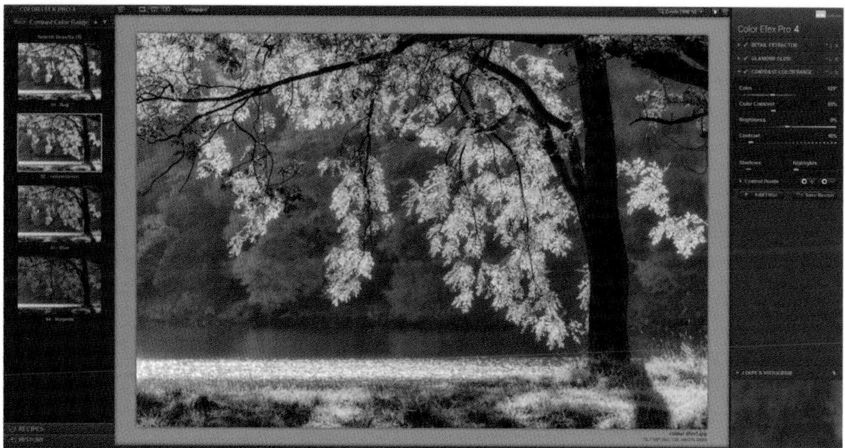

Fig. 11.11
Contrast colour range filter added.

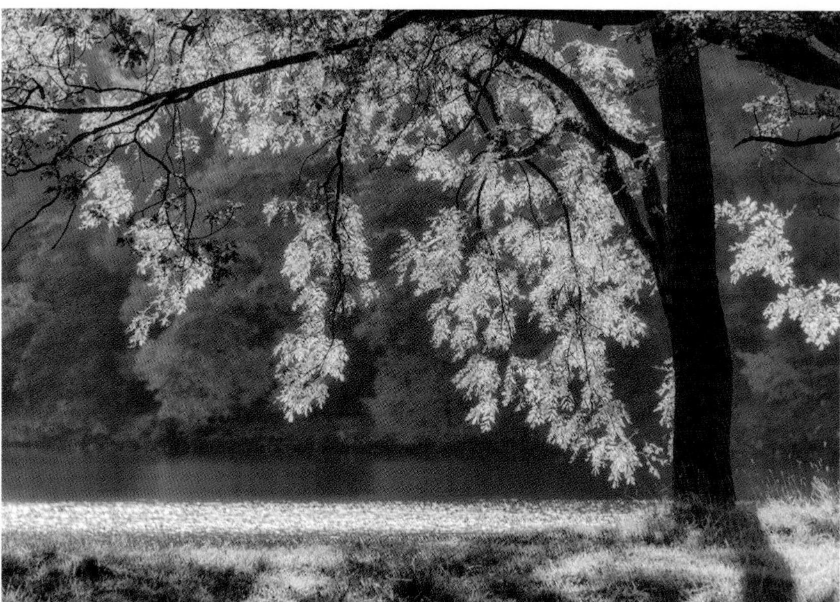

Fig. 11.12
Final image adding the glow and sparkle that seemed to be there when the image was taken.

Figure 11.10 shows the fourth option (cool glow) selected. The cool glow suited this image well, as it enhanced the blue tones in the background without cooling the leaves in the foreground. The default setting was a little strong, so the glow warmth slider was moved from its default setting of –54 per cent to –35 per cent, which still cooled the background a little, but retained more warmth in the foreground.

Finally, adding a 'contrast colour range' filter set to the second default option of yellow/green filter, with a little shadow recovery (shadow slider on the right side of the screen) retained the detail in the tree trunk.

By clicking on the OK button (lower right of screen) the three filters added are combined into a single layer on the top of the layer stack. If the adjustments you have set up using a series of filters is something that you might wish to add to a few photographs, the combined filtration can be saved as a custom filter simply by clicking on the 'save recipe' tab, situated next to the add filter tab on the right side of the screen.

Colour Efex has brought out the glow and sparkle that seems appropriate for the lighting conditions on the day.

The effects and adjustments that every filter within Colour Efex Pro 4 can make to images is far too extensive and varied to be fully covered within this (or indeed any) book. Only by practice and experimentation can the user get the most out of this section of the software.

SILVER EFEX PRO 2

Silver Efex Pro has rapidly established itself as one of the leading third-party black and white conversion plug-ins on the market. Many readers will be familiar with it, and the worked examples here serve to clarify some of its functionality.

One of the mistakes that many users make with Silver Efex Pro (and in fact with all the Nik Efex software) is that they tend to use it in place of any Photoshop work. Whilst this will often give very satisfactory results, the best results are often achieved by editing the image in Photoshop first, then applying the appropriate Nik Efex filter afterwards. Silver Efex Pro is a prime example of this.

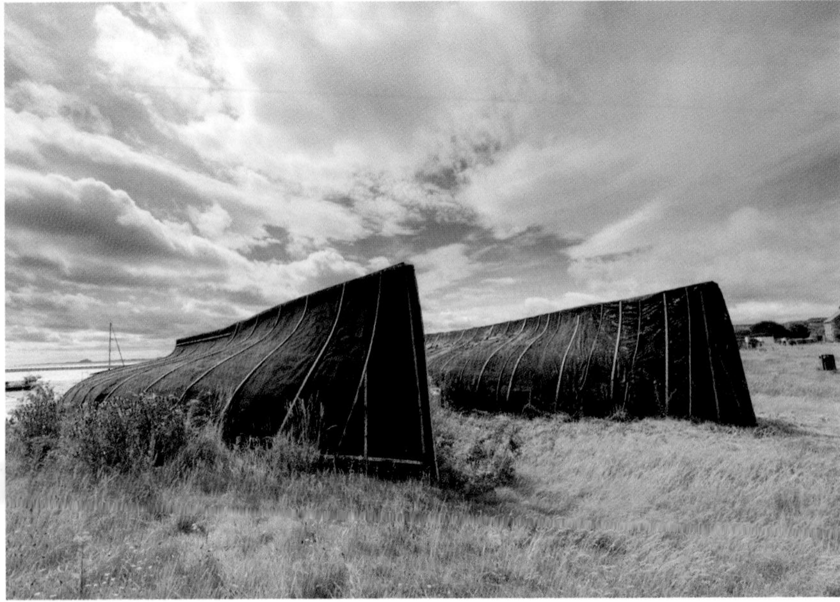

Fig. 11.13
Original image of boats/huts, Holy Island.

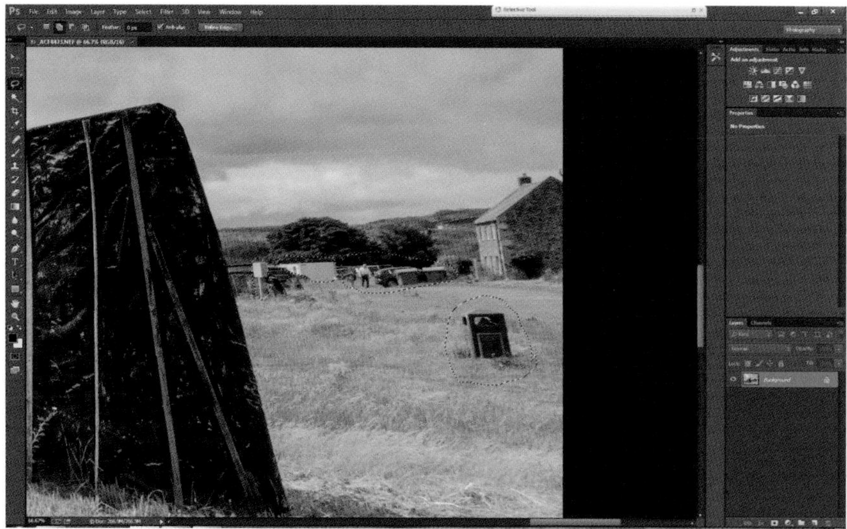

Fig. 11.14
Lasso tool drawn around distracting elements.

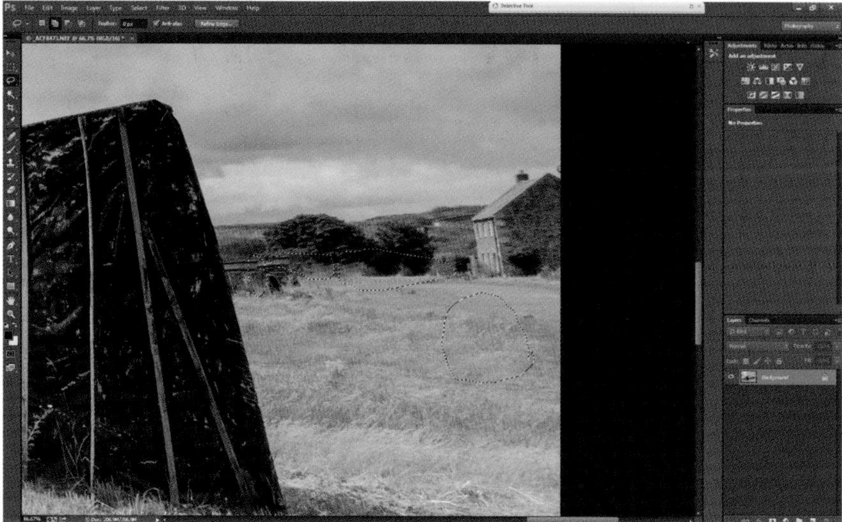

Fig. 11.15
Distracting elements removed using content-aware fill.

The worked example here is of a row of upturned boats/huts on Holy Island. These are iconic symbols of the area, boats that have been upturned, covered with roofing felt and have doors on their stern ends, creating huts used for stores or workshops. I had spent a couple of hours there waiting for the clouds to be right, the area to be reasonably clear of people and the lighting to be good (Fig. 11.13).

However, even after a long wait, there are things that appear in pictures that we have little or no control over. In this picture, there is a moored boat on the left edge, a mast sticking up from behind the stern of the left boat, a litter bin on the right foreground and large coloured bins in the background. A graduated filter was used to retain details in the highlight areas of the sky, while retaining as much shadow detail as possible in the boats.

Even with care in photographing, the grey box, square building, green and blue bins, parked car and rubbish bin are not something we have control over in our photography. A lasso tool around them and filling the selection with content-aware fill cleans them up pretty well. Any bits that don't work first time can either be refilled, or the use of a healing

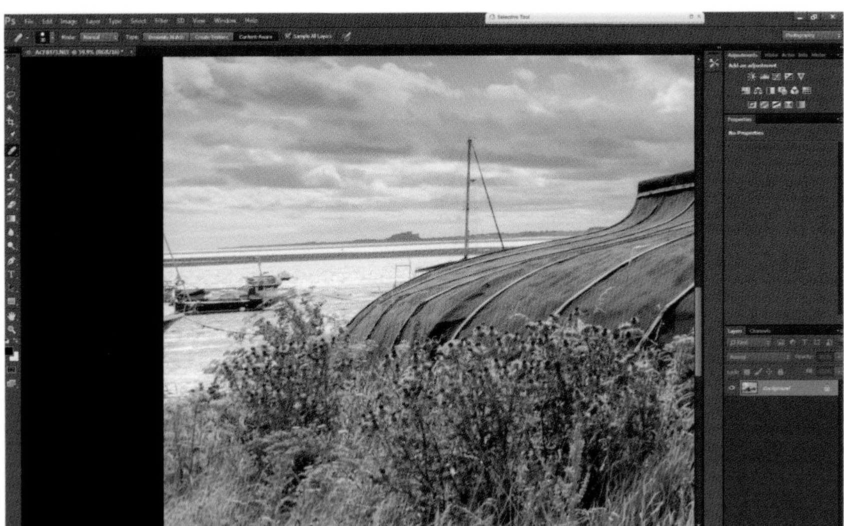

◀ **Fig. 11.16**
Mast and moored boat.

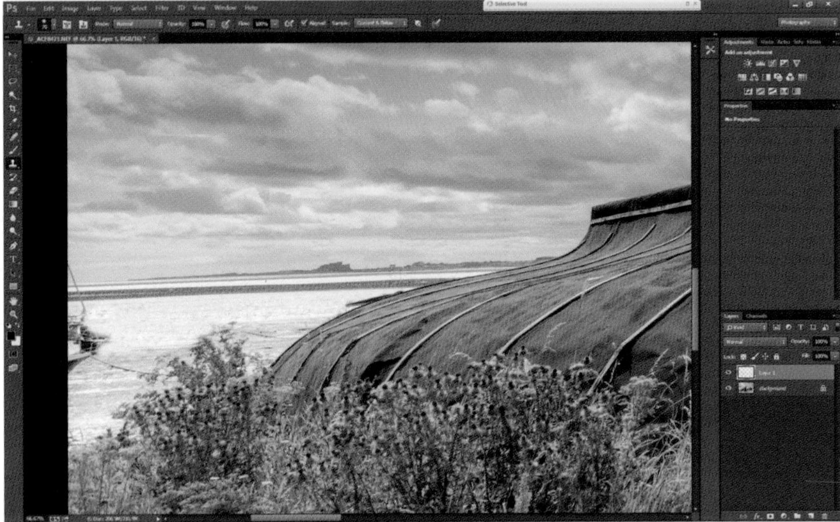

◀ **Fig. 11.17**
Cloning (on separate layer).

brush or even a clone stamp tool on a separate layer can tidy up fine details. (Do bear in mind when cloning that you might be working on a very small area of the image, and only you know where – often small flaws are not even visible to the viewer.)

On the left side, the mast and boat at the far edge (Fig. 11.16) didn't tidy up as well using content-aware fill (if filling a sky area right adjacent to the stern of the boat, it is likely to clone parts of the boat into the sky area) (Fig. 11.17).

The extreme left-hand side of the picture – the edge of the red boat – can be repaired using a mix of content-aware fill on the background layer and a touch of clone stamp and healing brush on layer 1. Continue building up the repair little by little until you are happy with the result. Don't forget to zoom out to full image occasionally to check it in relation to the whole picture.

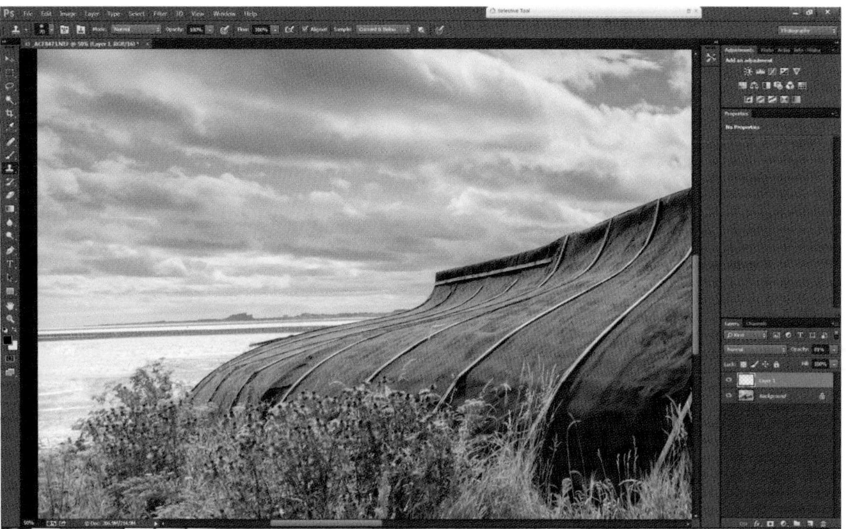

Fig. 11.18
Final cloning and healing.

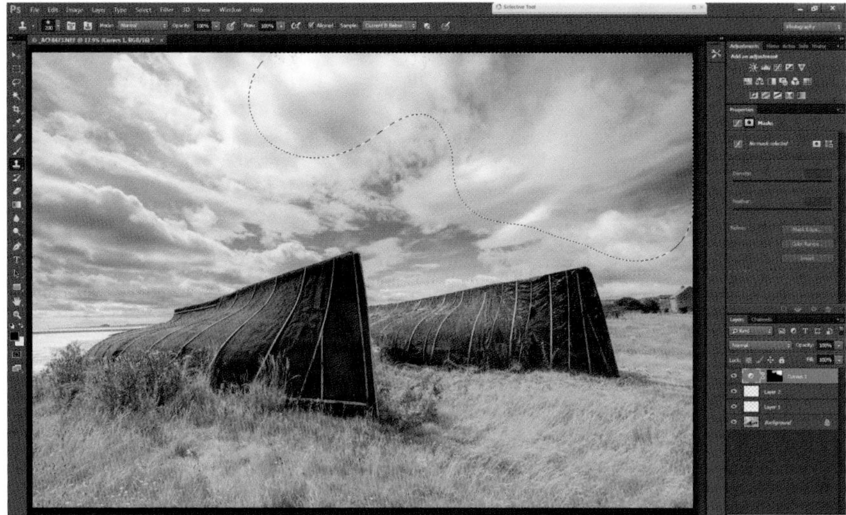

Fig. 11.19
Contrast increased in the sky area top right by using a curves layer.

With the picture finally tidied up (in this case layer 2 was added for some final spot healing) you should be ready for basic editing. The sky at the top right is a little flat in the original image, so a soft-edged selection (made using a large brush in quick mask mode) and a curves layer lifted the tones in this area (Fig. 11.19).

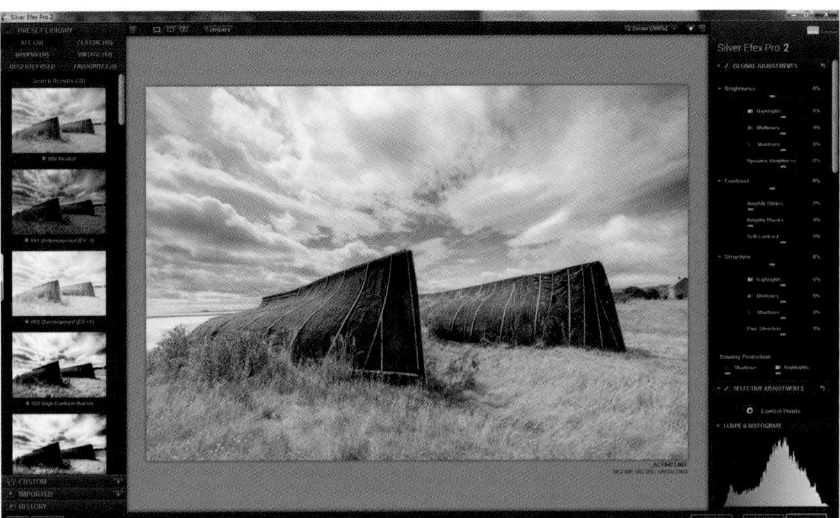

Fig. 11.20
Silver Efex main screen.

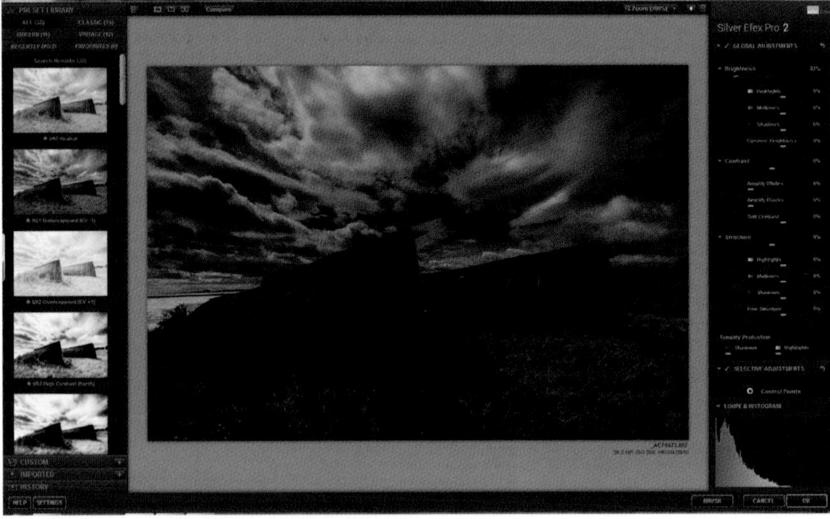

Fig. 11.21
Main brightness slider moved to the left darkens the image.

Having done the basic edit, clicking on the Nik drop-down menu and Silver Efex Pro 2 will open the Silver Efex main screen (Fig. 11.20).

The basic adjustments in Silver Efex are on the right side of the screen, and only need a little explanation.

Brightness: moving the brightness slider to the left darkens the image (Fig. 11.21), and moving it to the right brightens it (Fig. 11.22).

Within the brightness section, fine adjustments can be made for highlight, mid-tone and shadow brightness.

The next main group is *Contrast*. Moving the slider to the left will reduce contrast, while moving it to the right will increase it (Fig. 11.23). In addition to the global contrast adjustments, there are two sliders below, amplify whites and amplify blacks, that can be used to increase contrast within the upper

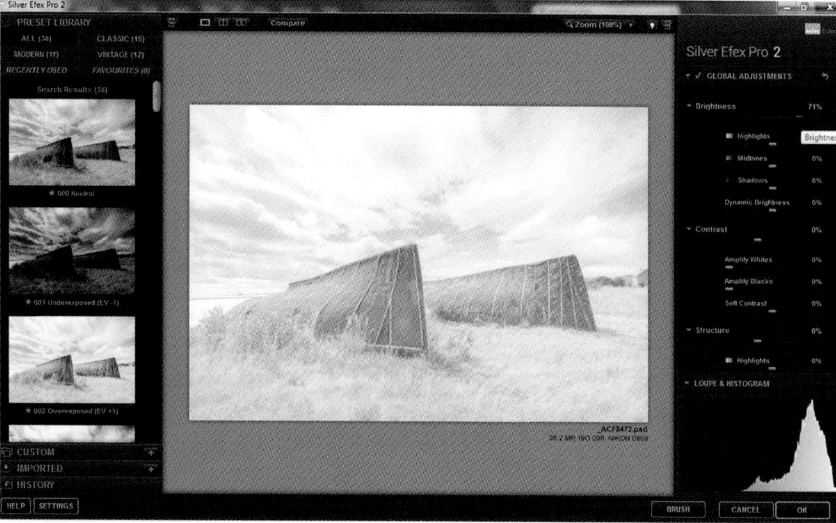

▶ **Fig. 11.22**
Main brightness slider moved to the right lightens the image.

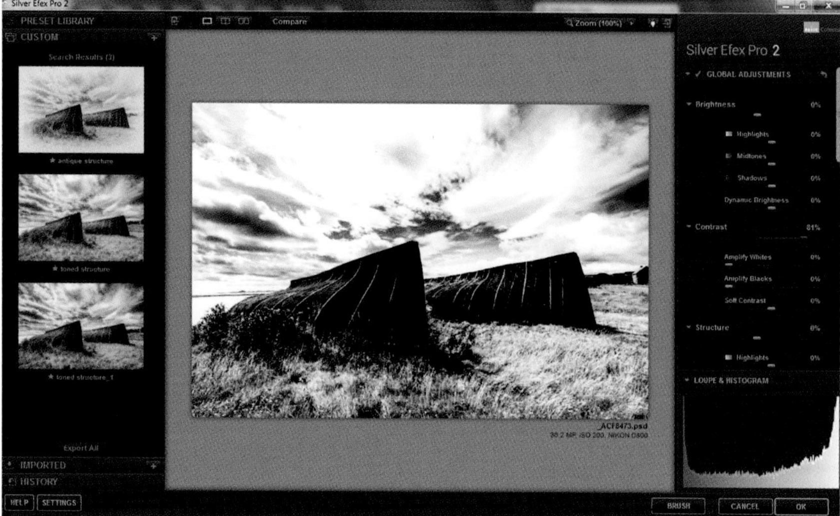

▶ **Fig. 11.23**
Contrast added globally with contrast slider.

and lower values of the brightness range. Fig. 11.23 shows the effect of increasing contrast globally. The shadow areas block up and the boats become black, while the sky and brighter areas become blown whites. Increasing contrast works well on images where the histogram is quite narrow, but on this image it is ineffective.

The third group of sliders are referred to within Nik Efex software as *structure*. Within Adobe Camera RAW or lightroom, it is similar to *Clarity*; within other software packages it is sometimes referred to as *micro-contrast*. It effectively increases the contrast of each brightness zone independently of other areas – so will increase the contrast of the tones within the boats, while simultaneously increasing the contrast of the clouds in the sky.

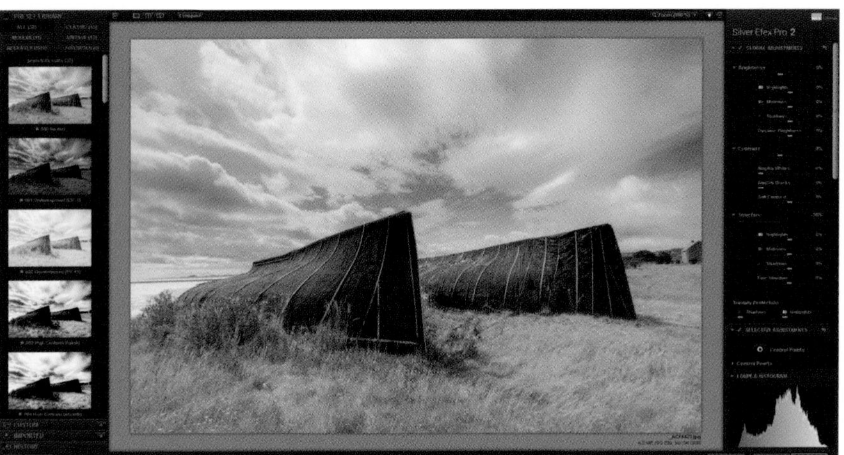

Fig. 11.24
Structure slider moved to the left reduces structure (texture).

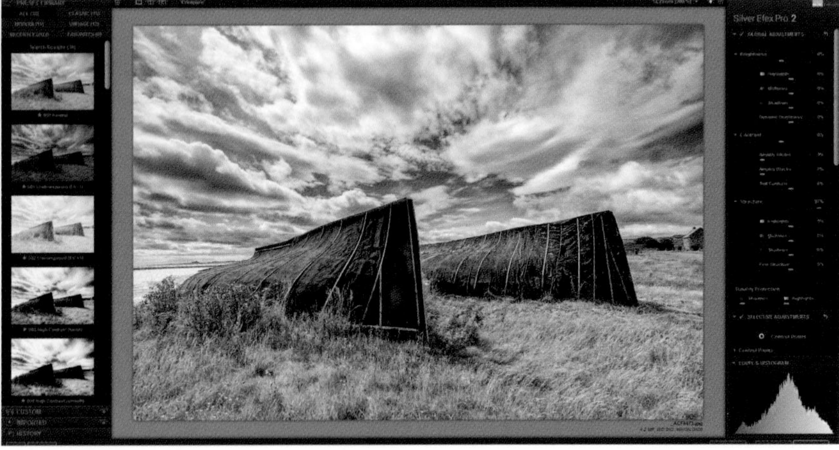

Fig. 11.25
Structure slider moved to the right will increase structure (texture).

Moving the structure slider to the left will reduce structure, and soften the picture (Fig. 11.24); moving it to the right will increase structure (Fig. 11.25).

One of the biggest mistakes new users to Silver Efex Pro make, is to overuse structure. Initially it does appear to be a really effective quick-fix to almost all photographs, and although most pictures will benefit from some additional structure, excessive use can result in black and white conversions that look more like etchings than photographs. Like the brightness sliders, structure also has individual sliders for each of highlights, mid-tones and shadows.

In addition to the three main adjustment sliders (and their sub-sliders), Silver Efex offers a default library, featuring a huge array of different monochrome effects.

Figs 11.26 and 11.27 show two of the default library presets of great use to landscape photographers. Fig. 11.26 shows *high structure (smooth)*, which takes global structure up to +20%, but moves the mid-tone structure up to +60%. The contrast controls show +20% on amplify black and amplify whites, which boosts the highlights and mid-tones a bit. This can be a good starting point for many landscape pictures, but keep an eye on clipping shadows and highlights on the histogram in the lower right-hand corner of the screen.

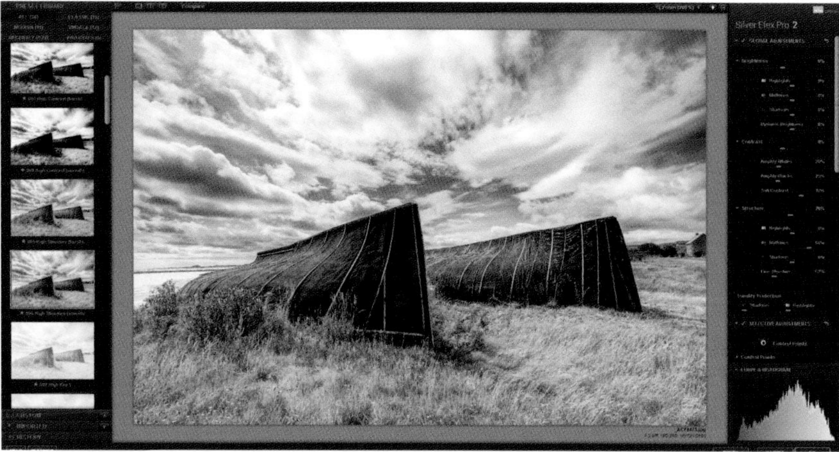

Fig. 11.26
Default preset *High structure (Smooth).*

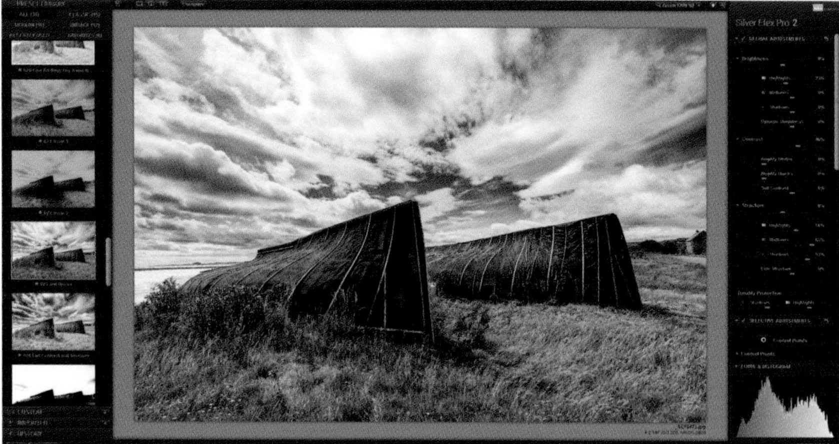

Fig. 11.27
Default preset *Wet Rocks.*

Fig 11.27 shows the *wet rocks* preset, only slightly different from the high structure preset, but with +40% global contrast added rather than amplify whites and blacks, and slight structure increases to highlights and shadows, but again with a big +66% on mid-tones.

The presets work really well as a starting point on adjustments, but always be prepared to fine-tune them.

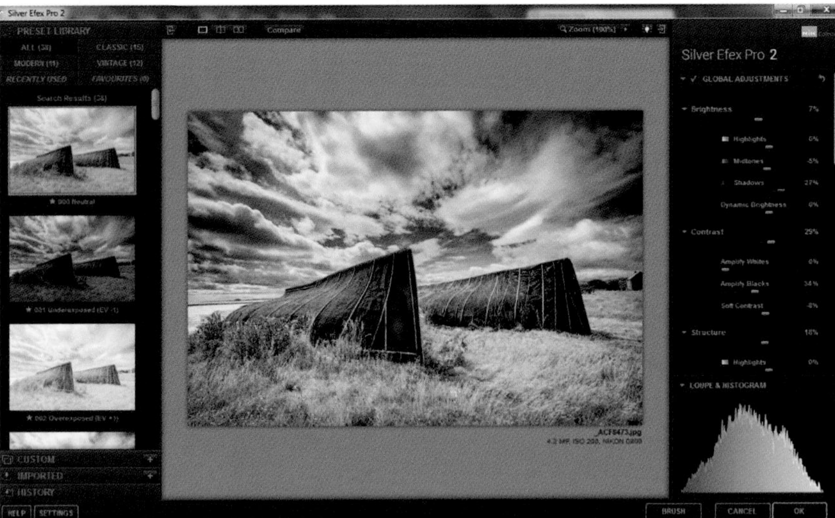

Fig. 11.28
Adjustments to the worked example starting with the *Neutral* preset and adjusting brightness and contrast.

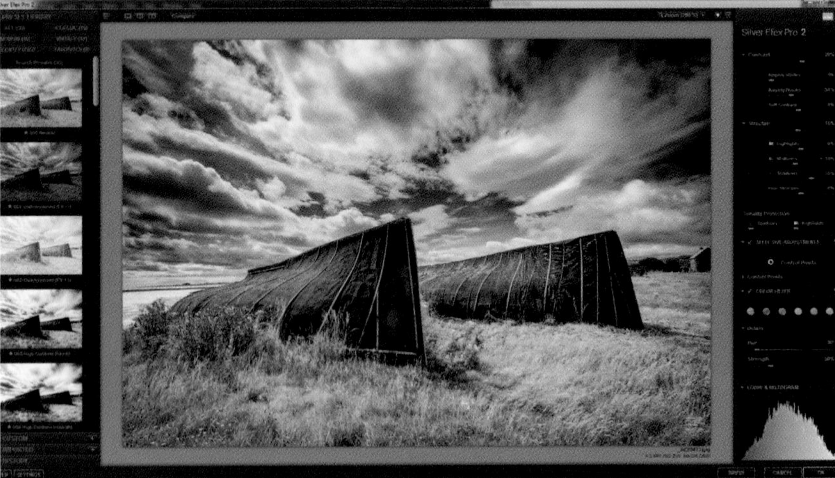

Fig. 11.29
Further adjustments, increasing structure, and adding an orange filter and a slight darkened vignette to the image.

On this worked example, the brightness of the shadows have been boosted slightly, contrast increased by +29%, and blacks amplified.

Scrolling further down the adjustments palette, Fig 11.29 shows adjustments to structure, and although it doesn't highlight as selected, tonal changes have been made by use of the orange filter. Darkening of the edges has also been created by a slight vignette of –21%, a technique often used in darkroom black and white printing, to hold the viewer's eye within the picture.

Having selected a range of adjustments that suits a photo taken on a particular day and location, and that also matches the style of the photographer, it would seem a long and arduous task to carry out the same modifications to other pictures, especially if your adjustments are very different from any of the Silver Efex presets. By clicking on the custom tab on the left side of the screen, there is a '+' icon just to the right of the word *custom*. Clicking on this will pull up a dialogue box (Fig. 11.30).

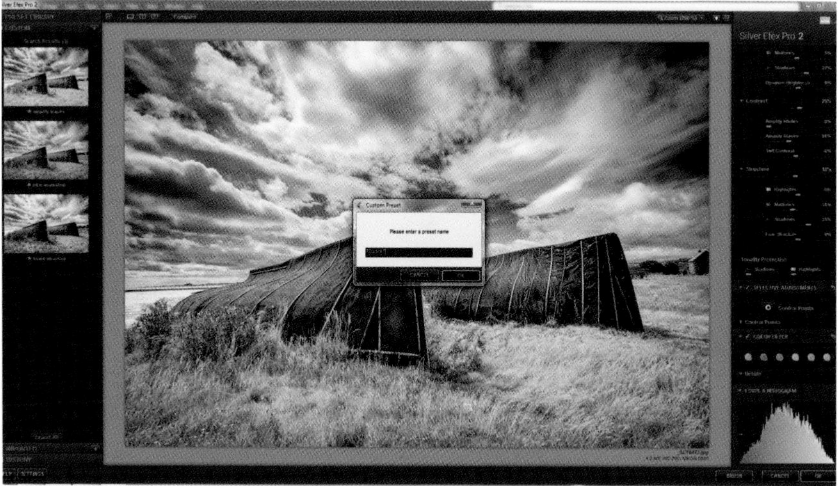

Fig. 11.30
Saving the adjustments as a custom preset so the same changes can be easily applied to other pictures.

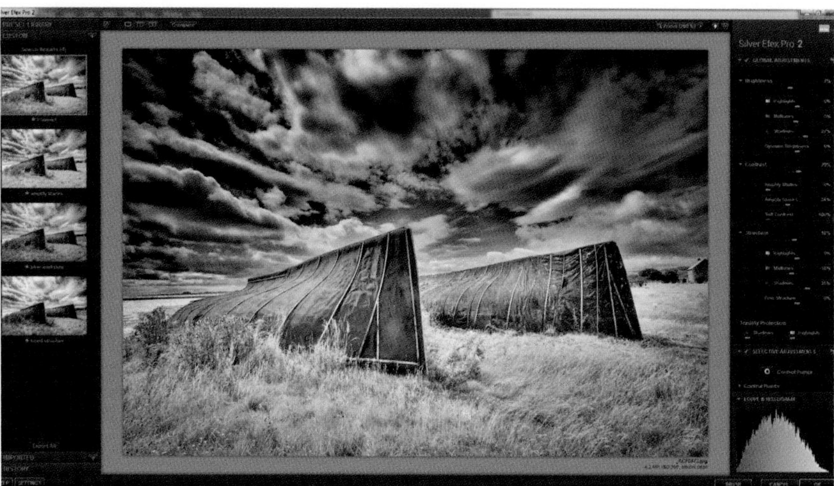

Fig. 11.31
Soft contrast slider set to minus (–) 100%.

Type a relevant title into the dialogue box and click on OK. This will save all your adjustments as a preset that you can call up on a single click.

A few more adjustments worth touching on include *soft contrast* and *toning*. At the bottom of the contrast sliders is one labelled *soft contrast*. This is much easier to demonstrate than to explain, but moving the slider to the left applies a unique type of contrast to different areas throughout the image (Fig. 11.31).

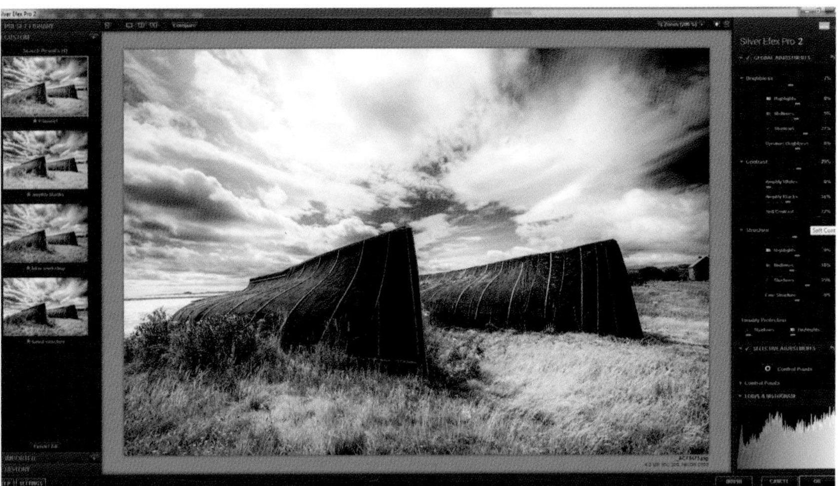

Fig. 11.32
Soft contrast slider set to plus (+) 100%.

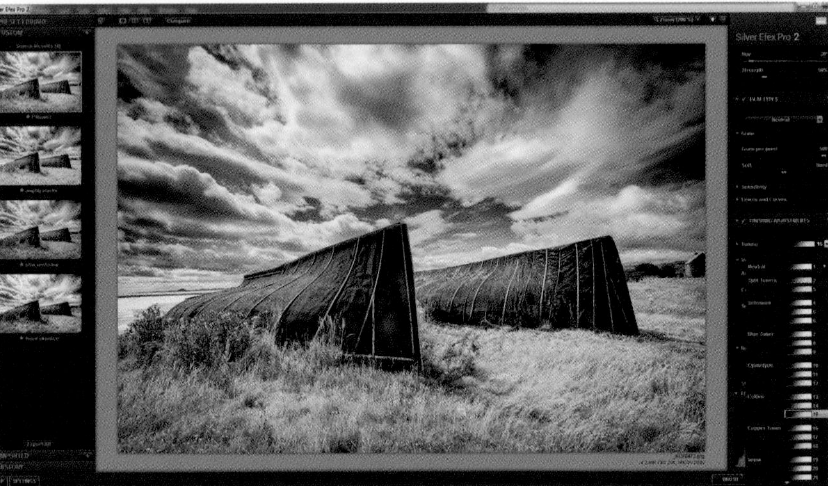

Fig. 11.33
Selection of a toning adjustment – No 15 *Coffee Toner* added (the strongest of the three coffee toners).

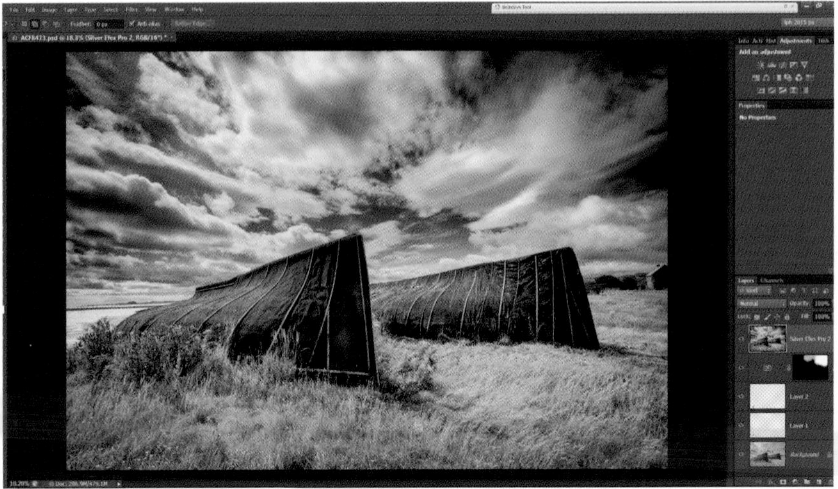

Fig. 11.34
Silver Efex Pro layer added to the Photoshop file as a separate layer over the original Photoshop layers.

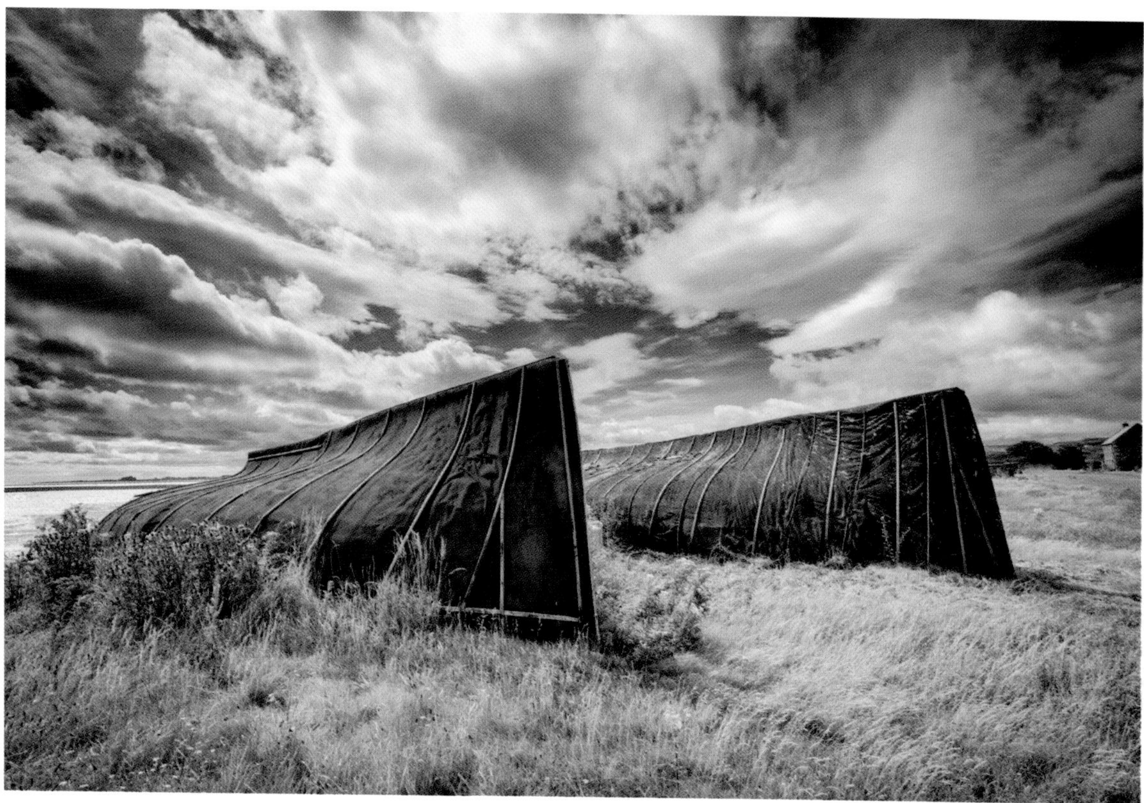

▲ **Fig. 11.35**
Final image of boat/huts.

Used too strongly, it can give the appearance of an over-worked HDR, but used with care, it can pull back shadow and highlight detail with great effect. Moving the slider to the right creates the opposite effect, by increasing contrast in a more traditional manner across the picture (Fig. 11.32).

Toning can be quite effective in conveying a mood to the picture. The range of available tones within Silver Efex pro is colossal, and these can all be individually fine-tuned to create custom tones. Fig. 11.33 shows the application of the No 13 coffee tone to the boat picture, which gives it a slightly more aged feel that suits the image (I was tempted to blue- or selenium-tone this image as well, to give it the feel of the sea).

Once all the adjustments are completed, click on the OK button at the lower right of the screen, and the Silver Efex Pro 2 conversion layer will appear as a top layer on the layer stack (Fig. 11.34).

The final image is shown in Fig 11.35.

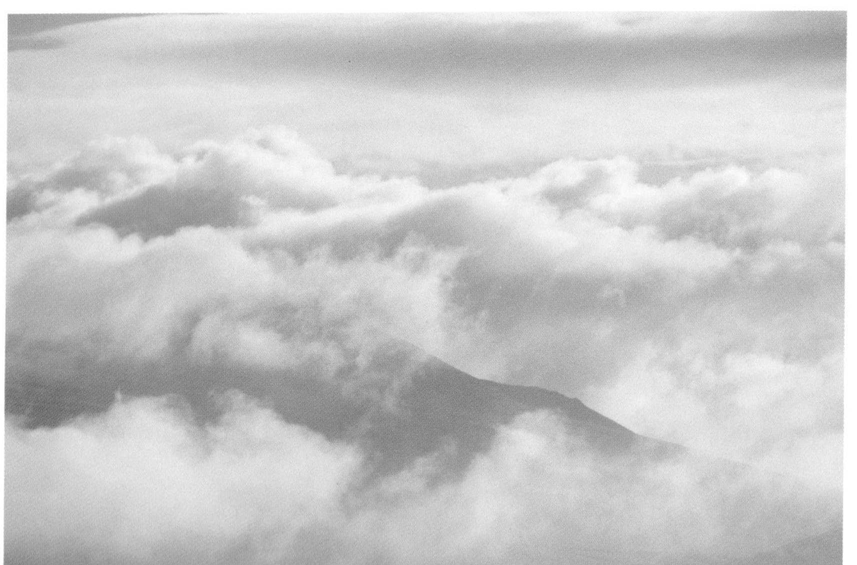

Fig. 11.36
Original image of clouds surrounding a mountain.

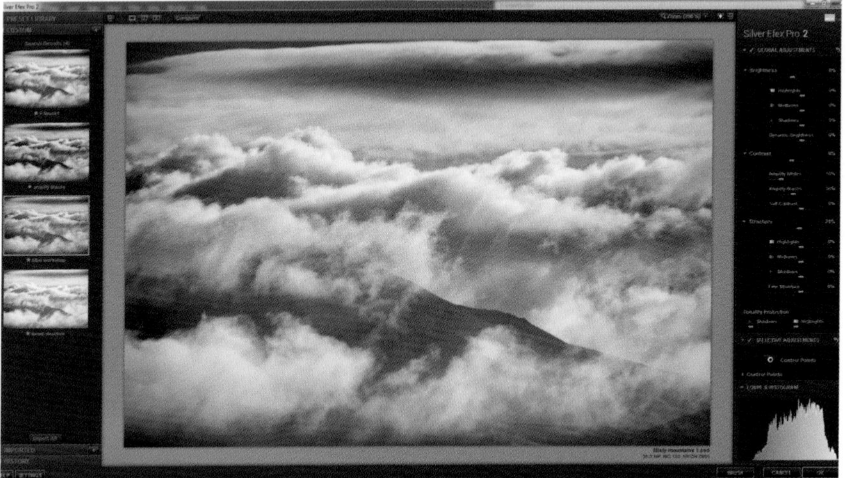

Fig. 11.37
Silver Efex Pro layer added, using a pre-prepared custom preset (any adjustments can be made).

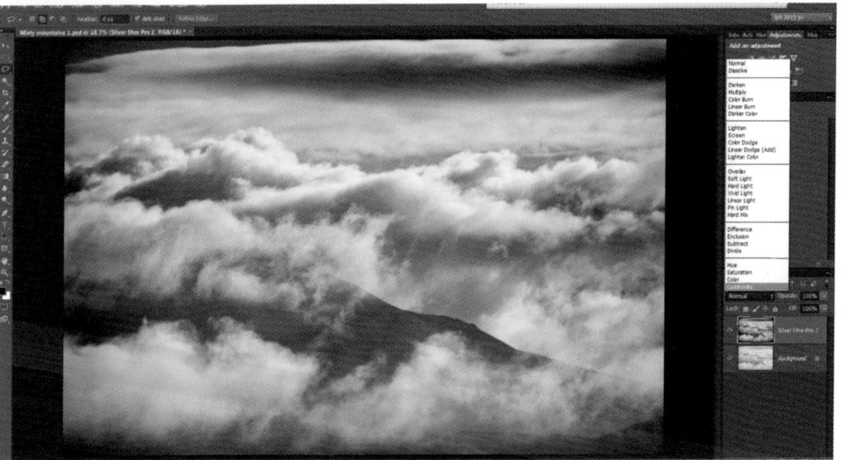

Fig. 11.38
Silver Efex Pro 2 layer added and blending modes drop-down clicked on to show all the layer blending modes available.

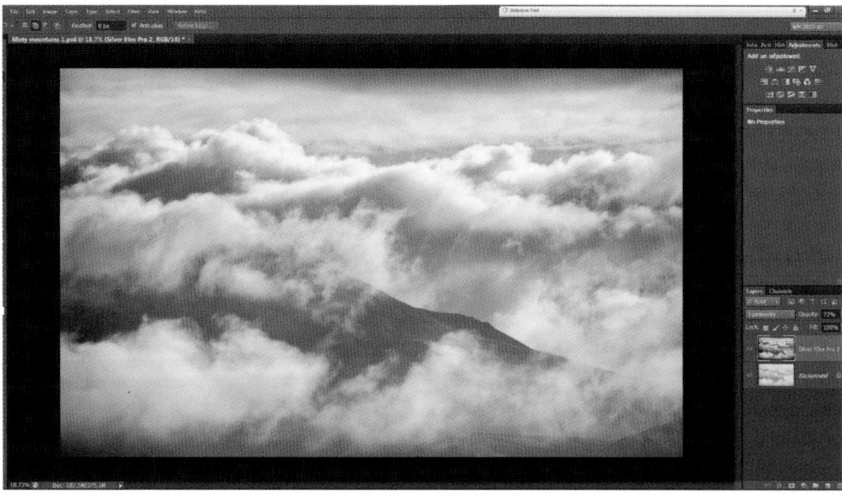

Fig. 11.39
Luminosity blending mode applied to the Silver Efex Pro 2 layer and opacity of the layer reduced to 72%

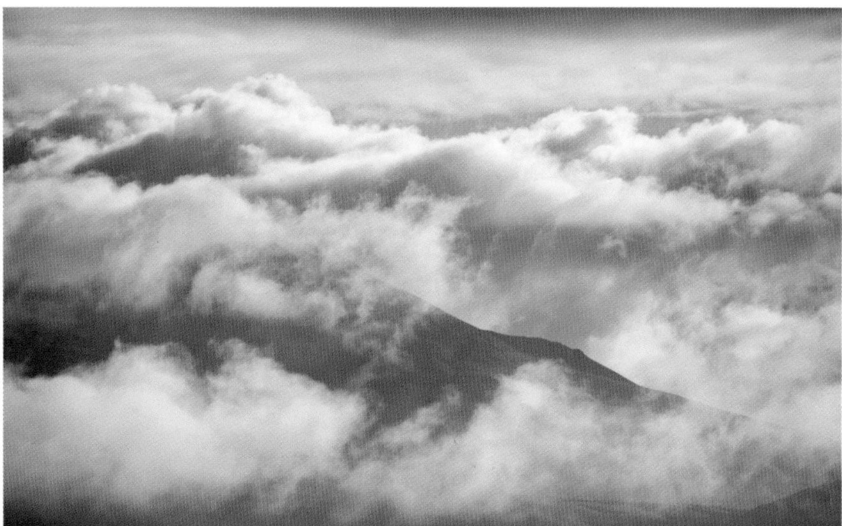

Fig. 11.40
Final cloudscape, showing more texture, definition and contrast than the original file.

As well as being a superb black and white adjustment application, Silver Efex Pro 2 can also be used to impart the same adjustments to a colour image. Take the picture of clouds surrounding a mountain peak (Fig. 11.36) for example; while the high-key effect suits the image, it might look more effective with a touch more 'bite'. This can be achieved quickly and easily with the help of Silver Efex Pro 2. Simply add a Silver Efex filter (Fig. 11.37).

Fig. 11.38 shows the Silver Efex Pro 2 layer as a separate layer over the background layer; this of course appears as a monochrome layer. However, by clicking on the blending mode pop-up (just next to opacity at the top of the layers palette) and selecting luminosity, it changes the black and white layer to a layer that applies the contrast (luminosity) changes to the colour layer below. At 100% opacity, the adjustments to the colour layer are a bit strong, so it is usually best to knock down the opacity of the Silver Efex layer until the adjustment looks more natural. Fig. 11.39 shows the same layer but with the blending changed to more luminosity and opacity reduced to 72%.

Fig. 11.40 shows the final image, displaying a marked increase in definition in the cloud textures.

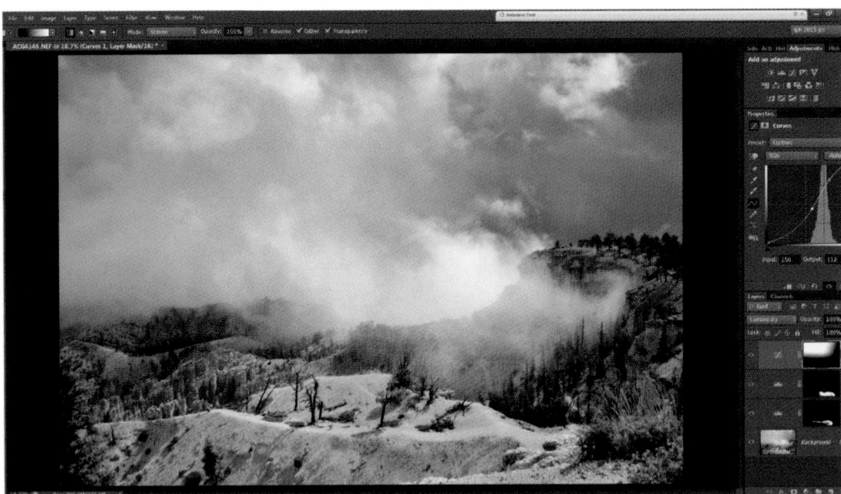

Fig. 11.41
Bryce Canyon image, with basic editing.

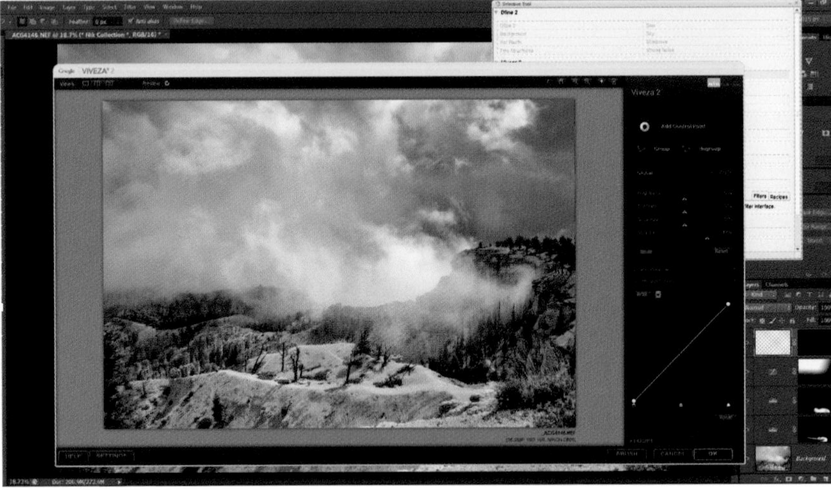

Fig. 11.42
Viveza main screen showing +45% structure applied to the whole image.

VIVEZA

A really simple, yet effective filter that allows subtle enhancements to all or part of the image in terms of contrast, brightness and most usefully, structure.

Fig. 11.41 shows an edited photo of clouds clearing in Bryce Canyon. This stands as a reasonable image without further editing; however, a slight enhancement of the cloud textures (and possibly greater texture within the sand) is achievable. Click on the Nik drop-down tab and select Viveza; the screen is fairly straightforward (Fig. 11.42)

Viveza can work either globally across the entire image, or using Nik's control points. While control points can be effective on some images, they are designed to work on circular selections, and you might find it easier to add layer masks within Photoshop to shape your selections more accurately. In this example, a global adjustment of +45% on structure brings out the details in the clouds, and enhances the textures in the land. Fig. 11.43 shows the final image. The effect is subtle, yet extremely useful on the right image. It doesn't make skies look too over-processed, as some other enhancements can.

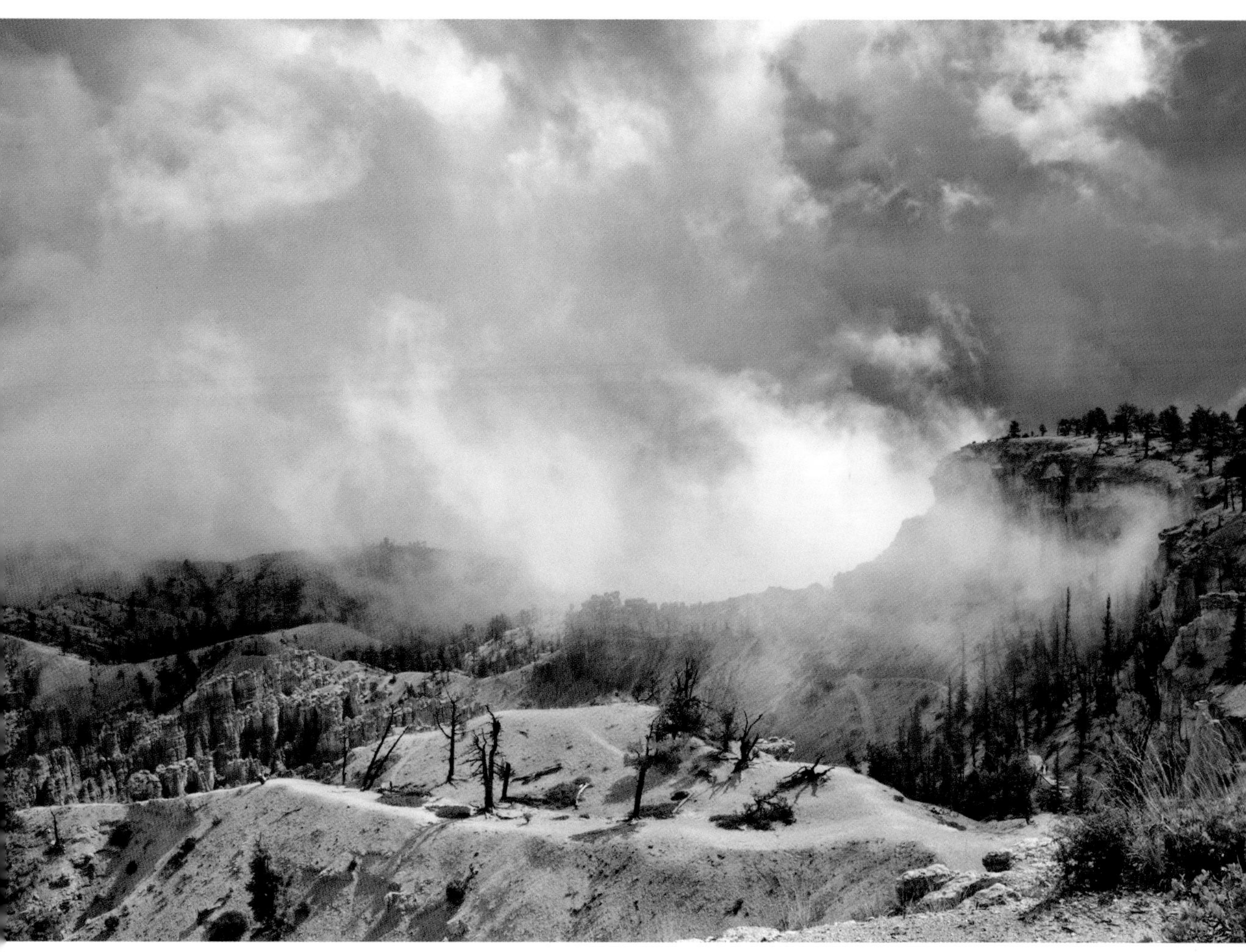

▲ Fig. 11.43
Final Bryce Canyon image

HDR EFEX PRO

The term 'HDR' can provoke much controversy among photographers. Many dismiss it immediately as a gimmicky, over-the-top effect, created to give graphic, extreme results; others use it as a matter of course on almost every image. In reality, properly used, HDR can give natural-looking results with detail retained in both highlight and shadowed areas of the image, where the dynamic range of the subject prevents detail being held in a single image.

While Photoshop has its own HDR application (which works very well), the Nik Collection also offers an HDR package. The purpose of featuring it here is not to compare or contrast it with the Photoshop HDR, merely to show its functionality. Many photographers use different HDR packages for different images or styles, as they will all give slightly different results due to the way the algorithms within them are worked out.

HDR Efex Pro is a fairly straightforward HDR application, and it has the normal two sections:

- Merge (Multiple image series)
- Tone Mapping (Single image)

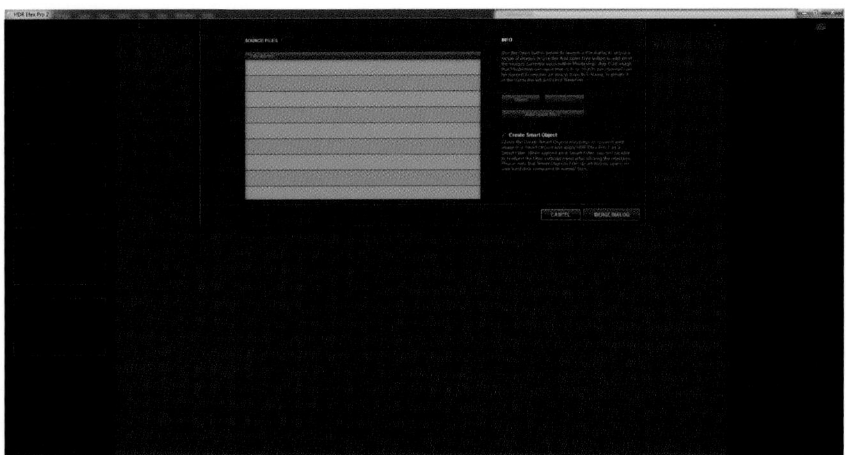

Fig. 11.44
Source files pop-up on HDR Pro.

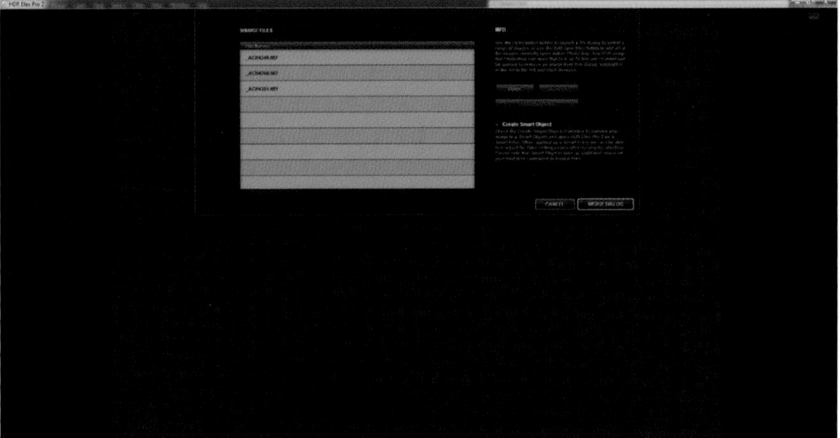

Fig. 11.45
Source file list showing the three files selected to create the HDR image.

The merge option is the more traditional HDR approach, done by merging together a range of exposures taken at different exposure settings to create a single continuously toned image. Without opening any images within Photoshop, just click on the Merge option, and the pop-up screen appears (Fig. 11.44). The buttons on the window are marked 'open' or 'add open files'. Simply click 'open' and select the appropriate bracketed files from your computer.

Select the source files and they are added to the source file window (Fig. 11.45).

Ensure the 'Create smart object' button is ticked (this will allow you to readjust settings even after closing the interface), click on the 'merge dialogue' button and the selected pictures will then be opened, and merged. Fig. 11.46 shows the next screen.

The merge screen in HDR Efex Pro is really straightforward. The white slider at the bottom of the image controls the overall brightness. Slide the white bar to the left, and the image will appear darker, as HDR Efex Pro will use more data from the darker image(s); slide it to the right, and the image will appear lighter. Just be careful not to lose highlight detail. The thumbnails at the top allow you to choose which of the bracketed images should be used as a ghost reference image. That is to say, if there are elements within the picture that have moved during

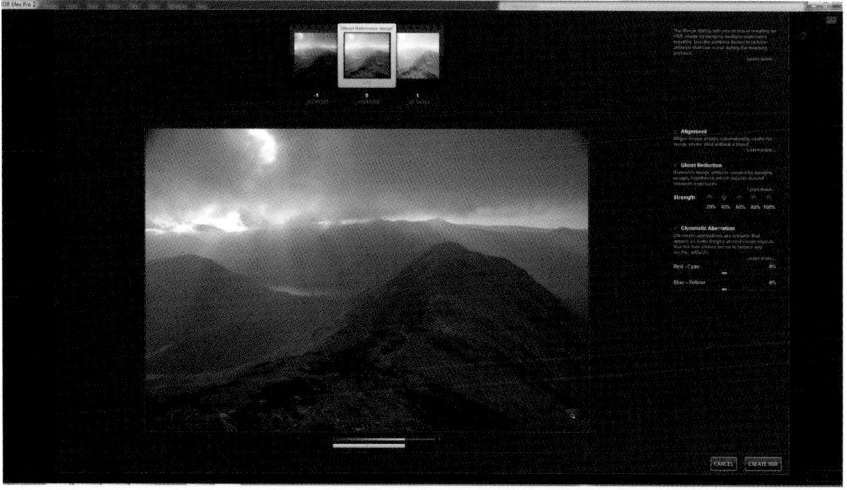

Fig. 11.46
HDR Efex Pro Merge screen showing the brightness slider immediately below the image and the Ghost source image at the top.

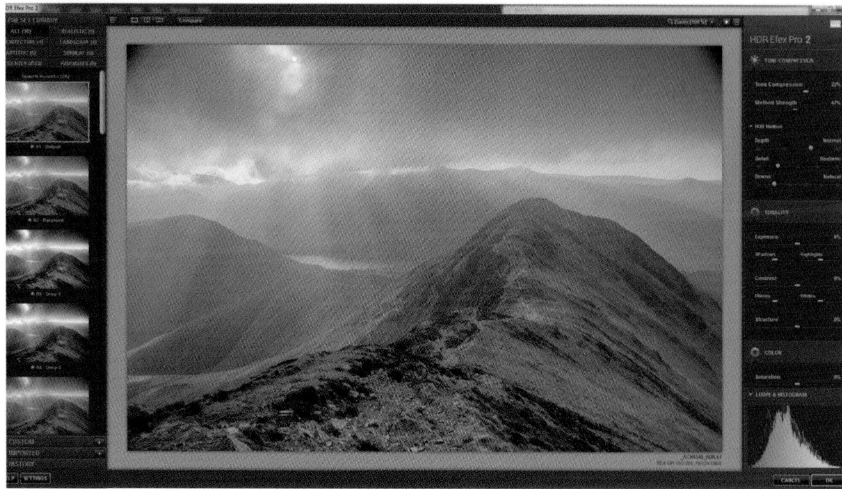

Fig. 11.47
HDR Efex Pro Main editing screen.

the various exposures (most commonly clouds, or tree branches), you can choose which one should take priority over the others. Ensure the alignment, ghosting and chromatic aberration boxes are ticked and click on the 'create HDR' button.

The images will merge and the main HDR screen will appear. As with many Nik Collection programmes, the layout has a series of thumbnails on the left of the screen, each of which can be adjusted and fine-tuned in the adjustment panels on the right of the screen for tone compression, tonality, colour and more.

The thumbnails on the left can be selected by group to suit your tastes; the default is for all twenty-eight HDR presets to be visible, but there are tabs for realistic, architecture, landscape, artistic and surreal, as well as recently used and favourites. Don't automatically assume that only the landscape presets are suitable for landscape photographs, however, as there are interesting alternatives in other groups. It's best to look through all the sections and remember which presets suit your tastes. Every time you enter HDR Efex Pro, it will automatically default to whichever tab you used last time. Once you have selected and ajusted the HDR file to give the most satisfactory result, click on the OK button. The HDR file is processed and creates a 32-bit image in Photoshop (Fig. 11.48).

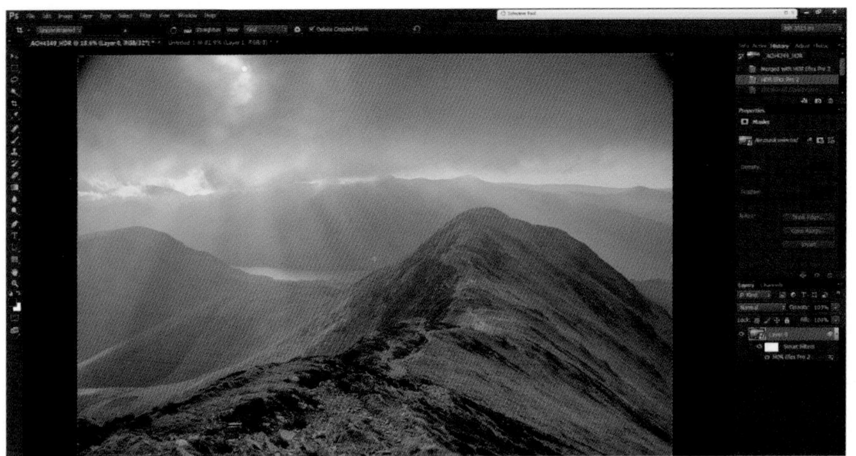

Fig. 11.48
32-bit HDR file created as a Photoshop image.

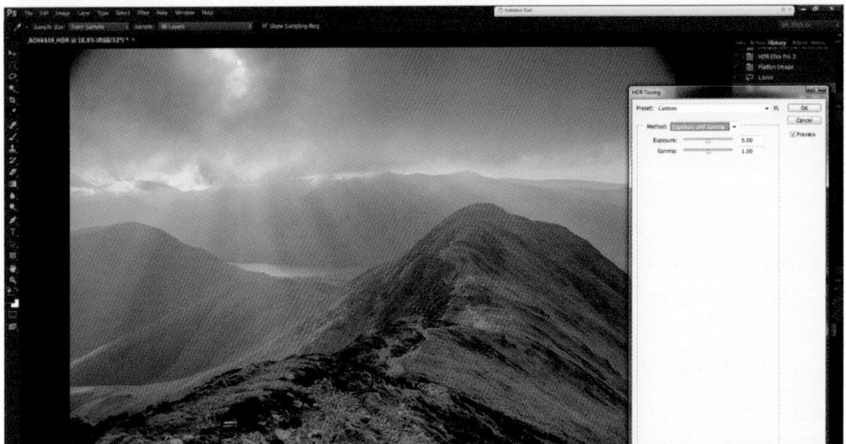

Fig. 11.49
Exposure and Gamma used as HDR toning to convert 32-bit file to 16-bit, preserving maximum tonality.

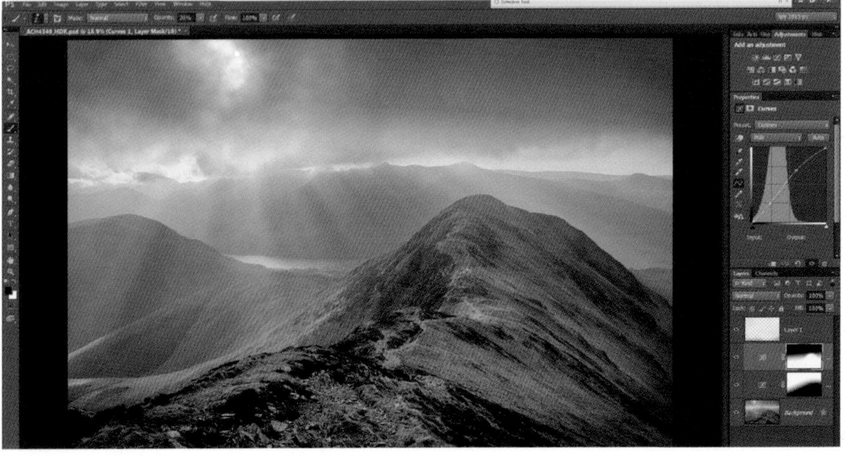

Fig. 11.50
Finally edited HDR image showing Curves 1 layer added to darken the sky and Curves 2 layer added to lighten the ground.

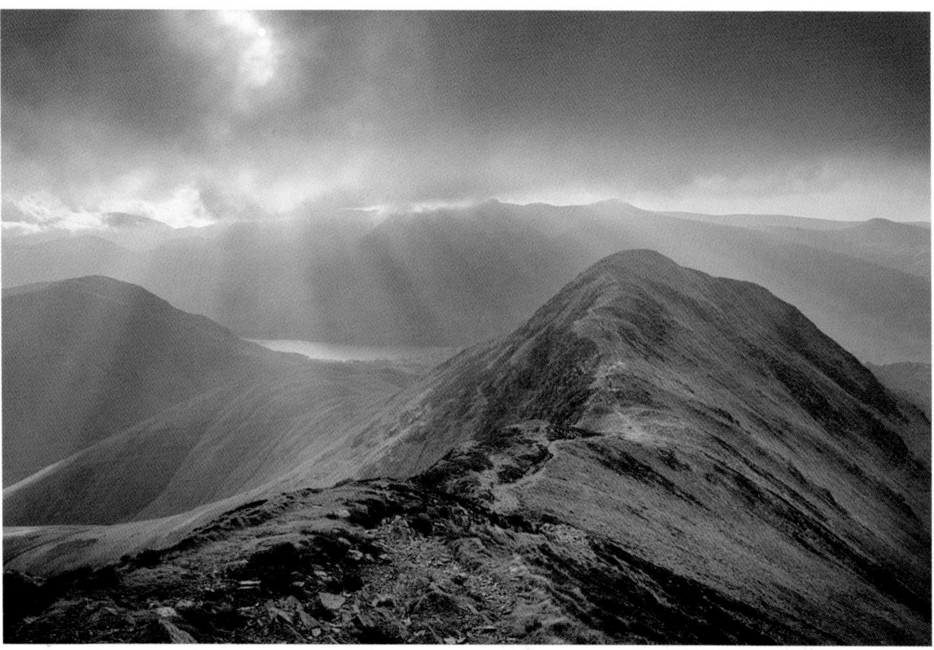

Fig. 11.51
Final HDR Image.

Although this file holds massive amounts of data, there is little further processing that can be done to a 32-bit image, although the 'exposure' adjustment layer, which is actually designed for 32-bit images, can be useful here, as it offers alterations to both exposure and Gamma correction. It isn't possible to add curves layers to a 32-bit file, so it is recommended that at this point the file is converted to a 16-bit file.

Image>Mode>16-bit will pull up a pop-up screen – the default setting of Local adaptation will change the image dramatically, but click on the drop-down next to 'local adaptation' and select 'Exposure and Gamma' as shown in Fig. 11.49.

This will convert the image to a 16-bit and retain the colours and tones comparative to the 32-bit file. You now have – as in the chapter on Photoshop HDR – a file of excellent data, with both shadow and highlight details. It is not yet necessarily a completed image, and further processing may be needed. Fig. 11.50 shows the changes that a few minor standard adjustments can have in the image: a curves layer on the foreground to lighten and separate the tones, a further curves layer on the sky creating a touch more tonality within the clouds and a soft-light layer to darken the lower edge of the frame and avoid the rough rocks from appearing too light.

Tone mapping single image option

Other than those who bracket almost all their pictures, it's not uncommon to open up a photograph and think 'what a shame I didn't bracket that, an HDR might just have given a little more in the highlights and shadows'. Fortunately, HDR Efex Pro 2 offers a tone mapping option for a single exposure. It won't work quite as well as a bracketed HDR, but it does a pretty good job.

The only thing unusual with the tone mapping single option is that, unlike almost every other function in the Nik Collection, it doesn't create its own layer, but works only on the active pixel layer. If you have an image that you have added an adjustment layer to, and not flattened (or upward flattened) you will see a pop-up message 'The command "HDR Efex Pro2" is not currently available'. Fig. 11.52 shows a photo taken of Castlerigg stone circle on an

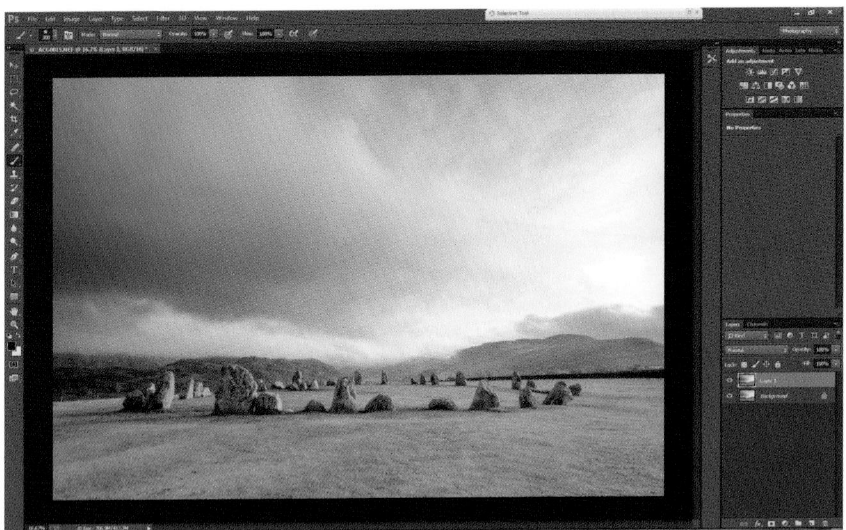

Fig. 11.52
Original Castlerigg Stone Circle RAW file opened in Photoshop and the background layer duplicated.

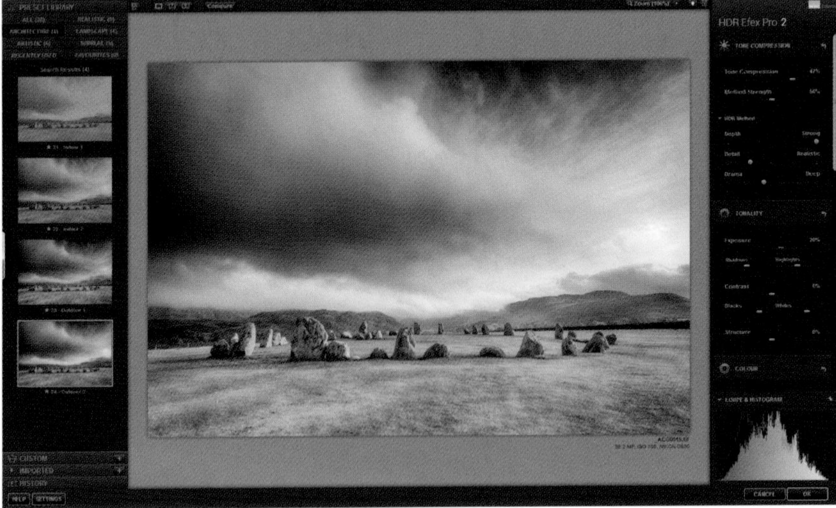

Fig. 11.53
Outdoor 2 tone-mapping preset applied.

overcast, drizzly day. The whole picture looks a bit flat and uninspiring. Textures in the sky in particular are fairly uniform.

Once the file is open on Photoshop, simply duplicate the background layer (Ctrl-J), which gives you a separate working layer to apply the tone mapping to, and click on the Nik Collection drop-down, then the tone mapping (single image) option (Fig. 11.53). The layout is identical to the *Merge* option described earlier. In this image, the sky was a touch lacking in separation and detail, and the foreground a little dark. Under the Architecture presets, *Outdoor 2* is an option that creates the effect of a graduated filter over the top half of the photograph. The intensity, angle and position of the graduated filter can be adjusted on the right-hand panels to tailor its position to each photograph.

The effect of the outdoor 2 tone-mapping preset on this image is rather 'over the top' for many tastes, but as you have the tone-mapped image on a separate layer, simply by using the opacity slider, you can change the intensity of the adjustment from none (at 0% opacity), through to full intensity (at 100%). The Castlerigg shot looked about right by taking the

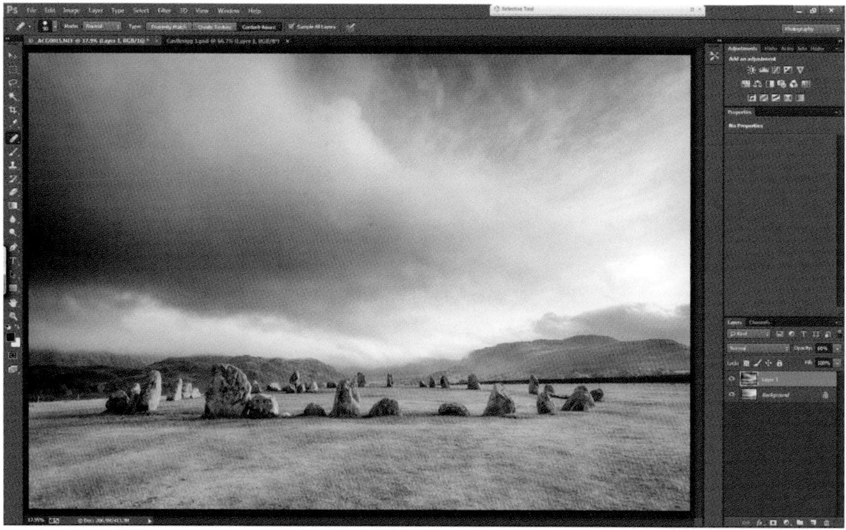

Fig. 11.54
Tone-mapped layer (Layer 1) reduced to 60% opacity to lessen the effect of the tone-mapped layer.

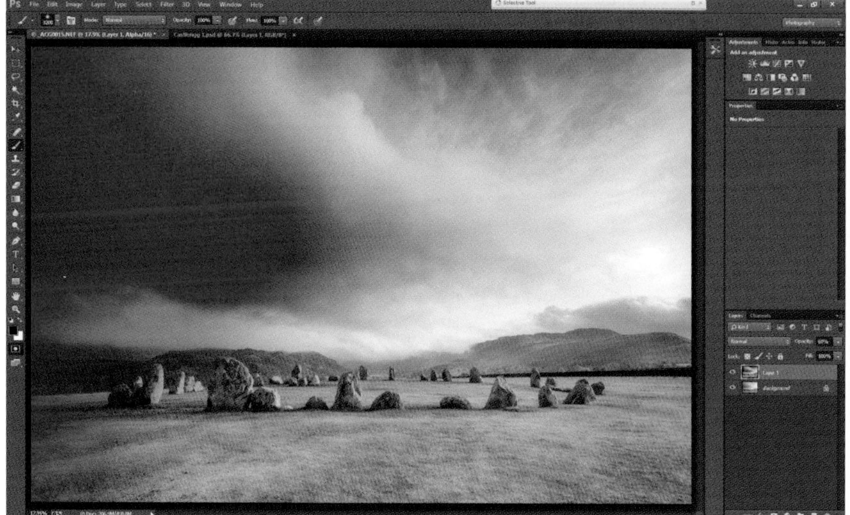

Fig. 11.55
Quick mask selection (made with brush tool set to 3200 pixels wide with a very soft edge) of dark cloud and left side of image.

opacity of the tone-mapped layer down to around 60% as shown in Fig. 11.54.

This adjustment on its own has improved the sky, although the clouds at the top left of the picture look a touch 'solid' and the whole left edge looks a little dark compared to the rest of the image. Select these quickly by using a large, soft, brush tool (B) in quick mask (Q) (Fig. 11.55). The grassy area has been selected using a large brush at reduced opacity, so adjustments on this selection will not be as strong on the grass as they will on the sky.

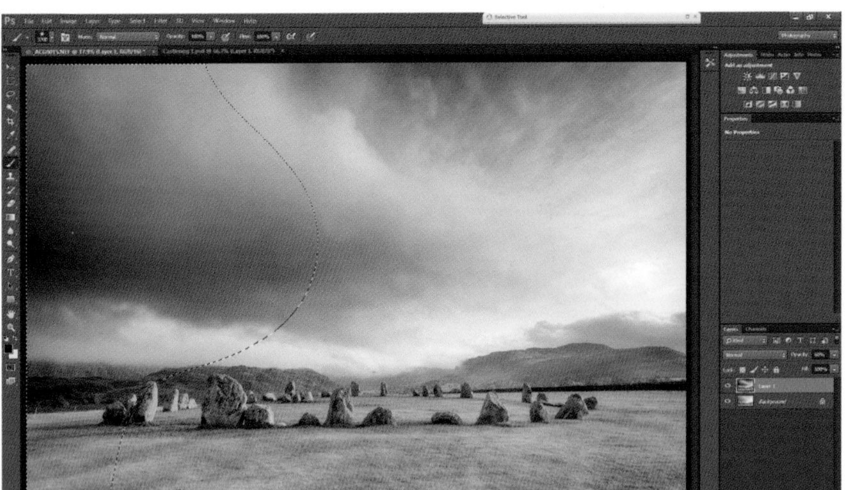

Fig. 11.56
Selection area shown by marching ants.

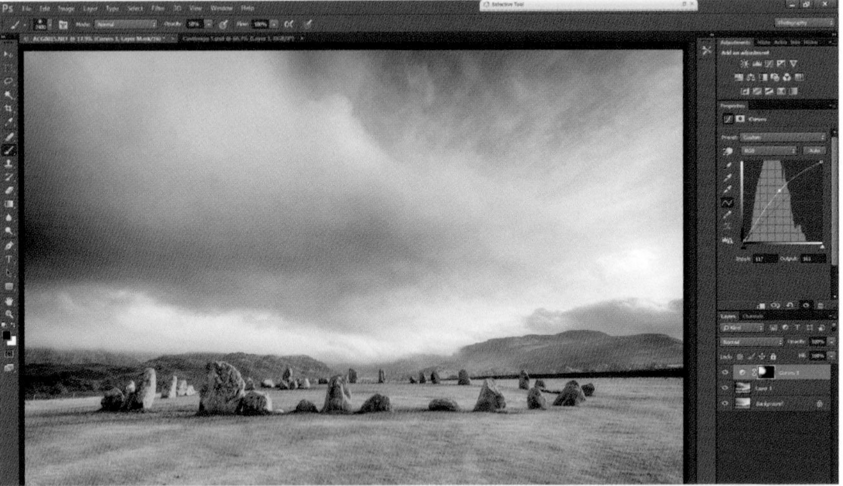

Fig. 11.57
Dark areas lightened using Curves 1 layer by lifting the central part of the curve.

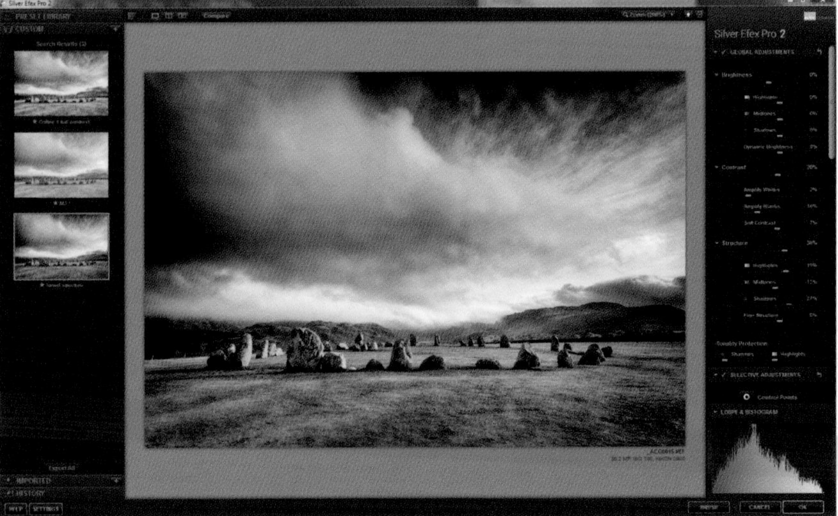

Fig. 11.58
Silver Efex Pro 2 added to the tone-mapped image, a custom preset applied.

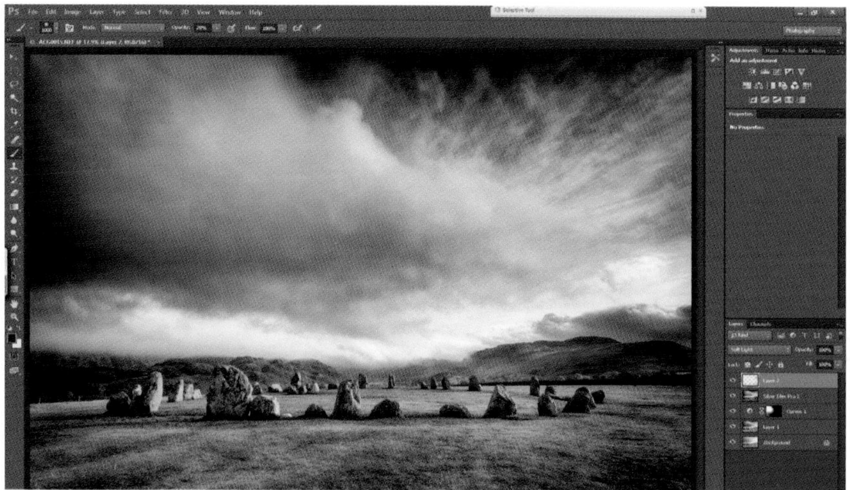

Fig. 11.59
Fully processed image with layers shown.

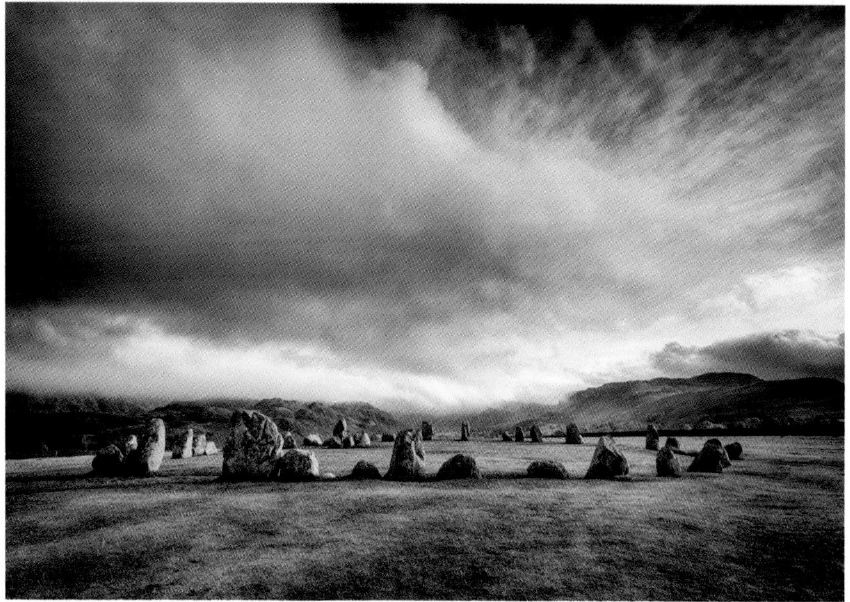

Fig. 11.60
Castlerigg Stone Circle Monochrome created using HDR Efex Pro 2 and Silver Efex Pro 2.

Exiting quick mask will leave a series of marching ants indicating the selection area (Fig. 11.56).

With the selection in place, adding a curves layer will create an adjustment layer with associated layer mask. Moving the centre of the curve up slightly will lift the tones in the dark areas leaving the sky looking more defined, yet natural (Fig. 11.57).

As the Castlerigg picture stands, the tones in the foreground grasses might not be as natural as some may like. This picture, however, would work wonderfully as a monochrome. One of the great things about the Nik Collection is that any number of Nik layers can be added on to other layers. So try adding a Silver Efex Pro 2 layer (Fig. 11.58).

Fig. 11.59 shows the final stack of layers in the complete image, which includes the original background layer, the duplicate layer with tone mapping applied (and reduced to 60% opacity), the curves layer and mask to lighten the clouds on the left side, the Silver Efex Pro 2 layer and a final soft light layer to dodge and burn selectively.

Fig. 11.60 is the final image.

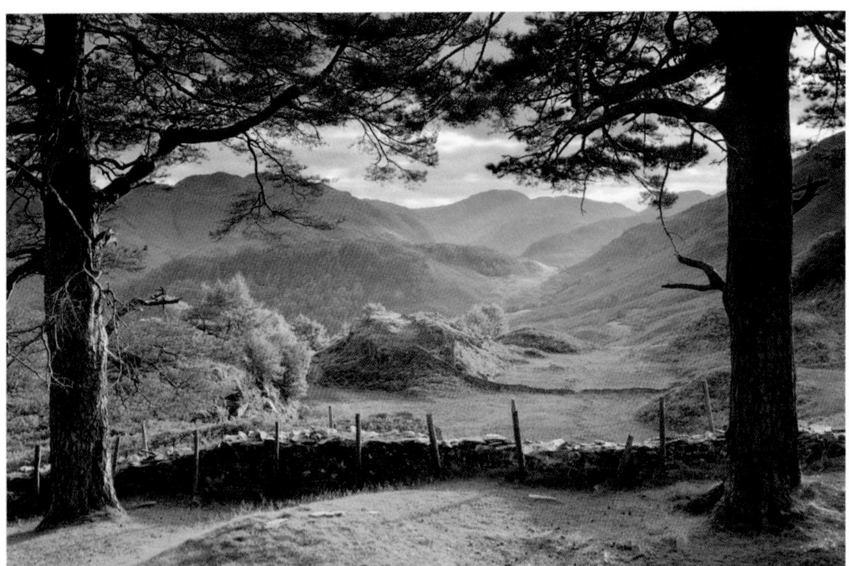

Fig. 11.61
Previously edited image of Trees on Castle Crag.

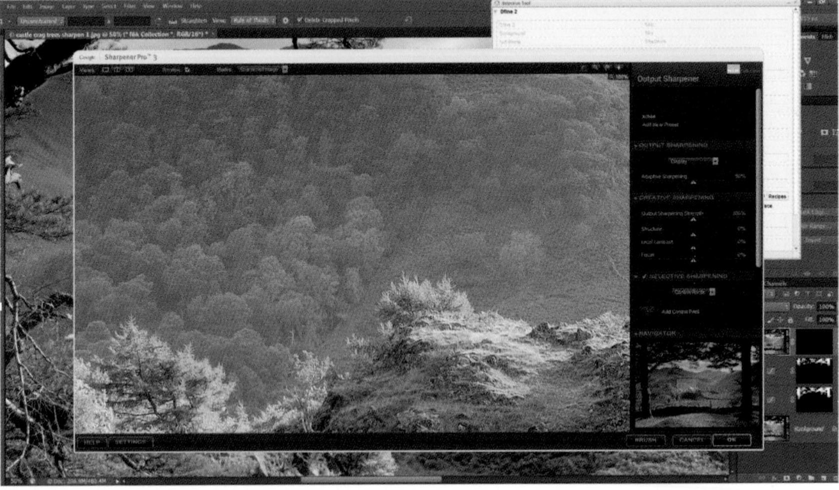

Fig. 11.62
Default Prosharpener screen showing output sharpening strength at 100% and all other adjustments at 0%.

Sharpener Pro 3

Sharpener Pro 3 is a fairly sophisticated sharpening application. It can apply output specific sharpening, whether your resultant image is going to be printed on an inkjet printer or will be displayed on the web. It also performs sharpening that can be applied to the image irrespective of output. Many get confused with the array of sharpening options it offers, but it can be quite logical.

Figure 11.61 shows the image used in an earlier chapter to show correction on grad darkening at the top of a picture.

The default screen on Sharpener Pro (output sharpening) is shown in Figure 11.62; it shows the four main sliders used in Sharpener Pro in their default settings.

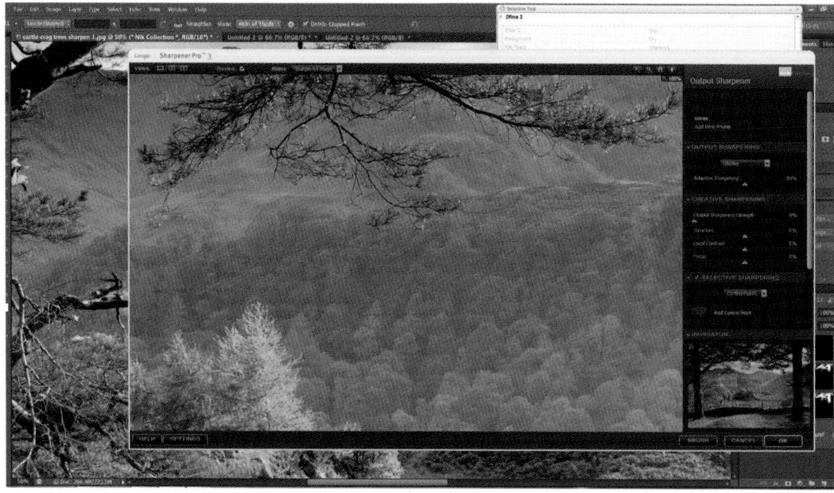

Fig. 11.63
Output sharpening strength reset to 0%.

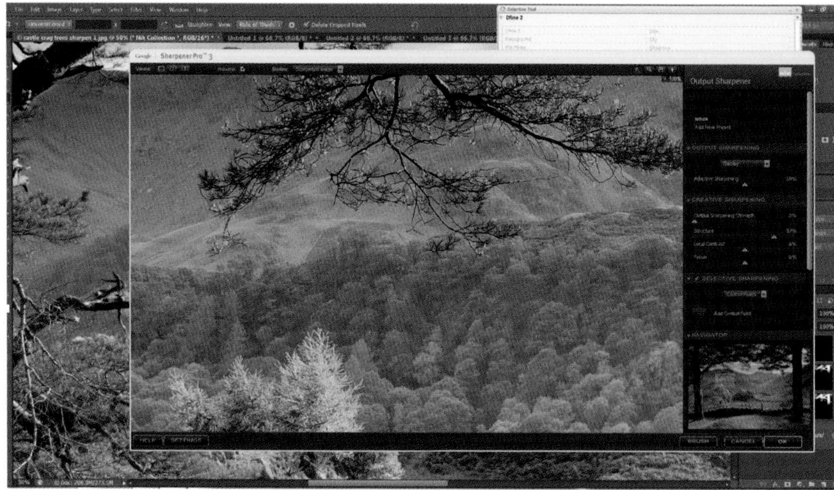

Fig. 11.64
Structure slider set to 57% enhancing texture across the entire image.

Output sharpener:	100 per cent
Structure:	0 per cent
Local contrast:	0 per cent
Focus:	0 per cent

The output sharpener should only be used when deciding what output the file will be used for – this means either screen, web, printer and so on. For basic sharpening it should be set at 0 per cent.

The three remaining sliders – structure, local contrast and focus – can be used individually or in combination to achieve the focus results you are trying to obtain. Figures 11.64, 11.65 and 11.66 show the effects of each slider individually; Figure 11.67 shows an adjustment using a combination of local contrast and focus.

The structure slider effectively enhances texture throughout the image, as can be seen in Figure 11.64. In particular the trees in the background appear crisper than in the unsharpened version.

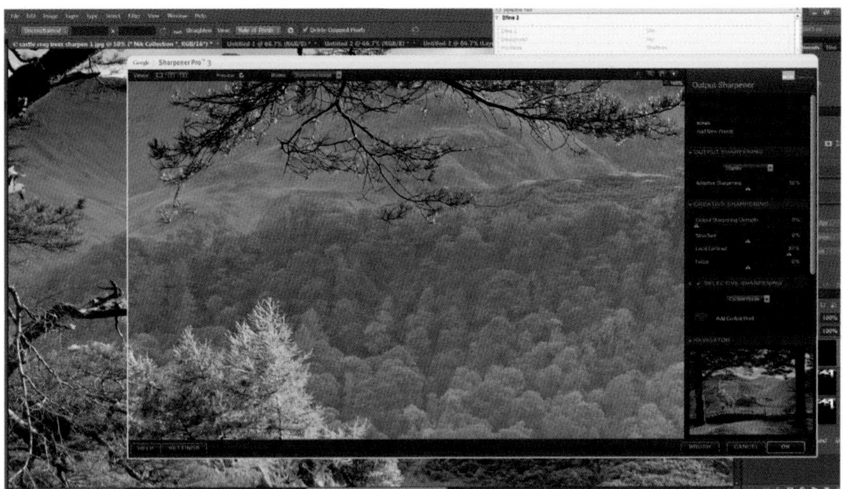

Fig. 11.65
Local contrast slider set to 81% to enhance separation between near and far elements of the picture.

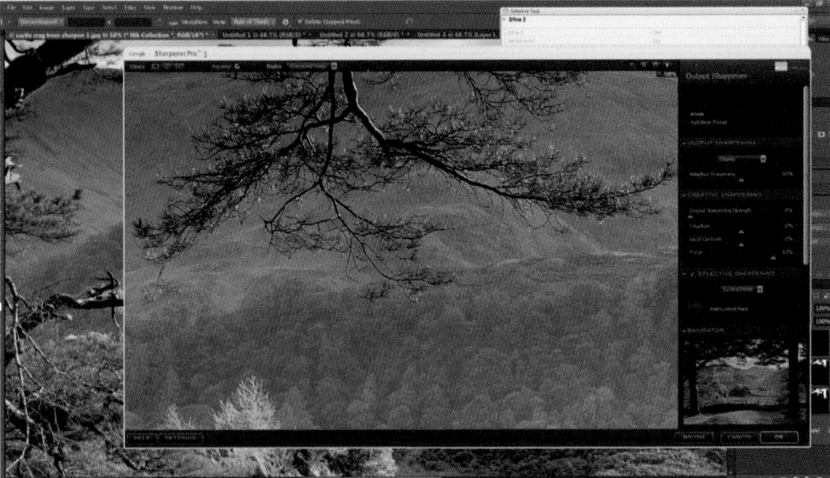

Fig. 11.66
Focus sharpening slider set to 63% to enhance edge sharpening across the image.

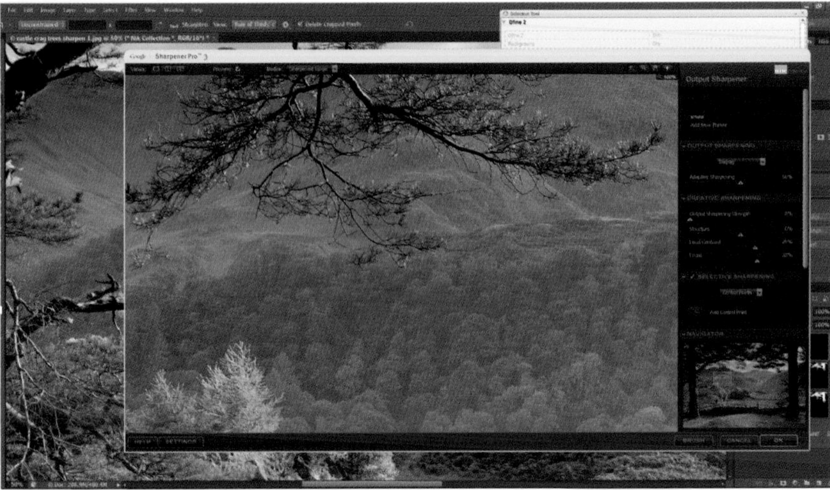

Fig. 11.67
Completed sharpening, using a combination of local contrast and focus sharpening.

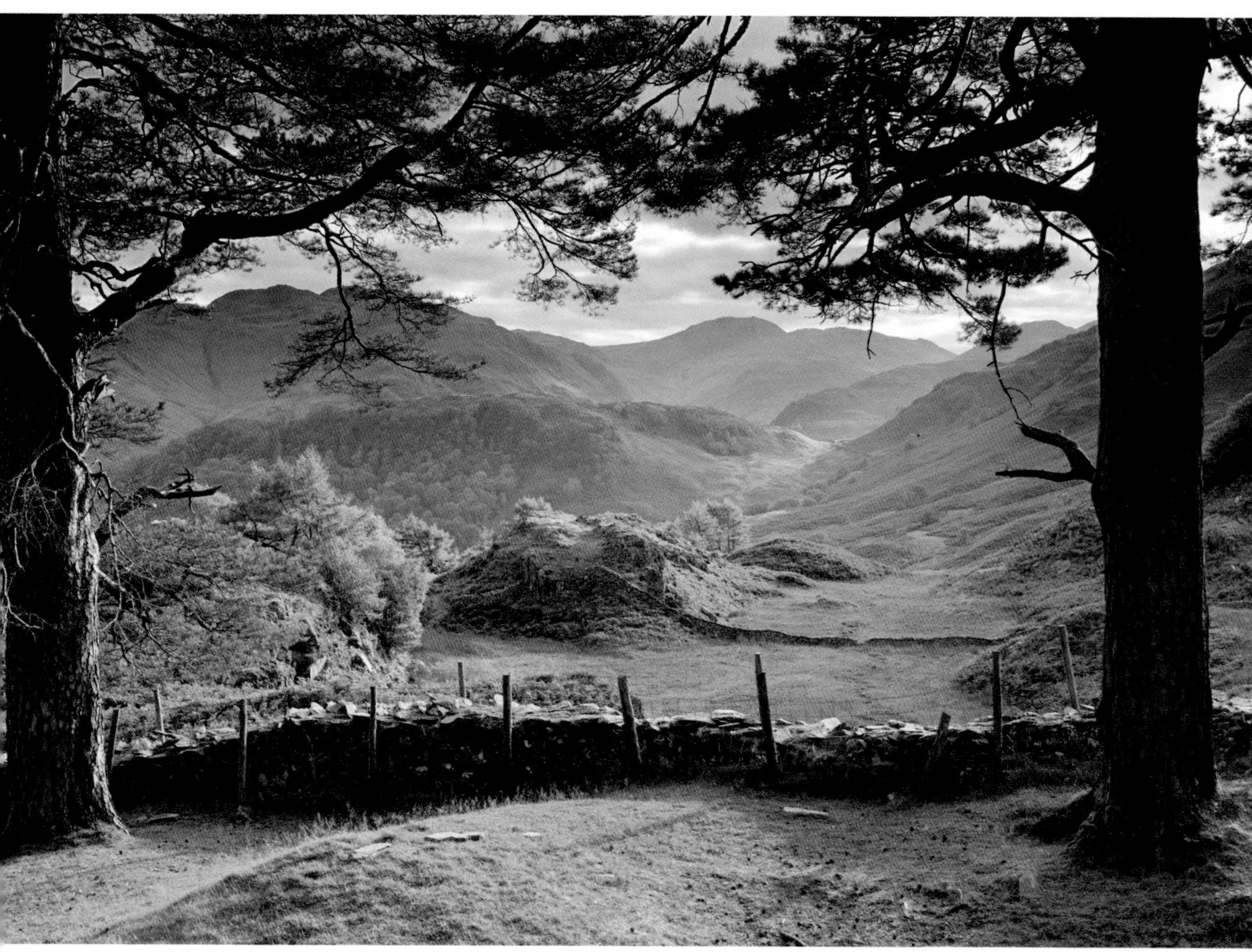

▲ Fig. 11.68
Completed, sharpened image, it is always important not to oversharpen, and this result gives a high definition, natural result.

The local contrast slider is a remarkable tool; it seems to have the ability to separate objects from other objects. By sliding the local contrast slider to the right, it has made the foreground trees stand out more from the trees in the distance.

The focus sharpening slider has a very similar effect to that of high-pass sharpening. It effectively finds all the edges within the picture, and on a pixel-by-pixel basis darkens the dark side of the edges and lightens the light side of the edges, which gives an excellent overall effect on edge sharpening across the image.

Of course, most images will work best with a combination of the sharpening tools here. In this picture (Figure 11.67), the separation of the foreground and background elements are of great importance, therefore enhancing the overall texture by increasing structure works against the concept of the image. A slight increase in local contrast helps separate the foreground from the background, and some focus sharpening tidies everything up perfectly.

The final sharpened image has great detail without looking oversharpened.

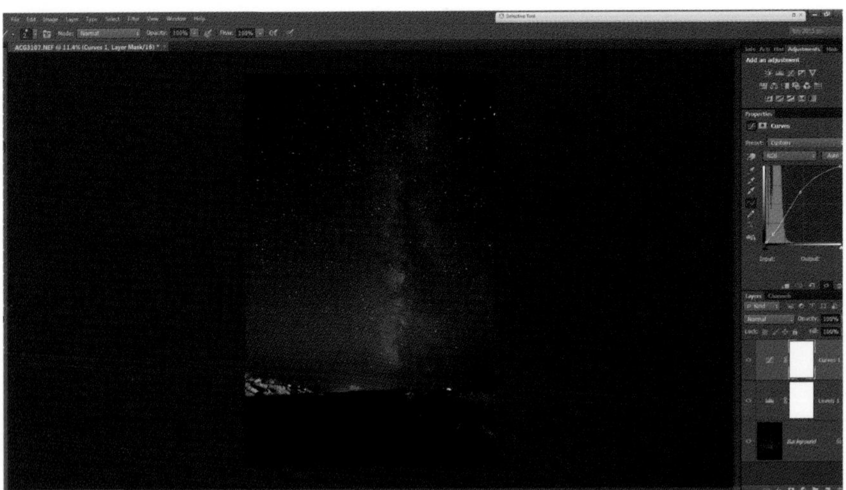

Fig. 11.69
Original, processed shot of the Milky way taken at 1600 ISO.

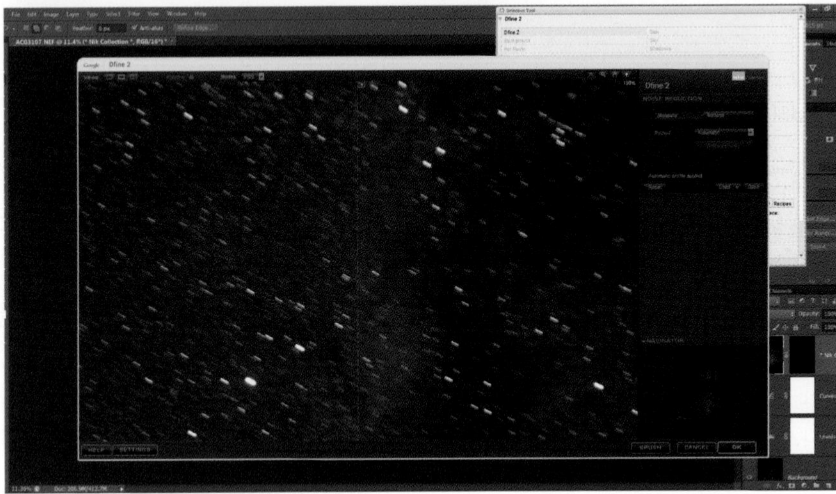

Fig. 11.70
Dfine 2 screen, with automatic noise reduction profile applied.

DFINE 2

Hardly a self-explanatory title, but a really effective noise reduction system. Now, opinions vary with noise reduction as to how much it softens the image, and in much of landscape photography, with the camera fixed firmly on a tripod, a low ISO can be used and noise reduction then becomes personal choice. However, if a high ISO has been called for as in the star shot (Fig. 11.69), where 1600 ISO was chosen to keep the exposure short enough to minimize star movement in the picture. The image has also been lightened with curves to create more detail around the Milky Way, which can accentuate noise, so some type of noise reduction is advisable.

As usual, click on the Nik Collection drop down menu and select Dfine 2. The software automatically analyses the data from the image and applies the appropriate amount of noise reduction in the areas where it is needed, and less noise reduction in the areas where it isn't. Typically, those areas of smooth tone, such as the night sky, will need more noise reduction than the more contrasting areas

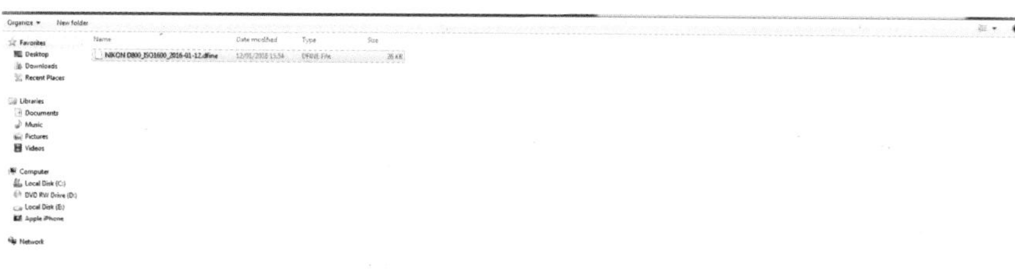

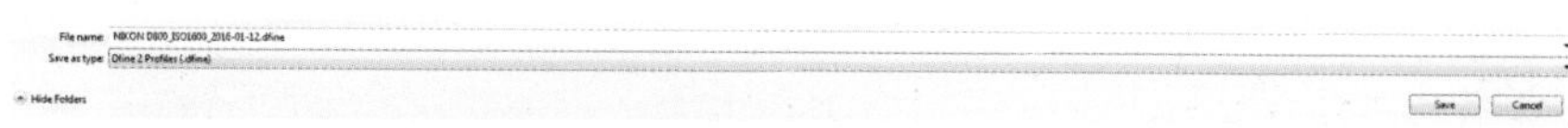

Fig. 11.71
Automatically camera-specific profile saved as a preset.

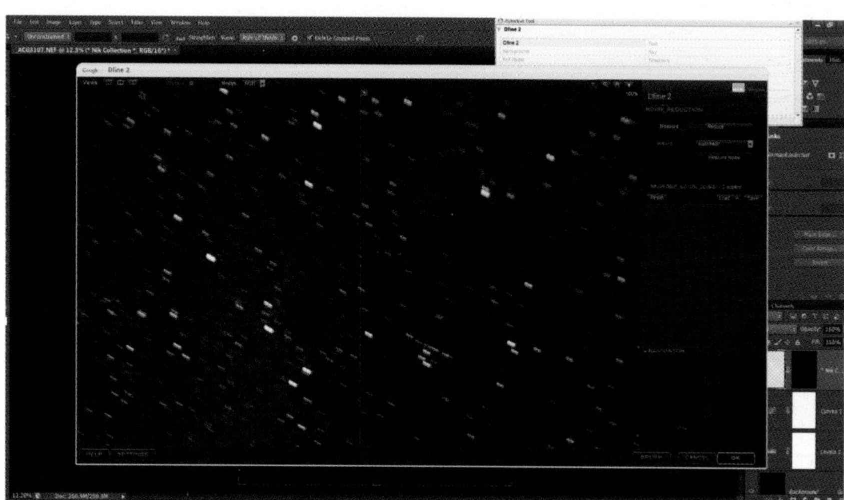

Fig. 11.72
Saved profile loaded as a preset.

of the illuminated sand bank at the side of the road (Fig. 11.70).

The automatic profile will have analysed the ISO and camera and applied the right amount of noise reduction. For 90 to 95% of pictures, this is all that you will need to do apart from click the 'OK' button. If you click on the 'save profile' button at this point, it will save the automatically generated profile as a preset profile for (in this case) a Nikon D800 at 1600 ISO (Fig. 11.71), which could, if required, be loaded at any time by clicking on the 'load' button (Fig. 11.72).

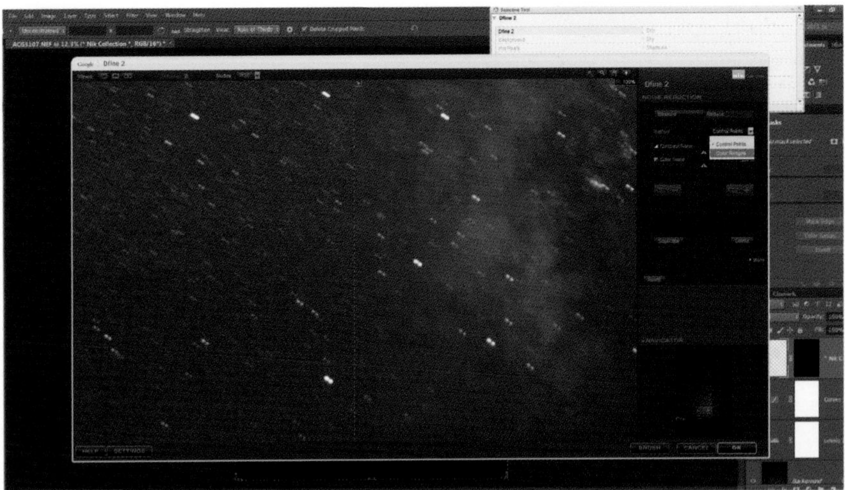

Fig. 11.73
Colour range menu item selected to further reduce noise in coloured areas.

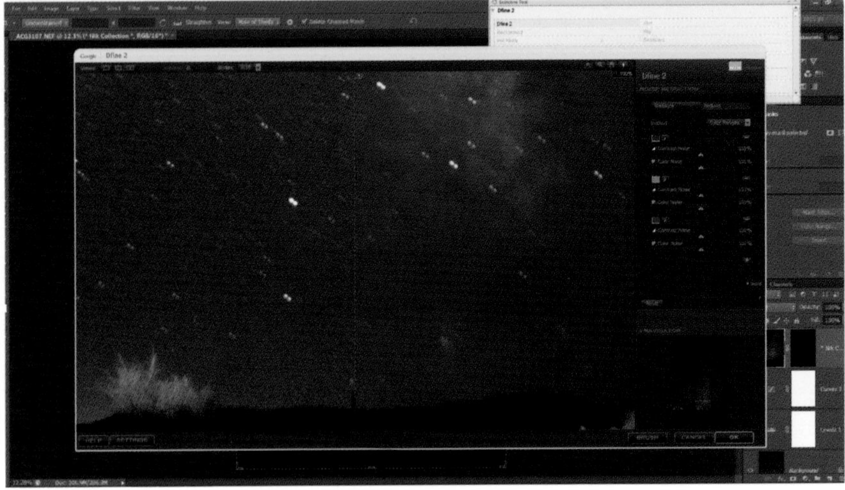

Fig. 11.74
Colour ranges palette open, allowing colours to be sampled from the image for further noise reduction.

On this picture, the noise reduction has worked very well in most of the sky areas, but there is still some noise visible near the horizon. Dfine 2 allows noise reduction by colour sampling, so it can perform more (or less) noise reduction on certain tones. Move the red navigator box down near the horizon, and click on the 'Reduce' button at the top of the noise reduction palette. The drop-down menu for method should then be clicked on and 'colour ranges' selected (Fig 11.73).

Once colour ranges is clicked, a fresh palette appears (Fig 11.74).

The colour ranges palette features three sample colours, the defaults are red, orange and blue, each of which has its own contrast noise and colour noise sliders. However, each of these colours can be sampled from the image. In this case, only one colour is needed, so by clicking on the pipette icon next to the red box, this will turn the cursor into a pipette, which can then be used to sample a colour from the

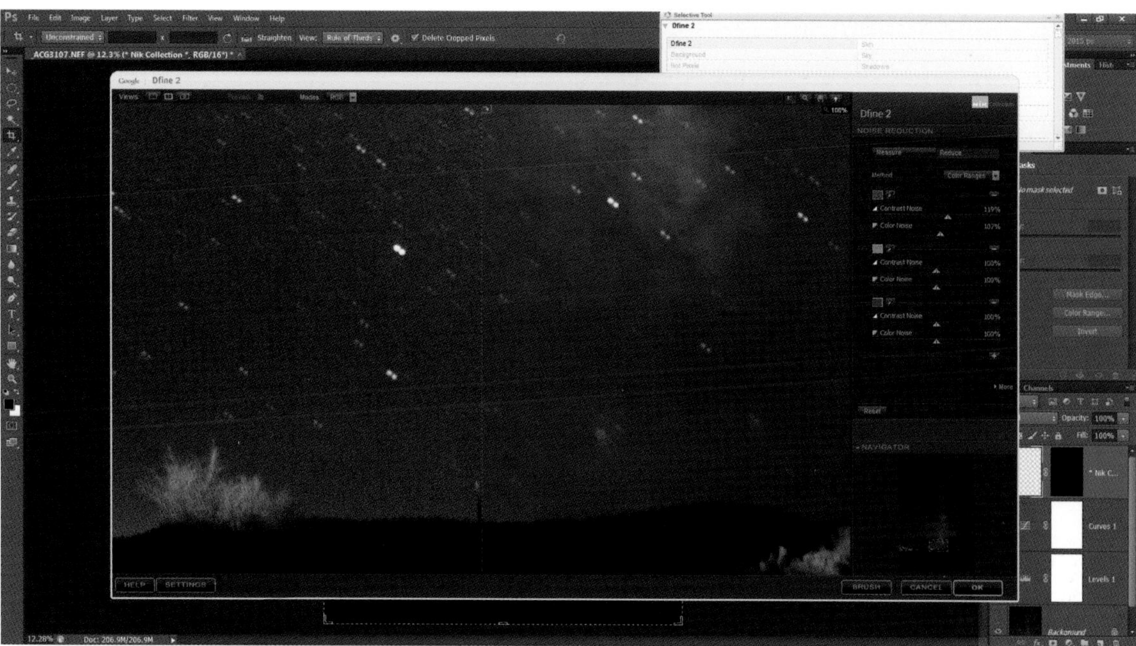

▲ Fig. 11.75
Noise reduction complete.

image. Fig. 11.75 shows the warm-toned sky colour sampled from the picture, and slight adjustments to contrast and colour noise used to smooth out the image noise in these tones.

While noise reduction may soften the image detail very slightly, the improvements it makes to image noise are substantial, and with the availability of Sharpener Pro after noise reduction has taken place, the inherent sharpness can be enhanced.

SUMMARY

The Nik Collection offers a few techniques that cannot easily be done in PhotoShop, and many that can. One of the main benefits of using the Nik Collection is speed and repeatability. The ability to do certain processes and save the settings as personalized presets is a huge advantage to the photographer; the amount of time that can be saved is enormous.

Appendix

A list of shortcut keystrokes

From the tool palette, remember, selecting a tool is not performing an action, so there is no need to use 'Ctrl', it is *just* the letter on its own – nothing could be easier:

Move tool	V
Temporarily invokes move tool while held down, can be used whilst any other tool is active	Ctrl
Marquee tool	M
Lasso tool	L
Wand tool	W
Crop tool	C
Eyedropper tool (Tab-I will eventually bring up the ruler tool)	I
Healing brush, spot healing brush	J
Clone stamp tool	S
History brush	Y
Eraser tool	E
Gradient tool	G
Blur, sharpen and smudge tools (no shortcut)	
Dodge and burn tool	O
Pen tool	P
Text tool	T
Path selection tools	A
Rectangle tool	U
Hand tool	H
Temporarily invokes hand tool when held down, can be used whilst any other tool is active	Spacebar
Zoom tool	Z
Temporarily invokes zoom tool when held down, can be used whilst any other tool is active	Ctrl-spacebar
Default colours (black/white)	D
Exchange foreground and background colours	X
Quick mask (toggle on/off)	Q
Screen mode, toggles through three screen appearances	F
Allows you to toggle through the various tools for each key – many tools have others located underneath	Shift-+ shortcut key

Other shortcut keystrokes – actions

Select all	Ctrl-A
Colour balance	Ctrl-B
Copy to clipboard (not recommended) – drag and drop less pixel-damaging	Ctrl-C
Deselect a selection	Ctrl-D
Merge down – merges one layer down into the layer below (lower layer has to be a pixel layer)	Ctrl-E
	Ctrl-F
Group layers (useful if you are working with many layers, they can be organized in groups)	Ctrl-G
Hides selection (retains the actual selection, but makes the marching ants disappear). Can be useful on very complex selections	Ctrl-H
Inverts	Ctrl-I
Duplicates active layer (or selection to another layer)	Ctrl-J
Opens preference dialogue box	Ctrl-K
Levels	Ctrl-L
Curves	Ctrl-M
New file	Ctrl-N
Open file	Ctrl-O
Print	Ctrl-P
Exit Photoshop (quit)	Ctrl-Q
Toggles rulers on/off	Ctrl-R
Save	Ctrl-S
Free transform	Ctrl-T
Hue/saturation	Ctrl-U
Paste	Ctrl-V
Close file	Ctrl-W
Cut	Ctrl-X
Toggles image to CMYK colour space	Ctrl-Y
Toggles undo one history state	Ctrl-Z
Toggles grid on/off	Ctrl-'
Fit picture to window	Ctrl-0
Zoom to 100 per cent	Ctrl-1
Views RGB channel	Ctrl-2
Views red channel	Ctrl-3
Views green channel	Ctrl-4
Views blue channel	Ctrl-5
Canvas size	Ctrl-Alt-C
Image size	Ctrl-Alt-I
Save as	Ctrl-Alt-S
Close all open files	Ctrl-Alt-W
Steps back in history palette	Ctrl-Alt-Z

Selects area of mask on layer mask/alpha mask or pixel layer	Ctrl-click on mask
Shows layer mask in red	\
Reduces brush size	[
Increases brush size	]
Decreases brush hardness (4-stages)	Shift-[({)
Increases brush hardness(4-stages)	Shift-] (})
Opens Camera RAW filter	Ctrl-Shift-A
Inverts selection	Ctrl-Shift-I
Fades last filter used	Ctrl-Shift-F
Colour settings	Ctrl-Shift-K
New layer	Ctrl-Shift-N
Save as	Ctrl-Shift-S
Close file and go to Adobe Bridge	Ctrl-Shift-W
Liquify filter	Ctrl-Shift-X

File commands

New	Ctrl-N
Open	Ctrl-O
Browse in Bridge	Alt-Ctrl-O
	Shift-Ctrl-O
Open as	Alt-Shift-Ctrl-O
Close file	Ctrl-W
Close all files	Alt-Ctrl-W
Close and go to Bridge	Shift-Ctrl-W
Save	Ctrl-S
Save as	Shift-Ctrl-S
	Alt-Ctrl-S
Save for web	Alt-Shift-Ctrl-S
File info	Alt-Shift-Ctrl-I
Print	Ctrl-P
Exit	Ctrl-Q

Edit commands

Undo/redo	Ctrl-Z
Step forward in history	Shift-Ctrl-Z
Step backwards in history	Alt-Ctrl-Z
Fade last filter used	Shift-Ctrl-F
Cut	Ctrl-X
Copy	Ctrl-C
Copy merged	Shift-Ctrl-C
Paste	Ctrl-V
Fill	Shift-F5
Content-aware scale	Alt-Shift-Ctrl-C
Free transform	Ctrl-T
Colour settings	Shift-Ctrl-K
Keyboard shortcuts	Alt-Shift-Ctrl-K
Menus	Alt-Shift-Ctrl-M
Preferences (general)	Ctrl-K

Image commands

Levels	Ctrl-L
Curves	Ctrl-M
Hue/saturation	Ctrl-U
Colour balance	Ctrl-B
Black and white	Alt-Shift-Ctrl-B
Invert	Ctrl-I
Desaturate	Shift-Ctrl-U
Auto tone	Shift-Ctrl-L
Auto contrast	Alt-Shift-Ctrl-L
Auto colour	Shift-Ctrl-B
Image size	Alt-Ctrl-I
Canvas size	Alt-Ctrl-C

Type commands

No default shortcut keys

Select commands

Select all	Ctrl-A
Select masked area on layer mask/alpha mask or pixel layer	Ctrl-click on mask/layer
Deselect	Ctrl-D
Reselect (last selection)	Shift-Ctrl-D
Select inverse	Shift-Ctrl-I
Shift-F7	Ctrl-I
Select all layers	Alt-Ctrl-A
Find layers	Alt-Shift-Ctrl-F
Refine mask	Alt-Ctrl-R
Feather	Shift-F6

Layer commands

New layer	Shift-Ctrl-N
Layer via copy (duplicate)	Ctrl-J
Layer via cut	Shift-Ctrl-J
Create/release clipping mask	Alt-Ctrl-G
Group layers	Ctrl-G
Ungroup layers	Shift-Ctrl-G
Bring to front	Shift-Ctrl-]
Bring forward	Ctrl-]
Send backward	Ctrl-[
Send to back	Shift-Ctrl-[
Merge layers (merge down)	Ctrl-E
Merge visible	Shift-Ctrl-E
\	Show layer mask in red

Filter commands

Fade last filter	Ctrl-F
Adaptive wide angle	Alt-Shift-Ctrl-A
Camera RAW filter	Shift-Ctrl-A
Lens correction	Shift-Ctrl-R
Liquify	Shift-Ctrl-X
Vanishing point	Alt-Ctrl-V

3D commands

Not applicable to this book

View Commands

Proof colours	Ctrl-Y
Gamut warning	Shift-Ctrl-Y
Zoom in	Ctrl +
Ctrl =	Ctrl-B
Zoom out	Ctrl -
Fit on screen	Ctrl-0
100.00 per cent (pixel size)	Ctrl-1
Alt-Ctrl-0	Shift-Ctrl-L
Extras (hide selection)	Ctrl-H
Target path	Shift-Ctrl-H
Grid	Ctrl-'
Guides	Ctrl-;
Rulers	Ctrl-R
Snap	Shift-Ctrl-;
Lock Guides	Alt-Ctrl-;

There is of course no way you will remember all these shortcuts and keystrokes, but the ones you use regularly will gradually creep into your memory. Within the keyboard shortcuts dialogue box itself (Alt-Shift-Ctrl-K) any action can have a custom shortcut allocated to it. There is no shortcut key for flattening an image (merge visible is closest, but will not flatten any layers that are not visible – in other words, that are switched off). I have allocated Ctrl-F2 to all the computers I use as a flatten image keystroke.

Index

Other photography titles from Crowood

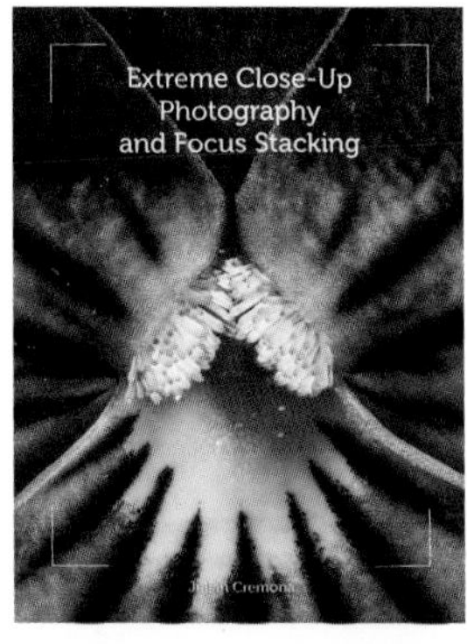

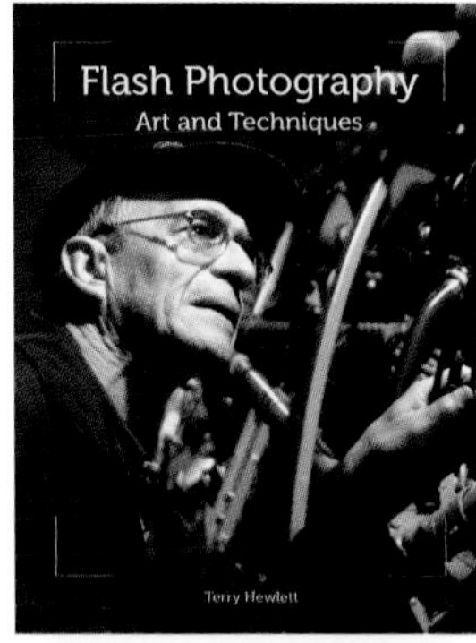

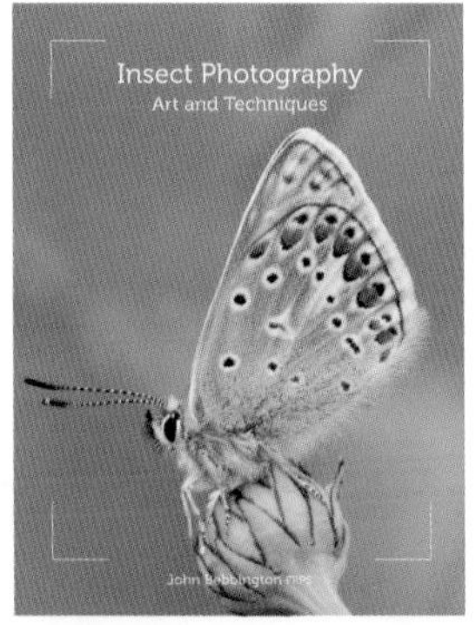

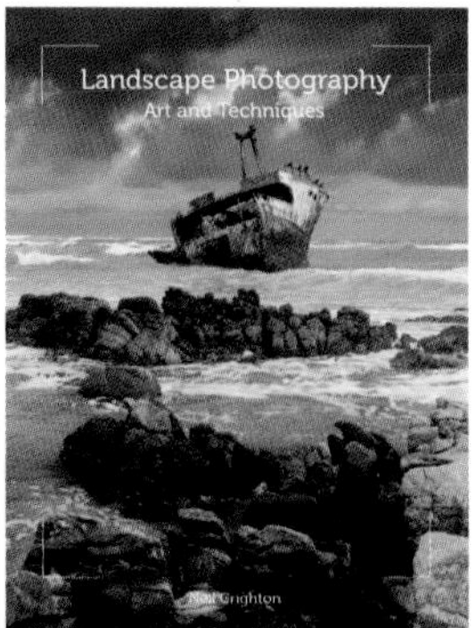

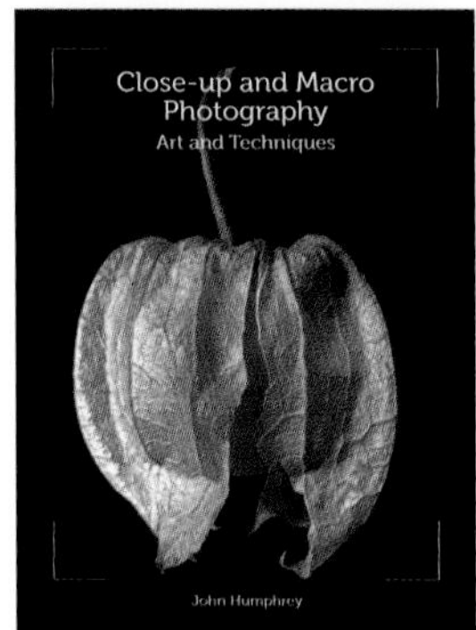

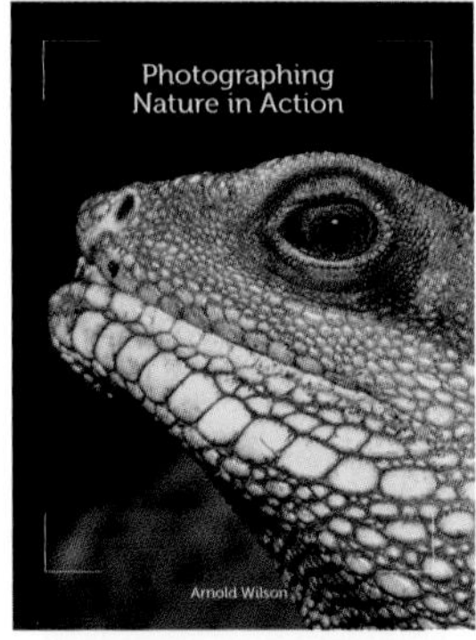

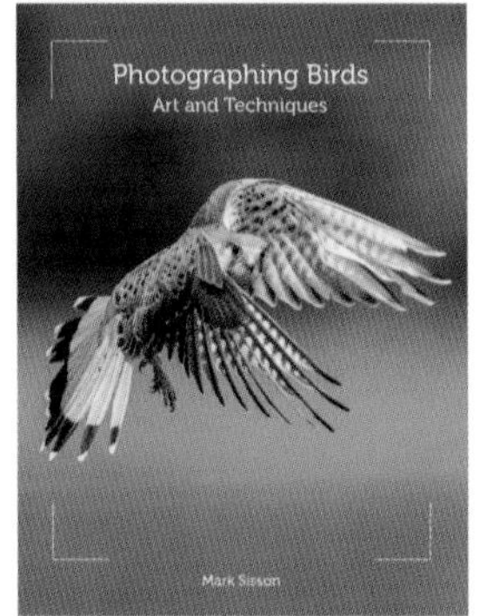

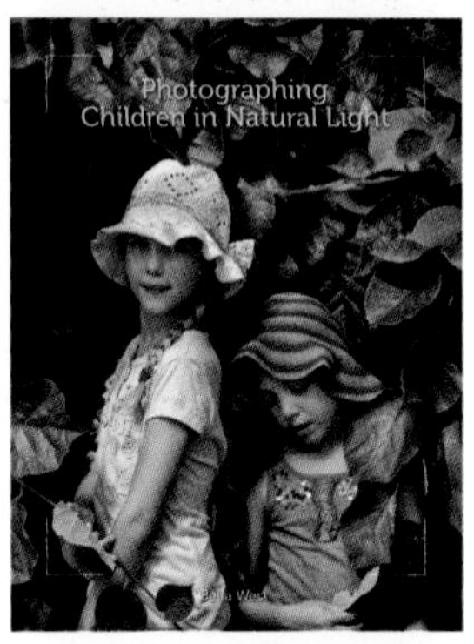

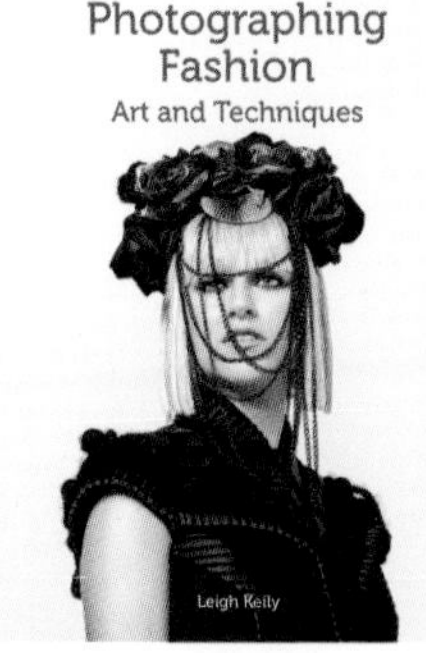

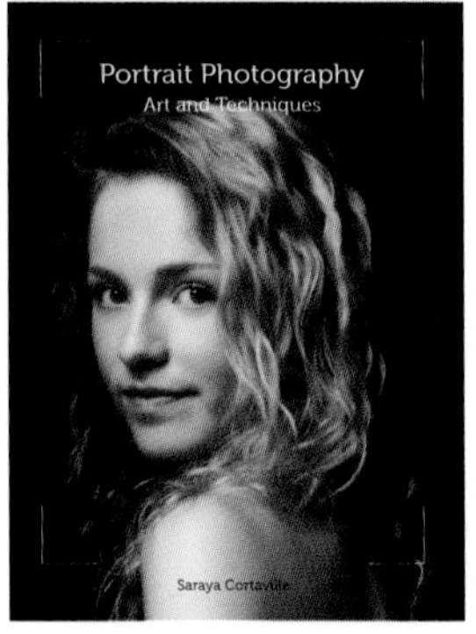

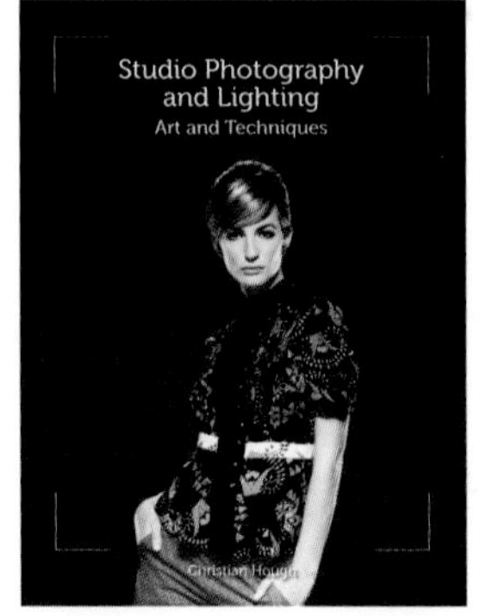

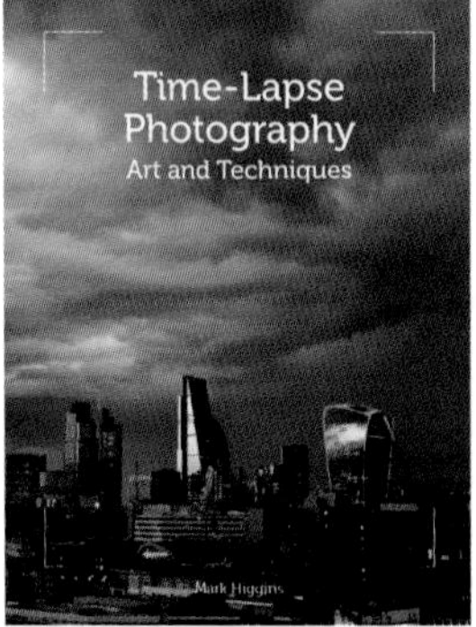

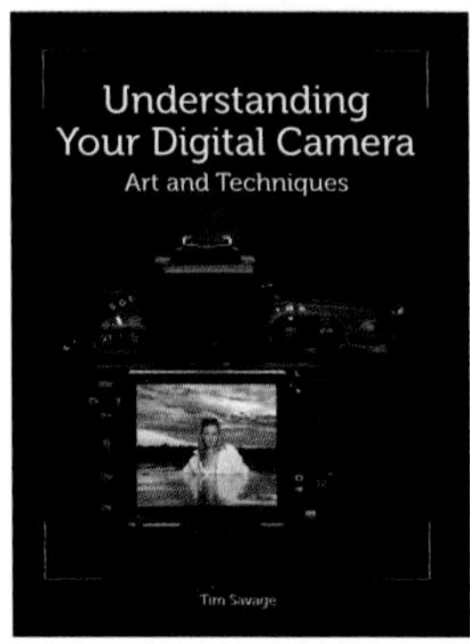

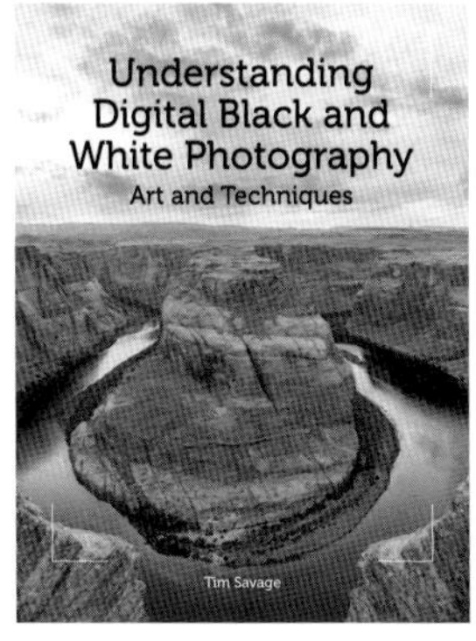

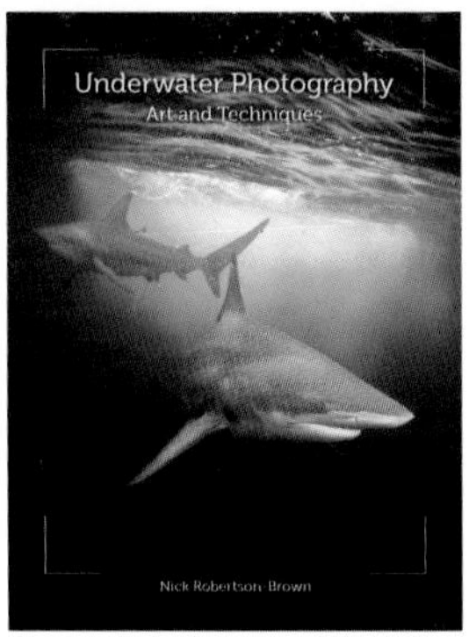

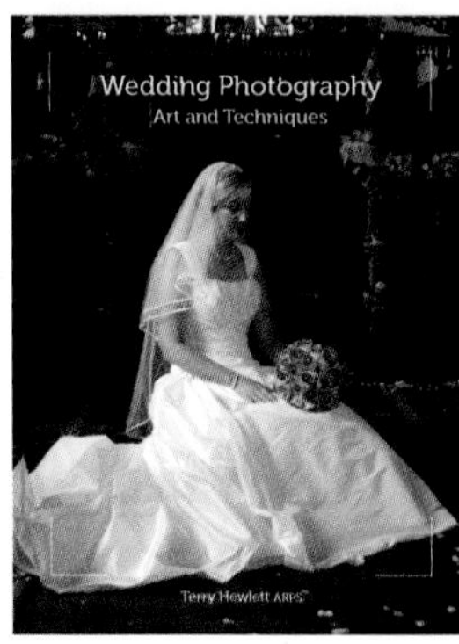